THE BOOK OF MAGNA CARTA

THE BOOK OF
MAGNA CARTA

Geoffrey Hindley

CONSTABLE · LONDON

First published in Great Britain 1990
by Constable and Company Limited
10 Orange Street, London WC2H 7EG
Copyright © Geoffrey Hindley
ISBN 0 09 468240 2
Set in Linotron 11pt Sabon by
Rowland Phototypesetting Limited
Bury St Edmunds, Suffolk
Printed in Great Britain by
St Edmundsbury Press Limited
Bury St Edmunds, Suffolk

A CIP catalogue record for this book
is available from the British Library

CONTENTS

ILLUSTRATIONS

Colour

between pages 16 and 17

'The Coronation of Edward the Confessor' (*English Heritage*)

Panel of four royal portraits from the Chronicle of Matthew Paris (*British Library*)

Chateau Gaillard (*Mary Evans Picture Library*)

'King John Hunting', from a thirteenth-century pedigree chronicle (*British Library*)

'Mouth of Hell', School of Winchester, mid-twelfth-century (*British Library*)

'The Church Militant and Triumphant' (*Scala*)

Blazons by Matthew Paris (*British Library*)

The Articles of the Barons (*British Library*)

Modern diorama of the scene at Runnymede (*Lincolnshire County Council*)

Sir Edward Coke (*Viscount Coke and the Trustees of Holkham Estate*)

King John's tomb (*Worcester Cathedral*)

Black and white

between pages 80 and 81

'King John and the Barons at Runnymede', Royal Exchange, London (*Copyright Guildhall Library*)

Writ and Seal of Edward the Confessor (*The Dean and Chapter of Westminster*)

William I's Charter to London (*Corporation of London Record Office*)

The Windmill Psalter c.1290 (*Pierpont Morgan Library, New York*)

Exchequer Memorandum (*Public Records Office*)

Magna Carta exemplification of the 1225 version, sent to the Sheriff of Wiltshire and held at Lacock Abbey until 1945 (*British Library*)

'The Court of the King's Bench' (*Masters of the Bench of the Inner Temple*)

Dorchester Crusader, Dorchester Abbey, Oxfordshire (*Photo copyright Reader's Digest*)

Sir Geoffrey Luttrell from the Luttrell Psalter

Coffin of Joan, wife of Llywelyn ap Iorworth (*National Monuments Record for Wales*)

between pages 144 and 145

Anointing spoon and ampulla (*Reproduced by gracious permission of Her Majesty the Queen. Photo: Dept of the Environment*)

A game of chess (*Mary Evans Picture Library*)

Seal of Winchelsea

The Battle of Sandwich, 1217, by Matthew Paris (*Corpus Christi College, Cambridge*)

Dover Castle

Lincoln Castle (*Lincolnshire County Council*)

Jew's House, Lincoln (*Lincolnshire County Council*)

Peasants and plough team, the Luttrell Psalter

Fourteenth-century windmill, the Luttrell Psalter

The Magna Carta Memorial, Runnymede (*British Tourist Authority*)

PREFACE

'. . . in the process of time, the facts embodied in [the Charter] and the circumstances giving rise to them, were buried or misunderstood . . . but the underlying idea of the sovereignty of the law, long existent in feudal custom, was raised by the Charter into a doctrine of the national state.'

Winston Churchill

'No freeman . . . shall be taken [i.e. arrested] or imprisoned or disseised . . . or outlawed or in any way destroyed, nor will we move against him nor send [our agents] against him, except by the lawful judgement of his peers or by the law of the land.'

Clause 39 Magna Carta 1215
Clause 29 Magna Carta 1225

Framed in Latin 775 years ago these words have provided a text for scholarly debate, a battle cry for civil war in England and a cornerstone for many an American state constitution. Four parchment copies of the text in which they first occur survive.

A charter was conceded by King John to a group of dissident barons, whom he met at Runnymede by the Thames in the month of June to agree a short-lived formula of peace on the 19th, and was superseded ten years later by a revised, shorter and altogether more king-friendly version in the year 1225. John had been dead nine years and the Charter was issued in the name of his son the young King Henry III.

This was the Charter which entered the statute law of England and was for generations of Englishmen *the* Magna Carta. A scholarly lawyer-contemporary of Shakespeare's writing in the early 1600s expresses mild interest that King John had, it seemed, issued a similar Charter. The dramatist did not think it merited even a mention in his play of *The Life and Death of King John*. The baronial opposition to John and their mentor Stephen Langton, archbishop of Canterbury, have enjoyed a mixed press over the centuries as has the king himself. The meaning and significance of the Charters of him and his son have been variously assessed too. But the ringing words at the head of this preface (given with technical additions in 1225), coined by a distant society in a half forgotten language, have been treasured by generations of men and women in the English speaking world as a safeguard of individual liberty.

Of all the documents surviving from the middle ages, Magna Carta 1215 has a unique fascination. In stolid legal Latin, some sixty-odd clauses regulate strange sounding privileges and harsh sounding obligations, order the abolition of fish weirs on the Thames, specify rates of composition payments for military obligations, lay down nation-wide standard weights and measures (a broadcloth to be two ells wide within the selvedges) and institute a Committee of Twenty-five barons authorized to raise the country against the king should he infringe the liberties granted. It was abandoned in the reissue of the Charter after John's death in 1216 and no such check on unbridled authority has ever since been seen in England.

Approaching the end of the twenthieth century, there are sections of British opinion increasingly uneasy that the United Kingdom, alone amongst the world's advanced democracies, is without a written constitution. Under certain management Westminster, which boasts itself the mother of parliaments, is liable to extend the metaphor towards an absolute and hectoring matriarchy. But in any case while parliament is sovereign there is no appeal against parliamentary oppression. Where the barons at Runnymede devised a novel instrument to limit the power of a king and where an American theorist can trace the very concept of human rights as it is understood today back to Magna Carta itself, Britain today has no appeal against a power potentially more absolute than John's. The crown in parliament, since 1688 supreme, combines in a single autocrat the two opposed powers which in former times acted as counterbalance to each other. Constitutional theory provides for the vote of the people, expressed at a general election, to oust any regime which is deemed to act against the general interest. But unfortunately, since British parliaments are habitually elected on a minority vote and since, in theory at least parliament could arbitrarily extend its term, there would in the last resort, be nothing – no supreme court, no written constitution – to maintain free institutions.

In the words of William Prynne, the great sevententh-century Parliamentarian, 'Parliament is the absolute sovereign power within the realm not subject to or obliged by the letter, or intendment of the laws, being in truth the sole law-maker, and having an absolute sovereignty over the laws themselves (yea, over Magna Carta and all other objected acts) to repeal alter determine and suspend where there is cause, as is undeniably its altering the very common law in many cases.'

Speculation as to the threats such a situation could pose is not entirely idle. In 1988 it was claimed that the Security Services could operate untramelled through the royal prerogative (long since appropriated by the government of the day in the name of parliament) in the interests of national security. Thus, not even the elected representatives of the free people in the High Court of Parliament are today permitted to question, let alone scrutinize the operation of 'services' whose sole reason for existing is the security of the community of the realm.

Historians, and especially medievalists, are sometimes asked to show what relevance their studies can have to the present day. As the most important single constitutional document in English history, Magna Carta needs, perhaps, little pleading. Besides its heroic part in struggles of the English speaking peoples for their liberties, it also offers through its detailed concern for the realities of daily living a rich variety of insights into an earlier way of organizing the business of human existence. And we need only try to imagine the formation of a Committee of Twenty-five to monitor and restrain the operations of a modern Westminster government and its agents to marvel at what things were once possible.

Anyone writing on this topic owes an immense debt to the great and classic commentary on the Charter by W. S. McKechnie, and to the work of the modern scholar J. C. Holt. For the reign of King John and his father Henry II, W. L. Warren is the acknowledged authority. My other chief debts are listed in the select bibliography. My wife Diana has helped me on this book, but it is for other, more important reasons, that this book is dedicated to her.

St Laurent-en-Caux, 21 March 1990

INTRODUCTION

'The ever-living fountain from which flow those liberties which the English world enjoys today' was just one of the pronouncements with which the American press greeted the arrival of the Lincoln manuscript of Magna Carta at the New York World's Fair of 1939. That manuscript has recently been once again on tour in the United States. It is one of four copies of the Great Charter of Liberties penned by royal clerks in the chancery of King John of England in June-July 1215 and surviving to this day. After more than seven and a half centuries their medieval lawyer's Latin, in clauses concerned almost entirely with the technicalities and social conditions of a world long forgotten, continues to proclaim a core principle of political life as we understand it: government shall, ultimately, be held responsible to the governed.

The society which established that principle, the struggle which led to its formulation, the history of the interpretations, misinterpretations and sometimes over-enthusiastic commentaries which enshrined it in the constitutional awareness of the English world provide the theme of this book.

The wording of the document itself has nothing flowery about it; almost nothing to indicate that those who framed it felt themselves part of an historic moment. Like all good law it aimed to be precise, and like all good law it had deep resonances for those who knew of what it dealt.

If anyone has been dispossessed or removed by us without the legal judgement of his peers from his lands, castles, franchises or his right, we will immediately restore them to him; . . . for all the things . . . from which anyone has been dispossessed or removed without the lawful judgement

of his peers by King Henry our father, or by King Richard our brother . . .
we will do full justice.

Those who forced the granting of the Charter may have been provoked
beyond endurance by the government of King John, but they recognized in
him only the latest, if perhaps the most ruthless, practitioner of an administrative system perfected more than half a century before by his father King
Henry II. Their ideal was to return to the 'good old days' of *his* grandfather
King Henry I or, still further, to the reign of the Anglo-Saxon king, Saint
Edward the Confessor, whose death in the year of Hastings was supposed
to have closed an idyll of royal justice and good government. Models for the
future were sought in an imagined golden age of the past. And if such
romantic dreams were beyond practical realization the Charter pinned down
workaday realities as firmly as words could.

It is hardly surprising that a document with such long-term effects as
Magna Carta had deep roots in what had gone before. One factor which,
unexpectedly perhaps, coloured the attitudes of the Anglo-Norman baronage
was that they looked on King John and his family as foreign interlopers.
That family derived its nickname of 'Plantagenet' from John's grandfather
Count Geoffrey of Anjou, who used to sport a sprig of broom flowers (Latin,
'*planta genista*') as a badge in his helmet. A turbulent warrior who married
much above himself when he won the hand of Matilda, widow of the Emperor
Henry V and daughter of King Henry I of England, he got the duchy of
Normandy for himself and a crown for his descendants. His son Henry II,
king of England and lord of half France, stands as one of the greatest rulers
in western European history. Yet at the time, some observers felt he never
did come to terms with the fact that his father was from the lower ranks of
the nobility.

By brilliance, an obsession with justice and an unequalled talent for the
business of government Henry, whatever personal hang-ups he may have
had, developed in England a governmental system without parallel in Europe
and a network of authority in his immense French territories which quite
overshadowed the kings at Paris. To understand the background to England's
constitutional crisis of 1215 it is important to see events in the context of an
emerging centralized state closely enmeshed in the affairs of continental
Europe. It was in the reign of Henry's son Richard I that affairs began to
develop into a pattern that would help to shape the future of France as well

as that of England, and it is with him, Richard the Lionheart, that we begin our journey into the world which gave birth to Magna Carta.

First, however, something about the structure of this book. To tell the story of the document various elements must be considered: how it came to be written, the nature of its contents, its subsequent history and its impact on the world. As a result, 'The Book of Magna Carta', is in four parts.

'The Road to Runnymede' (p. xvi), traces the generation that separates the coronation of King Richard I from the spring of 1215, the year of his brother's fateful encounter with his barons. For a time, royal power seemed threatened with terminal decay, for John found himself embattled against malcontents drawn from all sections of a society surly and discontented after years of often arbitrary rule.

'The Community of England' (p. 60), breaks the narrative with the competitors at the starting tape, so to speak, for a survey of that population as revealed in the Charter presented for the king's approval as the remedy to their grievances. Part Three: 'Crisis Charter to Legal Charter', resumes the narrative at quickened pace as the road from Runnymede leads through civil war to a new reign when, despite renewed turmoil, the Charter becomes part of the common law of England. Part Four: 'Law, Legend and Talisman', sketches something of the story of this remarkable document over half a millennium in which it served as battle standard of parliament, a talisman of independence against parliament, and a lawyers' text in cases ranging from civil liberties to commercial law.

THE ROAD TO RUNNYMEDE

In schoolbook history the middle ages were always the 'Age of Faith' – a time suffused with Christian religiosity or at least a devout belief in God. King Richard I 'the Lionheart' and crusader seemed a model. Brave he certainly was, and a brilliant soldier but his reign (1189–99) did little for the community of England except to add to its problems. Given the often almost pagan features of medieval folk religion, people were hardly more Christian than the average citizen of today. Better perhaps to call the period the Age not 'of Faith' but 'of the church'.

Churchmen were the mainstays of government. At a coronation, they were robed in the full aura of their priestly role. In the business of state bishops were often the crown's chief ministers and as such hated for oppressive policies. Sometimes they might be champions against the king; Archbishop Thomas Becket of Canterbury, murdered to please John's father Henry II, was England's most popular saint. Archbishop Stephen Langton takes the lead in the movement towards Magna Carta. The pope wields the sanction of excommunication, hoping to influence the course of events. Emperor and pope were major factors in political life – Richard surrendered his realm to the one, John to the other – they were also obvious metaphors for the rivalry of the spiritual and secular in human life. The English clergy were a major community of the realm but as members of an international allegiance they came to occupy centre stage in the diplomatic narrative. For this reason, though at the cost of some repetition the churchmen have their chapter in the section which follows.

THE BROTHERS PLANTAGENET

O N Sunday, 3 September 1189, a new king of England was crowned in Westminster Abbey. It was the first time in a hundred years that the crown had passed without controversy or warfare to the indisputable lineal successor. It is the first coronation for which we have an extended and detailed contemporary account. In broad outline it has served as a model for all subsequent coronations.

The participants would not have been surprised. The death of King Henry II two months earlier, lamented by some, had been a cause of joy for many more. The accession of Richard, his son, seemed the dawn of a new age, an end of royal extortions and a return to customs which the baronage of England liked to believe were rooted in an immemorial past. Yet within a year this new king's government, like that of his father, was at loggerheads with the realm, and a generation later his brother John was obliged to agree to a document which seemed an affront to the very idea of kingship. No doubt John himself was much to blame for the crises of his reign which culminated in Magna Carta, but it is also true that his brother fuelled discontents and resentments which it would have taken a more diplomatic and self-possessed monarch than John to resolve.

At the time of his coronation Richard Plantagenet, Count of Anjou and Maine, Duke of Normandy and Lord of Aquitaine by grace of his mother, the fabled Queen Eleanor, was in his thirty-third year. A handsome six-footer, with long, straight limbs, deep chest and reddish-golden hair, he had a surprisingly pale complexion and dazzling blue eyes. He looked the model of the knightly warrior. Violent in his rage and jealous of his honour, he could be generous. To a stark physical courage he joined an intellectual grasp of strategy, logistics and every branch of contemporary military practice which made him the most admired commander in Europe. Warfare was his trade. A contemporary monastic chronicler accused him of the 'immoderate use of arms from his earliest youth'. When he went to his crowning it was with the prospect of worthy employment. In October 1187 Jerusalem had fallen to the armies of Saladin and the following year Richard made his vows as a crusader. The English treasury was well supplied, thanks to the 'Saladin tithe' imposed by his father. But Richard's projected crusade would demand money, silver pennies by the barrel-load. The king had plans. No doubt his counsellors knew what was coming; intelligent courtiers no doubt guessed. But the Sunday morning celebrations of the coronation veiled the omens.

Attended at his lodgings by churchmen in purple silk vestments and priests bearing cross, candles and thuribles of smoking incense, the king was conducted to the abbey along the streets carpeted with finest linen cloth and resounding to 'the most glorious singing'. At the great west doors, a procession of nobles bearing the golden regalia of spurs, sceptre and verge fell in behind the royal party. Next followed three earls, among them the short, swarthy and somewhat foppish figure of John, Earl of Gloucester, the king's brother, and a score of other notables. The royal entourage halted at the high altar, where the king took the oath to protect the church, to exercise justice and to root out evil customs. He was now stripped of his clothes down to his undershirt and drawers. Taking the beautiful little silver spoon (last used at the coronation of Queen Elizabeth II in 1953), Archbishop Baldwin of Canterbury now anointed the king with the holy oil, smearing it on his head and naked shoulders and chest. This was the central ritual of the whole service; it was the act which was seen to imbue Richard with the semi-sacred aura of the kingly office. The actual ceremony of crowning followed. Approaching the altar, the king himself lifted the ponderous, jewel-encrusted crown and gave it to the archbishop, who placed it upon the royal head. Next the archbishop gave the king the sceptre and the dove-tipped verge and led him to his throne. As the archbishop conducted the mass of the day, the great crown was held over the king's head by two earls.

A coronation was the most important event in medieval political life. Richard had acted as king since the moment of his father's death, now he was confirmed in the exercise of supreme power in a ceremony which paralleled the consecration of a bishop. When the great barons swore allegiance to him it was to a man felt to have some of the attributes of the divine. In return he was pledged to do justice and to be a good lord to them. The only resort against a tyrannical monarch amounted to institutionalized rebellion. By a formal act known as *diffidatio* a baron renounced his allegiance and went to war. It was a perilous course. Except in the most extreme cases allies were hard to come by. A man who put himself outside the king's lordship was liable to find his lands assigned to others. The king's powers were immense and it required an extraordinary combination of oppression and mismanagement to provoke a general rising.

A successful king carried his great nobles with him in major policy decisions. They regarded themselves as his natural councillors, but the administration was generally headed by men of humble origins who had demonstrated their capacity as administrators and who were entirely dependent on royal favour. Two weeks after his coronation, Richard appointed the Norman clerk William Longchamp (who had already served him well in Aquitaine) as Bishop of Ely and Chancellor of England. Longchamp's enemies – he soon made plenty – claimed he was the grandson of a serf. The slander was almost certainly baseless. But the rise from unfree peasant to bishop in three generations was indeed possible. The church offered brilliant career opportunities to men of determination and talent from all walks of life. The minor clerical orders, badge of an educated man, were also the *entrée* to service in a great household or at court. For those who caught the king's eye, anything was possible.

Longchamp's appointment as Bishop of Ely was a classic instance of royal power in action. In theory bishops were made either by the election of their cathedral chapters or by the provision of the pope. In fact, the electors almost without exception confirmed royal nominees, while the pope intervened only if he thought the candidate outrageously unsuitable, or to arbitrate. The medieval bishop was a great landowner; his estates financed contingents of men-at-arms to the king's army, while their revenues would fund a handsome income to a minister of state at no expense to the crown. Piety, charitable works or theological profundity were rarely qualities a king looked for in his bishops: nor did he intend that a group comprising some of England's major landholders should be chosen by cabals of cloistered clerics. If contemporaries are to be believed, Longchamp looked like a cross between Shakespeare's Richard III and Tolkien's Gollum; he was low-born and avaricious, unscrupulous, inordinately proud and consumed by ambition. By general report he was also a pederast. Even if we discount a generous percentage of this as malicious slander, the man hardly emerges as an obvious ornament to the bench of bishops. Yet the timorous chapter at Ely did not dare gainsay the royal nominee and the pope acquiesced in the appointment.

The lay magnates also were subject to the royal will. If a wise king aimed at least for their grudging support he could back up persuasion with an ultimate resort to arbitrary power summed up in the uncompromising formula '*vis et voluntas*', 'power and will'. If he fell under the royal displeasure for any reason, the greatest noble could see his lands summarily confiscated and put in the hands of government receivers. The slightest hint of sedition; failure to meet feudal dues; the marriage of a ward without royal permission; all were misdemeanours which could bring crippling penalties. While men might complain at royal actions by *vis et voluntas*, no one questioned his right so to act. Naked fear of the king's power could shape the calculations of even the most obstreperous baron.

That such fear was fully justified is well demonstrated by the career of the king's half-brother Geoffrey Plantagenet. An illegitimate son of Henry II, he had remained loyal to their father while Richard and John had rebelled more than once. The old king called him 'my only true son', conferred the revenues of the bishopric of Lincoln on him, made him his chancellor and promised him the archbishopric of York. But Geoffrey, a few years older than Richard, had aspirations far beyond the church. Drinking with his cronies, he once settled a golden cup cover on his russet hair with the remark, 'Would not a royal crown look well on this head?' To scotch his ambitions, Richard ordered the canons of York Minster to elect Geoffrey archbishop. They complied, Rome having already waived objections to the candidate's illegitimate birth. Outraged protest rumbled through the English church for years. Geoffrey himself, not as yet even in holy orders, seemed to regard York and its revenues merely as a new power base, declaring that 'the king's grants in the province shall not stand except by my will and consent'. Acting by *vis et voluntas* Richard stripped him of his land and ordered him to be ordained as a priest. Three weeks after the coronation, 'unwilling and complaining', Geoffrey finally obeyed. His lands were restored only two months later on the promise of a payment of £3000 'to have the King's love'. With such power, both in church and state, pertaining to the monarch it is small wonder that a medieval coronation was a ceremony of high solemnity and deeply felt symbolism.

4

When the rites in the Abbey were completed King Richard, now sanctified in the awesome powers of his office, changed the heavy ceremonial robes for a richly elegant tunic and cloak and went to his coronation banquet in Westminster Hall. More than 900 sat down at table for this all-male occasion – by tradition women were excluded from the feasting. So too was a group comprising some of the richest men in the kingdom – the citizens of London. The nearest these merchant princes got to participating were the kitchen and the pantry, where the senior officers of rival guilds squabbled for precedence to serve at table. Yet men still richer than they were forbidden the very precincts of the palace.

From about the year 1100, when their ancestors came over from Rouen, the Jewry of London had played an ever-increasing role in the finances of England. Free of the Christian ban on usury, they were the linchpin of the still primitive banking system. They enjoyed the dubious privilege of coming under the special 'protection' of the king. We should understand the word in its Mafia connotation. Jewish moneylenders operated under tight royal licence; like the merchant community they were privileged to grant 'voluntary' gifts or tallages when required; but unlike Christians their heir at law was the king himself. When a Jew died his estate, including the bonds of his creditors, passed to the exchequer. (When Aaron of Lincoln died in 1186 a special department had to be set up to sort out his affairs.) However, vital though they were to his shaky revenues, Richard gave strict orders to the gatekeepers that such 'enemies of Christ' should be barred entry.

The great banquet was just beginning to swing when news came of a commotion at the gates. Unaware, one supposes, of the royal arrangements governing the guest list, a deputation of leading Jews, eager to honour their patron, had attempted to gain entrance with gifts and salutations. The guards had forced them back and the London mob, carousing outside the palace precincts, piled into the scrimmage. A bloody riot ensued. William Longchamp, Bishop of Ely and royal trouble-shooter, was sent to investigate. But mob rule prevailed. By morning the Jewish quarter and neighbouring districts were smoking ruins. Many leading Jews were dead. Richard was furious. The special peace surrounding the king's court had been grossly violated. People specifically under royal protection had been killed and, worst of all, their creditors' bonds had gone up in flames. Squalidly enough, the murderers saw their mayhem on the local 'enemies of Christ' as contributing to the royal crusade.

Money for the crusade was now Richard's overriding priority and the methods he used to raise it set new standards in royal rapacity. What we would now call government taxation policies were a major factor in the build-up to Magna Carta. In a decade as king, Richard extracted more money from England than had been taken in any previous ten years. On the Tuesday following the coronation Richard, we are told, 'put up for sale everything he had'. Estates from the royal domain, privileges of every kind, the profitable offices of county sheriffs, the high offices of state, all went on the market. Men already in place had to pay handsomely to keep their positions: new men bought in – William Longchamp paid £3000 for the chancellorship. Richard himself boasted: 'I would have sold London could I have found a buyer'.

In fact, a review of Richard's policy from the moment of his accession makes it clear that he regarded England merely as a source of funds. This attitude never changed. During ten years, of which he spent fewer than six months in England, he piled immense additional demands on the normal day-to-day outgoings of government. First the financing of the crusade itself, then the money for his ransom, finally funds for years of campaigning in France to defend his family's ancestral lands there against the designs of the French king. After ten years of unprecedented levels of taxation Richard left an empty treasury and a government encumbered by debt. His brother John entered on a soured inheritance.

However, in December 1189, as Richard embarked his crusading army at Dover, the prince had little cause for complaint. He had been created count of Mortain in Normandy, given a free hand in Ireland and granted numerous rich fiefs and castles in England. Ignoring church protests that the two were too closely related, Richard had allowed John's marriage to their distant cousin Isabelle, heiress to the great Gloucester estates. The revenues of Somerset, Dorset, Devon and Cornwall, Derbyshire and Nottinghamshire were all assigned to him. Here were the makings of a principality, and John prepared to rule it as a sovereign prince. One thing Richard had not done and that was to nominate his brother his heir. But crusading was dangerous work and Jerusalem was a long way from England.

Richard's generosity seems feckless: the family history may hold a clue. Their father's reluctance to delegate lands and responsibility to his sons had served as their pretext for more than one rebellion, while Queen Eleanor had eagerly abetted her sons. The feuding family was the wonder of Europe. It boasted the devil among its ancestors and intelligent observers were prepared to credit the legend. Philip of France, for his part, backed son against father at every opportunity. John, the youngest, had joined the last rebellion and, it was said, broken the old king's heart. Henry had not granted the boy estates to maintain his self-respect as a royal prince, and as John 'Lackland' he was a laughing-stock. But if Richard hoped to ensure his baby brother's allegiance by magnanimity it was faulty psychology. John had learnt disloyalty at his mother's knee; his brother had allied himself with the arch-enemy, France; and he himself was avidly ambitious. Later he was to reveal a fascination with and talent for government to match his father's. Now, in his early twenties, he wanted money by the sackful – and power.

To run his vast English territories John appointed an administration complete with justiciar, chancellor and seal-bearer, which mimicked the royal government. His chief adviser, Bishop Hugh Nunant of Coventry, had a reputation to match Longchamp himself. When he catalogued the sins of a lifetime on his deathbed no confessor would be found willing to absolve him. With Hugh at his right hand John stood ready to champion any baron with grievances against the royal chancellor. Longchamp obligingly provided them.

Nepotism was to be expected of a man with his power. Men sighed resignedly when the Norman upstart handed out profitable appointments to his relations. When he married them to great English heiresses whom he controlled as wards of the crown, resignation turned to fury. Longchamp boasted his contempt of the English and humiliated men appointed by Richard as his colleagues. Hugh le Puiset, Bishop of Durham, Earl of Northumberland and Justiciar for the North, was dispossessed and forced into retirement. William Marshal, one of Richard's most revered advisers, who was respected by the whole baronage for his knightly prowess, was relieved of the important castle of Gloucester. Bishop Godfrey of Winchester was forced to give up lands, castles and honours for which he had paid £3000 to the king only the year before. The chancellor added these to already considerable holdings and revenues which included the temporal revenues of the archdiocese of York. Geoffrey Plantagenet was still awaiting consecration, and while the see was vacant its non-ecclesiastical revenues went to the crown. Richard was opposing his half-brother's consecration, apprehensive of the use he would find for such resources. Many thought the chancellor a far greater threat.

In spring 1191 Longchamp came to a private understanding with King William 'the Lion' of Scotland. In March news reached England that Archbishop Baldwin of Canterbury had died on crusade. The 'temporalities' immediately fell under Longchamp's control, like those of York. Chancellor, chief justiciar and papal legate, he now aimed to become head of the church in England. But a stream of complaints about his deputy's high-handed behaviour was reaching Richard on the other side of Europe. Reversing his previous policy, he asked the pope to consecrate Geoffrey as archbishop of York. He also dispatched Walter of Coutances, Archbishop of Rouen, to England with letters authorizing him to partner Longchamp in administering the realm. But the chancellor-justiciar, with thousands of mercenaries and numerous castles at his command, ignored even the royal letters until their 'authenticity' could be proved. Archbishop Walter looked for an ally, and Prince John was the obvious candidate.

No one in England was more apprehensive of Longchamp's advance. The chancellor's seizure of Gloucester Castle was an overt threat to his lands in the west. Accordingly when Archbishop Walter approached him John eagerly sounded out the leading magnates. Most of them promised him support in the event of a confrontation. In this way, improbable as it may seem in the light of later history, Prince John became, briefly, the champion of the barons against the excesses of royal government.

The confrontation came when Longchamp demanded the surrender of the strategically important Lincoln castle by the sheriff of Lincoln, whom he also accused of corruption. The sheriff sought protection at John's court and left his wife Nicolaa de la Haye in charge of the castle's defences. They were in good hands. A castellan's wife was expected to know her husband's business, and Nicolaa was respected for her courage and competence. She held off the besieging army and Prince John took advantage of the breathing-space to seize the neighbouring castles of Nottingham and Tickhill. Longchamp decided to seek terms.

Under the mediation of Archbishop Walter, the two rivals, each backed by large forces of armed men including contingents of Welsh bowmen, met at Winchester. Fifty years before, in the turbulent times of King Stephen, such a confrontation would have ended in open warfare. But the strong rule of Henry II, coupled with the general desire among the baronage to avoid any return to anarchy, had altered the political atmosphere. Three senior bishops nominated arbitrators drawn from the rival camps. These were sworn to deliberate to 'the honour of each party and the peace of the realm' and to settle any future disputes. For their part the prince and the chancellor swore to abide by the arbitrators' decision.

Castles were a major concern. Lincoln, the cause of all the trouble, was returned to the sheriff of Lincolnshire, though he was to answer charges of corruption. Prince John surrendered Nottingham and Tickhill to Archbishop Walter, but they were to be returned to John should the chancellor cause further trouble. Longchamp remained in office but was forced to accept the archbishop as his colleague in government. The treaty at Winchester dramatically curbed his powers in another matter also. Henceforward no one, whether bishop, earl or simple freeholder, was to be dispossessed merely 'at the pleasure of the justiciars or ministers of the lord king'. Any such case was to be settled in the courts 'according to the legitimate customs of the realm', or by the king himself. No one dared question the monarch's personal exercise of his '*vis et voluntas*'. It was another matter altogether when royal ministers invoked it as a routine procedure of government. The very idea of such arbitrary powers was beginning to seem anachronistic: a famous clause in Magna Carta would abolish it altogether. The Winchester meeting provided other anticipations of Runnymede. The opponents of the royal government based their case on an appeal to the ancient custom of the realm; a senior churchman acted as mediator; and the treaty set up a committee to monitor the government's observance of the treaty terms and enforce redress if it broke them.

In September, Geoffrey Plantagenet, at last consecrated archbishop of York in fact as well as name, landed secretly at Dover despite an order banning his entry by Longchamp. The chancellor's sister was also wife of the constable of Dover Castle. It was probably she, fanatically loyal to her brother, who forced events. On Wednesday 18 September, in the sanctuary of Dover priory, the archbishop was ordered to leave the kingdom. When he refused, armed men dragged him from the church by the feet, his head jolting over the mud and cobbles of the ill-made streets. Imprisoned in Dover Castle, he solemnly excommunicated his abductors. It was barely twenty years since Thomas à Becket, archbishop of Canterbury, had been martyred on the steps of his own altar. It was useless for Longchamp to protest that he had not ordered the sacrilege: the country was united against him and his supporters. In effect, the royal government was under siege from popular opinion.

John leapt to his half-brother's defence. He sent to Dover to demand his release. The castellan refused without direct orders from Longchamp. Together with Archbishop Walter, John rallied the guarantors of the Winchester treaty. Bishops, barons and the chancellor himself were summoned to assemble at Loddon Bridge between Reading and Windsor, to deliberate on 'certain matters concerning the lord king and the realm'. Now Longchamp did order Archbishop Geoffrey's release. The wronged prelate relished a triumphal progress to London where he preached opposition to the chancellor. When he finally rode into the pavilioned camp at Loddon Bridge John welcomed him with effusive displays of brotherly love. The next morning, majestically attired in cope and mitre, the archbishop, tears in his eyes, fell to his knees to implore the assembled magnates to right his wrongs. Next, Archbishop Walter read the king's letter empowering him to supervise the election to the see of Canterbury and to depose the chancellor should he refuse to consult with his fellow justiciars. It was all very affecting and, for Longchamp, ominous.

On the way to the conference, at the last moment he had turned away and was now at Windsor. In desperate straits he sent William de Braose to Prince John with offers of a handsome bribe for his support. It was the right idea – John rarely refused money – only the timing was wrong. Enjoying his unaccustomed role as champion of an oppressed nobility, John was also anticipating the removal of his rival. The bribe was virtuously rejected and Longchamp summoned to answer the charges formulated by the conference. 'Sparing neither horse nor spurs' the chancellor raced for London, even then the key to England.

City politics meant that there was a faction in favour of the chancellor, but the mood of the time was against them. To support Longchamp would mean shutting the gates against England's most popular archbishop and most powerful man – both brothers of the king himself. The chancellor and his party ran for safety to the Tower, while the citizens went out with torches and lanterns to welcome Prince John. The next day, summoned by the bells of St Paul's, the citizenry assembled to hear again the wrongs done to Archbishop Geoffrey and the misconduct of the chancellor, mewed up in his 'refuge' by bands of citizen militia. To general acclaim, Longchamp was pronounced deposed from office and Archbishop Walter chief justiciar in his stead. As for Prince John, he was hailed as *rector totius regni*, 'governor of the whole realm'. In return, London was recognized as an independent 'commune'.

Longchamp's humiliation was not over. Attempting to escape from England disguised as a woman, he was fumbled, and rumbled, on Dover sands by a fisherman. On 29 October 1191 John authorized a ship to take him to France.

Having seen off his chief rival in England, John was ready to try his luck in France. The time was opportune. In December King Philip returned from the crusades. Leaving Richard of England to champion the cause of religion in the Holy Land, he saw the chance to take over his lands in France. His plans to invade Normandy failed when the French barons refused to make war on a crusader. Philip calmly turned to the crusader's brother. For years he had pitted the Angevin brothers against their father; now he confidently expected to play the same game between the brothers themselves. As overlord of the family's French territories, he offered them to John. Fascinated by the prospect, John assembled a force at Southampton. By mid-February 1192 all was ready, but the expedition never sailed. Queen Eleanor had got wind of the plan and, braving the wintry waters of the Channel, she crossed to England. Convening four successive meetings of the Great Council, she forced John to abandon his treacherous scheme under threat of confiscation of all his English lands.

Having mobilized the lay magnates against her unscrupulous son, the ageing but imperious queen next turned her attention to conditions in the English church. Here the air was thick with ecclesiastical thunderbolts of excommunication. Once out of England Longchamp, in his capacity as bishop of Ely, had appealed to the pope. By return of post, so to speak, he received bulls against the archbishop of Rouen, the bishops of Winchester and Coventry – John's adviser – and against John himself. Meanwhile in the north the bishop of Durham had been excommunicated in the course of a local dispute by Archbishop Geoffrey of York. Not even Hugh of Lincoln, reckoned the most saintly of the English bishops, paid any attention to the papal thunderings. Archbishop Walter confiscated the revenues of Longchamp's Ely diocese and he, in retaliation, laid the diocese under an interdict. None of his clergy could celebrate mass and bodies lay unburied in the fields. Visiting some of her manors in the diocese, Queen Eleanor learnt about conditions at first hand.

Deploying their awesome spiritual sanctions like the cumbersome siege weapons of battle commanders, the church's 'fathers in God' seemed oblivious of the eternal fate of the souls in their charge. Superstitions rooted in the pagan past thrived in the folk ways of medieval peasant religious life. In the higher social ranks the manoeuvres of ecclesiastical power politics invited disillusion with religion as such. In the next reign the whole kingdom lay for years under a papal interdict. John's policy as king was the direct cause. Yet among the accusations and abuse hurled at him by the monastic chroniclers the jeopardy of Christian souls hardly features. The episcopal wars of '92 encouraged scepticism. Eleanor was able to force a reconciliation among the southern bishops; Durham and York continued hostilities, but by the end of the year the kingdom was troubled by rumours of more serious events.

In October, King Richard sailed from Palestine. He had recaptured much territory for the Christian kingdom of Jerusalem but the Holy City itself remained in Moslem hands. The king had won a hero's reputation, but affairs at home demanded attention. To avoid the hostile territory of France he took ship up the Adriatic and then made his way through the Alpine passes into the lands of the empire. Even here he travelled in disguise, for the route lay through the lands of Leopold of Austria, a fellow crusader whom Richard had insulted by removing his standard from the walls of Acre when the city was captured. Such was the affair of honour which brought the crown of England into pawn and the diplomacy of Europe into frenzy.

It seems it was the king's great height that gave him away. At all events he fell into Leopold's hands, a candidate for ransom. Leopold soon sold his prisoner to the emperor Henry VI, who found he had an auction on his hands. Philip of France put in bids, first for custody of Richard (the price of release would have been the renunciation of the Angevin French inheritance), later to persuade the emperor to hold the prisoner for a year after terms had been arranged with the government in England. In that time, he reckoned, he could overrun the Angevin lands with John as puppet vassal. In January 1193 John hurried to Paris to do homage, then bustled back to England to foment civil war, confident of help from France. The modern rehabilitation of John's record as a king has revealed his talents for administration, his concern for justice and his capacity for hard work. To contemporaries he seemed devious, untrustworthy and, in the last resort, cowardly. In a world where character counted for more than competence, these things mattered. When we consider that while John was negotiating with his brother's enemies the English government was straining its resources to ransom its king, we can perhaps understand why John earned his unsavoury reputation.

The ransom had been agreed at 150,000 marks – a sum almost beyond the range of contemporary accounting. It was impossible to audit the returns of the collectors. Extortion and embezzlement were rife. A country drained by demands to finance the crusade was now ransacked for cash for a king who, some may have thought, should have had more sense than to get captured in the first place. Yet the first massive instalment was found, and in February 1194 Richard was back in London. The honour escort of German knights who had accompanied him were stunned by the city's opulence and reckoned their emperor would have pitched the price higher had he been better informed.

John had fled to Normandy. His grandiose treason had collapsed from lack of support. In March the king presided over a Great Council which stripped him of his lands. John Lackland once more, he was to stand trial in forty days for treason. It never happened. Travelling through Normandy in May, Richard gave him the kiss of peace with the words: 'Think no more of it, brother: you are only a child who has had evil counsellors.' His lands, however, were not at once restored. Taught loyalty at least for the time being, he displayed considerable ability as a captain of mercenaries in Richard's campaigns against Philip of France. At home, the exchequer toiled at its familiar task, extracting money from an ever more fractious baronage to send overseas.

Forty years old, Richard was in his element. In September 1198, commanding a small force of his battle-hardened mercenaries, Richard routed the main French army near Gisors. The king led the flight across the River Epte and, as the bridge broke under the weight of the French knights, Philip himself 'drank of the river'. For his part, though unhorsed, Richard captured three French knights while Philip was hauled up by his heels on the opposite bank. Four months later he signed a five-year truce with Philip. New trouble was looming among his fractious vassals in the duchy of Aquitaine. Adhémar, viscount of Limoges, was among the ringleaders. On 26 March, directing the siege of the viscount's castle of Chalus, Richard was fearfully wounded by a crossbow bolt. The wound festered and on 6 April, after days of agony, Richard died, the victim of gangrene. He bequeathed his jewels and the bulk of his personal treasure to his German nephew, Otto of Brunswick; the remainder of this treasure he left to be divided among his servants and the poor; the 'realm of England and all his other lands' went to John.

The will of a dying king weighed heavily in the choice of his successor; especially when, as in this case, the law was not clear. Richard's territories, stretching from a northern frontier with Scotland to the foothills of the Pyrenees and a border with Spanish Navarre in the south, were held by a cluster of titles and governed by a patchwork of local customs and traditions. The crown of England was the prize title, followed by the golden rose ducal coronet of Normandy and the great ducal sword of Aquitaine. It was as count of Poitou that Richard claimed the allegiance of Adhémar of Limoges; in the family's hereditary land of Anjou itself he ruled by virtue of his title as count. And the law governing the succession varied from territory to territory.

In England there was no accepted consensus. Fashionable legal opinion was tending to the view that descent of the crown lay in the senior male line, what today we would call strict primogeniture. On this basis the haughty, twelve-year-old Arthur, posthumous son of John's older brother Geoffrey duke of Brittany, had the better claim. Archbishop Hubert Walter of Canterbury urged that it be accepted. The other chief adviser of the dead Richard, the justiciar William Marshal, declared for John. By the ancient custom of Normandy 'the younger son is nearer to the land of his father than is a nephew'; moreover, their dead master King Richard had made his will plain. The archbishop warned him he would live to rue the decision, we are told. But the choice was inevitable. Arthur, a ward of the king of France, had never been to England and despised the English.

As soon as news of his brother's death reached him John rode straight to Chinon on the Loire, the traditional treasury of the Angevins. Arthur's mother, Constance of Brittany, entrusted her son to the care of King Philip, raised an army of Bretons and at Angers on Easter Day convened an assembly of the barons of Anjou, Maine and Touraine, who pledged their allegiance to Arthur as their count. On 25 April at Rouen John was solemnly invested as duke of Normandy while in England a council of the nobility held at Northampton under William Marshal and the archbishop declared for John as their king. He was crowned in Westminster Abbey on 27 May 1199. Significantly, Isabelle of Gloucester was not at his side. The church had always contested the legality of their union and John now wanted freedom of manoeuvre in the royal marriage market. Two panels of bishops were appointed, one in England and one in Aquitaine: both ruled the king to be a single man. At this time he was contemplating a Portuguese marriage, to counterbalance the friendship between Philip of France and Navarre which threatened Aquitaine in the south.

The immediate problem in the summer of 1199 was the rebellious condition of Anjou, Maine and Touraine. The territories divided Normandy from Aquitaine, held for John by his famous mother the septuagenarian Queen Eleanor, and had to be secured. Volatile and moody, John was a sound strategist and capable of vigorous military action. This the English barons would one day learn to their cost. Now he ignored a French raid into Normandy and campaigned southwards into Maine so successfully that in September Constance and Arthur signed peace terms at Le Mans. Outmanoeuvred, Philip also came to the negotiating table. At the Treaty of Le Goulet on 22 May 1200 John was recognized as heir to Richard's territories in France, in return for the homage due to King Philip as his overlord there and the payment of a relief (a standard feudal inheritance tax) of 20,000 marks. John was now undisputed lord of the Angevin lands in France; Portuguese ambassadors were at his court and prospects for the southern alliance looked promising. Above all it seemed that the French king had abandoned his attempt to drive the Angevins from France. But Philip was a man dedicated to a mission.

In more than two centuries his family had amounted to very little. The founding father, Hugh Capet, had been tolerated as king by men more powerful than he and determined to remain sovereign in their own lands. While the Capetians held small domains around Paris, Norman dukes proud of their Viking ancestry controlled northern France, while the dukes of Aquitaine ruled an immense territory which had once been a kingdom in its own right. Lesser men like the counts of Anjou rapaciously extended their own bailiwicks with barely a nod in the direction of Paris.

Yet all these ambitious barons honoured the fine old political fiction that, as heir to the great Charlemagne, the Capetian at Paris was their feudal overlord. Almost all went through the ritual of homage; some even paid reliefs to enter on their inheritances. Meanwhile, the Capetians methodically produced sons, had them crowned in the sacred city of Rheims with the holy oil presented in legendary times to St Rémy by the Blessed Virgin, and stolidly extended their modest influence wherever possible. By degrees they accumulated attributes of actual power to the aura of kingship which none denied them.

Then, in the mid-twelfth century Henry of Anjou, father of Richard and John, united north and south, Normans and Aquitainians, and added them to the crown of England. Half of France was under western Europe's strongest ruler and he the king of a foreign power. This was the nightmare clouding the inheritance of Philip when he came to the throne, just 15 years old, in 1180. His own insignificant appearance and youthful inexperience suggested that the dynasty was doomed to mediocrity. But the slow seepage of custom and precedents accumulated by his forefathers had filled a reservoir of royal prestige and power, and Philip soon revealed qualities of political cunning and determination fully equal to the sometimes neurotic brilliance of the Angevins. The destruction of their power in France was his lifetime's work. It was John's misfortune to face the first king with the resources, ability and tenacity of a world-class statesman.

The treaty of Le Goulet was a classic Capetian stratagem. Couched in traditional feudal terms which no reasonable man could dispute, in fact it strengthened a legalistic obligation which could be developed as a lever of power. Even King Henry II had done homage for his French lands. Homage was, after all, the cement of feudal political society. Should he refuse it to his French overlord, his own barons might jib at swearing allegiance to him. But neither Henry nor Richard had dreamed of paying any reliefs. Money always had to be extracted and no French king of their acquaintance had dared raise the matter. At Le Goulet, for all its conventional technicalities, King John made a binding admission of the French king's once theoretical overlordship which was sealed for the first time in cash.

English critics of the treaty dubbed their king John Softsword. The borders of Normandy gleamed garishly with the fresh-hewn stone of his brother's new castles, with Château Gaillard, Richard's 'saucy castle' on the Seine, the queen of them all. To replace the often reluctant and amateurish feudal levies Richard had mobilized flying columns of professional mercenaries. Breaking the convention of spring-and-summer fighting he had waged war all year round, looming up out of winter mists to steal unfair victories from startled and indignant enemies. But Normandy had been temporarily bankrupted in the process. As Richard cheerfully bragged, 'there's not a penny left in Chinon', and John discovered how nearly the jest spoke the truth. Richard's five-year truce with Philip of France had died with him, and John still needed the time. 20,000 marks paid of necessity by the long-suffering English would anger the taxpayers and might be a legal hostage to the future. It was, however, a small price to pay compared with the costs of continuing the war. To quote a modern biographer, 'if John had tried a firm sword it would have shattered in his hand'.

'The Coronation of Edward the Confessor', E. W. Tristram's reconstruction of the thirteen-century original from a watercolour copy of 1819. The original was part of a series of wall paintings in the Painted Chamber, Westminster destroyed by the fire in the Palace of Westminster in 1834. The room with its decorations had been the bedchamber of King Henry III who was a devotee of his saintly English predecessor, canonized in the 1160s. The caption is in the royal language, French; the scene one of regal splendour as much as pious devotion.

Hen. secundus

Johes Rex

Henricus III

Chateau Gaillard, a fine nineteenth-century watercolour view of one of Europe's most impressive fortified sites. Built by Richard I in the 1190s, it originally commanded an extensive complex of defences, causeways, river barrages and towers, which virtually covered this stretch of the Seine valley.

(*Left*) Henry II; Richard I with the leopards of England; John; and his son Henry III who built a shrine for Edward the Confessor. Matthew Paris (d. 1259) who painted this as one of the illustrations for his St Alban's Chronicle, systematically blackened King John's name. A staunch partisan of the baronial cause, Paris depicts John, alone of the four, sitting not on a throne but a folding campaign stool, his crown very precariously perched over one ear, and half blocking the view of the church. He looks altogether a shifty and disreputable character.

'King John Hunting'. The artist of this delightful thirteenth-century illumination shows the king riding to hounds with, apparently, his hawk returning to her master even as the dogs prepare to pull down a stag. This laudable, if not actually realistic, drive for comprehensiveness gives us a well-populated rabbit warren in the foreground and, in the background, trees pruned to yield specific types of timber.

This 'Mouth of Hell' comes from a manuscript produced for Henry of Blois, Bishop of Winchester, some time in the 1150s, in the cathedral's renowned scriptorium. The caption reads: 'Here is Hell and the Angel that closes the Gate.' The theme was a favourite one with medieval patrons but the dire forecasts seem to have had little effect on people's conduct. During the reign of John, the realm of England was for years under a papal interdict, with little sign of protest.

'Pope and Emperor' detail from Andrea di Buonaiuto's fresco for the Spanish Chapel, Florence, done in the fourteenth century to celebrate the Dominican Order, founded by St Dominic. This majestic allegory of the medieval world view, although painted a century or so after John's death, interprets to us how the upper echelons of the social order, at least, liked to see themselves. Side by side sit the spiritual and temporal powers – the Pope supported by cardinals, archbishops and abbots, the Emperor by kings and

counts and other great lords. At their feet the community of Christendom is portrayed
as Christ's sheep, looking for guidance and prey to heretical wolves. Round about snap
the hounds of God (Dominicans – Latin 'Domini canes'). This was the world in which
the thunderbolts of King and Pope sought to intimidate English society at the time of
Magna Carta.

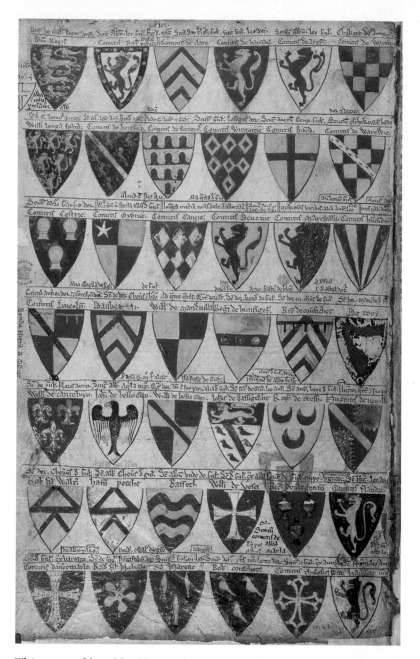

This page of heraldic blazons by Matthew Paris starts with the royal arms. Also identifiable are those of the earls of Pembroke (William Marshal), Salisbury (William Longsword), Surrey (de Warenne) and d'Aubigny, as well as those of Ranulf, Earl of Chester, all of whom were John's supporters. Among his enemies, Essex (de Mandeville), Hereford (Bohm), and Clare are represented.

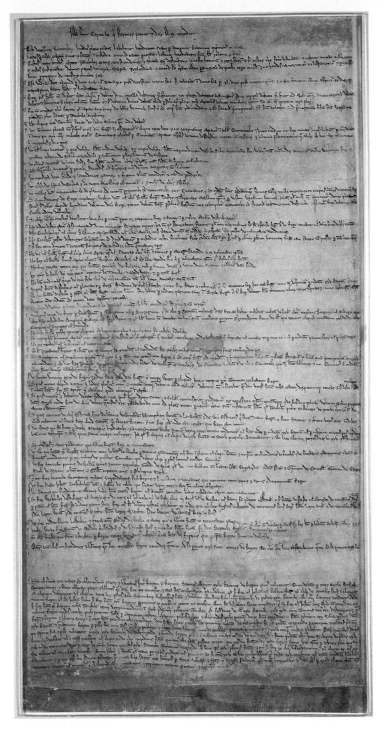

The Articles of the Barons, which formed the basis for negotiations leading to Magna Carta itself.

A modern diorama reconstruction of the scene as it might have appeared at Runnymede.

Sir Edward Coke, James I's chief justice of the common pleas and then of the King's Bench (1606–16) and from 1620 MP. His *The Institutes of the Laws of England and Reports of Sir Edward Coke Kt. in English in Thirteen Parts* . . . made Magna Carta central to the English Civil War and later to the struggle of the American Colonies against Parliament.

By his own wish, King John was buried in Worcester Cathedral before the altar of St Wulfstan, the last English bishop (seated here at the king's left shoulder). At his right is an earlier English saint, Oswald. Considering the trouble St Edward's memory had caused him, it is not surprising that John wanted nothing to do with him. Nevertheless, this tomb slab is not the only hint that John shared his subjects' fascination with the old English past. With his son it became something of a mania.

Peace in the north seemingly assured, in July John embarked on a progress through Aquitaine, southwards towards the Pyrenees. He commissioned a return embassy to the Portuguese court. As he moved south, receiving homage from counts and nobles, inspecting castle garrisons and relishing the luxuries of southern cuisine, the city of Angoulême in central Aquitaine was preparing for a brilliant marriage between Isabella of Angoulême and Hugh le Brun, lord of Lusignan and of La Marche. The marriage could have dire consequences, for their united lands would form a block of territory stretching from royal France in the east to the Atlantic coast and splitting the duchy of Aquitaine virtually in half. The Lusignans were no friends of the Plantagenets and John had cause to worry.

He was well south of Bordeaux when, in mid August, he retraced his route to arrive at Angoulême in time to join the throng of fashionable guests at the wedding. The bride was a dazzling young beauty, barely in her teens. John's first sight of her, we are told, was as she was led into the church by her father. By his authority as overlord of both Angoulême and Lusignan he stopped the proceedings and took the bridegroom's place at the altar rail. So goes the story, and the actual events may have matched it. Certainly John and Isabella were married only days after his arrival in the city. John had broken the dangerous Angoulême-Lusignan accord and acquired a bewitching bride: passion and policy seemed married that day. People were to say he had, literally, been bewitched – even historians think he was in love. But he had won, too, a remorseless enemy. Count Hugh left Angoulême swearing vengeance.

John felt in control, always a dangerous mood for him. He had won himself a beautiful child-bride, forced Philip of France to terms and cowed the troublesome lords of Poitou. In the first year of his reign he had toured most of his continental lands; the Angevin realm was at peace. But in Aquitaine Queen Eleanor's agents reported renewed discontent among the Poitevins. She sent couriers across the Channel, urging her son to come and rally his supporters. John, in characteristic style, preferred instead to humiliate his enemies still further. He ordered his officials to harry the Lusignans and 'do them all the harm they could'. Punitive measures of this kind were the standard way for an overlord to discipline unruly vassals. In England, as yet, there was no one to contest such overbearing action. In France the case was different. The Lusignans appealed against John as duke of Aquitaine to their supreme overlord, the king of France himself.

It seemed, however, that John had correctly assessed the political situation. King Philip had domestic problems and did not wish to undermine his treaty with John. He had the power to summon him, as lord of Aquitaine, to answer the complaints of his under-vassals in the royal court of France. Instead he accepted an assurance that the Lusignans would receive a fair hearing in the Aquitainian court. Confident that the situation in France was back to normal, that he like his brother and father before him could flout the theoretical supremacy of Paris as an outmoded legal quibble, John went back on his assurance. Seething with frustration, Philip recognized that he now faced the great showdown with the Angevins at a time not of his own choosing. If he left the Lusignans to their fate Capetian claims to the sovereignty in France would be exploded; if he challenged John war could be guaranteed and victory was far from certain.

Grasping the nettle, Philip did issue a summons against John to stand trial as a vassal of France for failing to render justice to his sub-vassals of Lusignan. Although it was issued against him in his capacity as the duke of Aquitaine, Philip's summons to John as a vassal fascinated contemporaries. Whatever the legal technicalities, here was a king solemnly claiming jurisdiction over another. At Le Goulet John had formally acknowledged Philip to be his overlord in France, but that was a very different matter from standing in the well of his court as an accused lawbreaker. The hearing was set to open on Tuesday 28 April 1202. The barons of France assembled in formal session, for the duke of Aquitaine could only be tried before a court of his peers. The appointed time came and went.

John had promised to attend the hearing and even to hand over two castles as security. He fulfilled neither undertaking. Now, at the behest of King Philip, the barons formally pronounced him contumacious for failing to obey the citation of his liege lord. He was declared to have forfeited his fiefs of Aquitaine, Poitou and Anjou; the king proclaimed that the mutual ties of feudal obligation between him and John were severed. Next he knighted Arthur of Brittany and invested him with Angevin lands which the court had adjudged forfeit. In July 1202 Arthur did homage. Meanwhile, French troops invaded Normandy.

There was no legal justification for such an attack. It was not John 'Duke of Normandy' but John 'Duke of Aquitaine' who was contumacious. But Normandy was the keystone of Angevin power. John was confident that the great border castles would protect the duchy and marched south to deal with the Lusignans, now fighting alongside Arthur, who were converging on the small force led by his mother. Approaching eighty, the shadow of her legendary beauty still able to inspire men to follow her imperious will, Queen Eleanor had raised herself from her sickbed in defence of the Angevin heartland.

On 29 July, just south of Le Mans, John was met by a desperate courier with news that the Queen was in imminent danger of capture at the castle of Mirebeau, eighty miles to the south. Forty-eight hours later, at the head of a crack body of horsemen, John had raised the siege and was master of the place. His mother freed, all the rebel leaders, Arthur at their head, were his prisoners. Contemporaries considered it near miraculous: as in 1200, King Philip withdrew from Normandy. Angevin power had never seemed greater. It was a triumph to match anything achieved by Richard. John threw it away.

Vindictive in victory and mistrustful of loyalty, he shocked opinion with the ill-treatment of the prisoners and drove new men into rebellion by insulting those who had helped him to his triumph. As for Arthur, he was never seen in public again. Given the temper of the times, he could hardly expect liberty. The legendary name he bore made him a hero to the Celtic Bretons; King Philip had dubbed him lord of John's French inheritance; having made war on his own grandmother, this arrogant fifteen-year-old was clearly no plaster saint. He had played an unscrupulous hand for high stakes and lost. Rumour soon reported that John had killed him. Evidence was never produced, though it seems that William de Braose, one of John's cronies, later claimed to have been present at Rouen castle on the night that the king murdered his nephew in a drunken rage. Not even Philip ever formally accused John of the crime, contenting himself with pointedly agreeing to talk terms when Arthur was produced. Few mourned, and none was surprised at the disappearance. Yet the killing of a kinsman was dirty work for a king and John's reputation fell another notch.

By the autumn of 1202 John was master of all the rebel strongholds in Poitou. Many of the minor leaders of the rebellion had died in England in an attempt to take over Corfe castle, where they were incarcerated. Arthur and the two chief Lusignans were closely confined. But a new threat was posed by John's former allies of Mirebeau, entirely alienated by his contemptuous treatment of them. To counterbalance this he now reinstated the Lusignans in exchange for hostages and oaths of allegiance. With John, such cynical horse-trading passed for statecraft. William Marshal and other advisers looked on, horrified, as he resurrected the rebellion buried only months before. Abandoning their hostages, the Lusignans were soon hunting once again with the Bretons, leaderless but united in fury by the rumours now circulating of Arthur's murder.

John never learnt to win the loyalty of his barons, whether English or French, and he lacked the force of personality and habit of success with which Richard had held men loyal even against their will. The triumph of Mirebeau was followed by months of desultory, ill-directed activity. In the spring of 1203 King Philip was able to make a progress down the Loire through the heart of Angevin territory, supporting the rebels against John and enjoying the tribute due to a liege lord. Returning to the attack in Normandy, he won still more startling successes; Vaudreuil, a key fortress only a few miles down river from Rouen, surrendered with scarcely a fight.

So far John's strategy in France had been based on the assumption that Normandy was secure. Its castles were up-to-date and the defenders were, for the most part, hardened mercenaries. Rouen, one of the greatest cities in all France, was steadfast in its loyalty, thanks to the civic and trading privileges guaranteed it by ducal charters. Many of the duchy's great barons held lands in England, just as English barons had family lands in Normandy.

Yet the old ties, dating from the time of the Norman conquest of England, were seriously weakened. The proud days when Norman dukes of the old line boasted a royal crown as well as the ducal coronet were long past. The Angevin house, mere counts by origin, were considered outside upstarts who tyrannized over the duchy as they did over the kingdom. Richard compelled loyalty by force of character and military prowess. His use of mercenaries was resented but had to be borne as a military necessity. But John, 'that feckless young man', openly favoured his mercenary captains above the Norman nobility. He preferred their company, appointed them to positions of trust and responsibility and allowed them to pillage the countryside to pay their men. 'King John lost the love of his people here in Normandy', wrote a contemporary, 'because that wolf Lupescar [the most hated mercenary captain] treated them as though he were in enemy territory.' In place of the honoured lord protecting grateful vassals against the invader, John himself seemed like a hostile commander fighting to maintain a beachhead in no man's land. In the autumn of 1203 King Philip prepared for the final offensive.

With all the ceremony such an occasion demanded, and with a vast train of siege engines, he led his army to the walls of Château Gaillard.

The great castle was well supplied, well garrisoned and commanded by a professional English castellan utterly loyal to John as his commander-in-chief. By this time the duke-king was travelling everywhere with a heavily armed escort. He found little support among his barons and announced his intention of going to England to raise an army, certain that Gaillard would hold out until his return in the spring. On 3 December he slipped out of Rouen before daybreak; on the 5th he took ship from Barfleur.

John spent Christmas at Canterbury with his young queen. Men said that his infatuation with her sapped his energies, but in January he was presiding over a council of barons at Oxford. Many held lands in Normandy; a few who did not privately wondered whether their duty to aid the king in his wars entailed service overseas. Almost all held their lands in return for obligation to supply armed knights when required. As always, John preferred money to pay professionals, but he was granted by the assembled magnates a composition payment (called '*scutage*', literally 'shield money'), at the rate of two and a half marks per knight's service owing. It was the highest such grant ever made. Levies on towns and merchant shipping and the sale of honours and privileges brought in further funds, and supplies were sent across the Channel in preparation for the spring campaign.

The king seemed in confident mood. On 6 March he gave orders for the trapping of game in the New Forest to be shipped over to Normandy with his hunting gear, dogs and falcons, to ensure his sport during lulls in the fighting. Château Gaillard had held out for six months and was provisioned for a few weeks more. Rouen was heavily fortified and the west of Normandy as yet untouched by war. It was here that John planned to mobilize his counter-attack while Philip battered the walls of castle and city. The strategy was nullified by the shattering news that Gaillard had fallen – on the very day, in fact, that John was arranging his sporting facilities.

The siege and capture of Château Gaillard is one of the epics of medieval history. At the end of six months and two weeks the garrison numbered just 156 effectives. Even then the stubborn and emaciated defenders refused to make a formal surrender and had to be systematically disarmed. Worse was to follow. With a surprising flash of insight King Philip by-passed the heavily fortified defences of Rouen, marched through southern Normandy and joined forces with his Bretons in the west. By June he had taken most of the strongpoints of the duchy and, by promising to confirm the town's privileges, had won the submission of Rouen itself.

The loss of Normandy would haunt John for the rest of his reign. Perhaps it was, in the long perspective of history, inevitable. But whereas King John was across the Channel laying sophisticated strategical schemes, his brother Richard would undoubtedly have been on the spot, directing the action and leading the assault. Over the next ten years John was to devote much of his time to recovering his family's position in France, to little effect. The English found themselves taxed as never before to replenish an exchequer emptied by Richard and strained by wars. The end of the Norman connection meant that the baronage were less willing than ever to assist John's war overseas. The king's favouritism towards his mercenary captains, tolerable when exercised to the discomfort of Norman lords in time of war, became insufferable when those same mercenaries were given positions of profit and honour in England. Above all, the loss of Normandy and the French occupation of much else of the Angevin territory overseas meant that the king was in England most of his time, directing the government in person and intervening at will in his barons' conduct of their affairs. Almost all the excesses of royal power complained of in Magna Carta had been committed by the governments of King Richard. But while he remained out of the country opposition could press home its case without resorting to rebellion. With John the king was always present and became the target of discontent.

The roots of the great charter of liberties were traced even by contemporaries back to the authoritarian but efficient rule of John's father. The systems of government then introduced were developed to the point of excess by the harassed officials who governed England under incessant demands for cash from his brother. In an age when office-holders were expected to recoup their expenses and to make a comfortable profit from the revenues they collected, corruption, as we understand the term, was built into the system. Within their own domains the great magnates had nevertheless enjoyed a pretty free hand, despite encroachments made by the establishing of a royal, national regime of law. When financial exactions, central administration and royal justice were pressed with ever greater efficiency under the personal direction of a king whom few had cause to respect and many had cause to fear, repetitions of the baronial solidarity which had brought the humiliation of William Longchamp were, perhaps, predictable. That they produced a constitutional upheaval whose tremors are still detectable today was the result of events and developments some of which are traced in the next few chapters.

2

THE SMACK OF
FIRM GOVERNMENT

WITH the Norman ports in French hands, John had to rethink his entire strategy. Moreover, King Philip was renewing his attacks into Aquitaine. Poitou was quickly overrun up to the walls of La Rochelle before the French advance faltered. While the port held for John a major English expedition was still a practical proposition, but this would take time and in the meanwhile a French advance into the bordering territory of Angoulême was the logical military move. Politically, however, it was impossible. John held the territory by right of his wife Isabella, a peeress of France, and any intervention by Philip would be met by the outraged opposition of the French baronage, many of whom also held land by marriage.

South of Angoulême the minor lords of Aquitaine were rallying to John. There was no special love for the king of England, merely alarm at the prospect of exchanging his distant rule for the intrusive administration of Paris. English treasure, proceeds of the funds collected for the aborted Norman campaign, now poured into Bordeaux to pay for a Gascon army to hold the line and spear a counter-attack.

The loss of Normandy had altered the logistics as well as the strategy of overseas campaigning. For well over a century, what we might call the Anglo-Norman Channel had been the effective preserve of the king-dukes. Merchant shipping was commandeered as need arose for military expeditions. Henry II had a fast royal galley in constant readiness and the Cinque ports were required to provide a military service of fifty-seven ships for fifteen days a year. But such ad hoc arrangements could not cope with the new situation. Having lost command of the seaways John needed an effective naval force of his own – a royal navy, in short. He set about raising one with an energy and attention to detail which characterized his whole conduct of government business.

In 1205, he granted the Cinque ports a charter which confirmed their privileges, but also restated their military obligations. The ports remained an important element in coastal defences but were less effective as an aggressive force. The ships they provided were, after all, merchantmen and their brief period of wartime service was bound to be somewhat amateurish. Preparing for his land campaigns John always, so far as possible, aimed to substitute professional mercenary soldiers for the feudal levies owed as part of their tenure by his tenants-in-chief. So now, reshaping England's naval forces, he wanted custom-built fighting units at sea. Keels for several new galleys were laid down at London yards in 1205 and building continued apace throughout the reign. Between 1209 and 1212, for example, twenty new galleys and thirty transports and other ships were launched at the king's expense. For the first time in her history England was a maritime power.

A stream of orders and directives, still filed away in London's Public Record Office, reveal the urgency and efficiency with which the new force was built up. Harassed minor officials found themselves ordered 'in the same hour that these letters reach you' to labour night and day in the king's service to see to the completion of the job specified. At the head of the hierarchy chief keepers of the ports maintained supervision of the merchant arm of the services, acted as overseers for the technical specifications of the royal naval establishment and, in short, fulfilled many of the functions of an admiralty. Richard had established a maritime depot near the royal castle of Porchester on the Solent. John developed it with magazines to house stores and a new breakwater to harbour his valuable fighting ships. For 750 years Portsmouth held pride of place among England's royal naval dockyards.

The chief commander of the battle fleet was William Longsword, earl of Salisbury and half-brother to the king – the only one of his barons, it has been said, with whom he was on back-slapping terms of intimacy. In May 1212 at Damme near Bruges the royal navy, commanded by Longsword, destroyed an immense invasion fleet assembled there by Philip of France. It had taken John barely seven years to create this new and formidable force which now delivered England's first great naval victory.

While we can admire such efficiency – it did, after all, play a vital role in the country's defence – it reflected a growth in government bureaucracy which men at the time resented as much as the citizen of today does the intrusive apparatus of the modern state.

Even before John's accession, England was the most thoroughly governed state in Europe. Chancery officials had perfected formulas for royal writs, based on sophisticated Anglo-Saxon examples, which were models of brevity and precision. Officials throughout the country, from humble port-reeves responsible for harbour dues and customs, to sheriffs administering whole counties, implemented central directives with an effectiveness unmatched by continental regimes. The legal system applied routine procedures or 'writs of course', to matters once ruled by traditional local custom. The court of the exchequer administered royal revenues with an efficiency which, it has been said, was 'the wonder and envy of Europe'.

John's great officials of state – chancellor, justiciar, treasurer – were professionals fascinated by the possibilities of the machine they controlled. Lucid and detailed handbooks of procedure from his father's time, while displaying a characteristically English respect for tradition, set a pattern for pragmatic innovation. The servants of the king began to acquire the esprit de corps of a true civil service. The best efforts of an unruly baronage would prove unable to strangle the sturdy infant. It was during John's reign that the royal chancery began the most characteristic practice of bureaucracy – the systematic keeping of records.

The machine creaked occasionally. While functions of government might be clearly distinguished, the personnel that carried them out were not. All ministers were officials of the royal court and dealt with business of all kinds as it came to hand or as the king directed. Government was the monarch's personal business, and where functions were not clearly defined confusion could arise. The fact remains that any English king interested in administration had a powerful apparatus at his disposal. To his subjects' great dismay John loved the work. As the abbot of Coggeshall in Essex noted, 'the king governed indefatigably'.

In the months immediately following the collapse of Normandy and in the midst of planning the expedition to Gascony, he initiated a full-scale reform of the currency. At the same time, he issued a tariff of standard fees payable at the chancery for the issue of documents under the Great Seal. Authenticated charters and a variety of other official documents were increasingly valued as titles to lands and privileges, but for years past the charges made by the clerks had risen extravagantly. John made reductions by as much as 90%

but in return ruled that only charters he had confirmed would be accepted by the courts.

A copy of every document was kept, each parchment sheet being stitched to the foot of the one before. Swelling relentlessly, the royal archive rolls, carried on packhorse or wagon, like so many short lengths of piping, were just part of the baggage train of miscellaneous paraphernalia – kitchen stoves and utensils, the king's bed (and dressing-gown – John is the first Englishman known to have worn one), the chalices and furniture of his chapel, his bathtub and personal wardrobe – which followed John from royal manor to castle on his incessant tours of England. This was personal government in action. For all the divinity that hedged a medieval king a surprising number of his subjects could have glimpsed John of England at least once in their life.

Not the least unusual aspect of John's reign, compared with those of his predecessors, was the fact that after 1204 he was in England most of the time. His father had followed a yearly itinerary which included half France, while his brother spent most of his reign in Palestine, in an imperial gaol or on campaign in Normandy. By contrast, John barely seemed to leave the country. Law cases which had been settled in the justiciar's court in Westminster under his predecessors were now heard by the king himself *in coram rege*, the royal quarters wherever the king happened to be at the time.

Administrative acts and rulings were all now registered in chancery documents – little was left to memory and nothing left to chance. Thanks to the efficient management of the royal exchequer, John was able to keep a firmer grip on the royal finances and on the sheriffs who administered them in the regions than ever before.

The revenue was run on what, in modern terms, amounted to a franchise basis. The sheriffs were rewarded not by a salary but by the difference between the dues they were able to collect and the annual levy demanded by the exchequer. This levy or 'farm' fixed under John's predecessors remained unchanged for year after year while, because of inflation, the money value of the services due to the king in the shires naturally increased. Thus the sheriff's profits increased. In an attempt to restore the situation Richard's government had charged certain sheriffs a crementum over and above the fixed farm.

At a time when the concept of inflation was barely understood, the royal claims to need increasing revenues merely to keep pace with legitimate expenditure tended to be regarded as evidence of irresponsibility, extravagance or simple greed. Moreover, given his ambitions to reconquer his lost French lands, John's revenue needs were increasing in real as well as relative terms. He extended the demand for the crementum to all the shires and imposed additional incremental payments. The sheriffs' response was predictable – to meet these new obligations they increased their exactions wherever they could. Thus in clause 25 of Magna Carta we find: 'All counties, hundreds and trithings (i.e. the ridings of Yorkshire and Lincolnshire, etc.) excepting those of our demesne manors (those directly owned by the king himself) shall remain at the old rents without any additional payment (incremento).'

There was no doubt about the profitability of the office of sheriff, men paid well for the appointment. The problem was that no one was clear as to the real value of shire revenues, since the farms had been established in the reign of Henry II. The country was clearly prospering, but despite the measures by the administration to increase yields the king's share of the revenues was less than it should be. The royal administration introduced various reforms to increase the yield to the exchequer.

One outcome of the loss of Normandy was to increase the effectiveness of the government machine in England. Clerks who had held jobs such as castle paymasters in the duchy returned to appointments in the English administration, some of them as joint sheriffs of the larger or more populous counties. One such was Brian de Lisle, who in 1205 was appointed castellan of Knaresborough and rose to become chief forester of Nottinghamshire and sheriff of Yorkshire. De Lisle appears to have been nothing more than a loyal if tough government servant. But as baronial opposition mounted John began to give shires, castles and forest wardenships to another group of French refugees – the mercenary captains whose professional support had proved more reliable than the feudal loyalty the king reckoned he could demand from his barons.

Their job was to clamp down on any hint of rebellion. Like the sheriffs they displaced they took their pay by ruthless exploitation of shire revenues. It was an example of the way in which John managed to transform accepted operations of government into apparent tyranny. Traditional though it was, the system of farmed revenues tended to oppression even in the hands of reasonable officials; by handing it over to men whose profession had hardened them, whose ambition encouraged them and who as foreigners were doubly open to hostility, he ensured that his government, from being resented no more than any other medieval government, earned particular loathing. While the populace feared them as they did all royal officers, the baronage hated them as foreign newcomers who had edged them out of their natural preserve as king's servants.

Few of these interlopers were more hated than the clan of Gerard d'Athée, named in Clause 50 of the Great Charter itself, in which John promised to remove them all from any office in England. Appointed sheriff of Gloucester and Herefordshire, in 1209 Gerard was succeeded by his nephew Engelard de Cigogné, who later became constable of Windsor Castle and warden of the nearby forest of Odiham. A more distant relation of Gerard's, Philip Marc, possibly provided the ballad-mongers with a model for the sheriff of Nottingham in the Robin Hood legends. His appointment as sheriff ran concurrently with the career of Robert Hod, 'fugitive', recorded in the Yorkshire county rolls and proposed by one modern historian as the origin of Robin himself. Marc was appointed sheriff of Nottinghamshire and Derbyshire and castellan of Nottingham in 1209 and had custody of Sherwood Forest itself. Strategically well placed for the north of England and North Wales, Nottinghamshire was also rich in royal demesne lands and forests. As a provincial treasury Nottingham Castle received the proceeds of the levies made in Ireland, Yorkshire and Northumberland for the campaign year of 1210 and would be a vital royalist strongpoint during the civil war.

Up to the middle of John's reign cash revenues, accounted for at the exchequer in Westminster, were stored in the ancient treasury of the Saxon kings at Winchester. The needs of the travelling court had to be supplied by cumbersome and costly convoys of wagon-loads of silver pennies trundling along England's inadequate and often dangerous roads. In 1207 John began a modest policy of decentralization with provincial treasuries at towns such at Bristol in the west and Nottingham in the midlands.

At the same time, the streamlining of government procedures and the placement of John's household officers in positions of administrative responsibility made for an ever tighter royal grip on finance. It became increasingly common for the king's accounts to be heard by officials of the chamber, that is, at the court where the king happened to be, rather than in the exchequer. More and more money accounted for in this way tended not to be convoyed on to Winchester, or even one of the new treasuries, but to be diverted to the king's immediate use. In place of silver pennies, the treasurer received chamber receipts, or writs of liberate – he knew where the money had gone but was of course that much the worse off when having to meet accounts presented by merchants or landowners whose goods or services had been requisitioned in the royal service.

The chamber, once the private accounting department of the royal household but now in process of becoming a department of state, sometimes took receipt of major nation-wide taxes, and it was common for church revenues to be paid into it. Above all, it was to the officials of the chamber that feudal levies, like those paid for the wardship of heirs and heiresses, were handed over. Access to cash was the constant objective of government. The flexibility and quick returns of chamber accounting offered very real practical advantages; the drawback was that it personalized public administration at its most sensitive point – the raising of money.

Taxation is generally resented, even when its objective may be popular, and, as the historian Frank Barlow has observed, John's purposes were seldom popular. From that fateful year of 1204 his overriding objective, amounting almost to an obsession, was the recovery of his family's hereditary lands in France. The English baronage had little interest in the project. Although proud of their Norman descent, very few families still retained actual property interests in the old duchy. The king's oppressive efficiency at raising money was the more resented because of its objective; the fact that the money itself was actually handed over to his personal officers of the chamber merely rubbed salt into the wound of baronial indignation.

So far, it may seem that the chief reason for John's evil reputation was, to use the modern jargon, a matter of perception. There was, unfortunately, rather more to it than that. Vindictive by nature, he could also be brutal. The classic case concerned the fate of William de Braose and his family.

Ruthless and unscrupulous, de Braose held large estates on the marches of Wales where he summarily dealt with any Welsh troubles on his borders. A loyal henchman to King Richard, he was quickly favoured by John, who in 1201 granted him the vast lordship of Limerick in Ireland against 5000 marks to be paid in easy instalments. As a royal favourite William could reasonably hope not to be pressed for payment. The next year William did John a signal service at the capture of Mirebeau when he personally handed over the young Prince Arthur to the king. But he was too close to the royal councils for his own good. The death or disappearance of Arthur under mysterious circumstances started ugly rumours that the king had had him killed, even murdered him with his own hands. It is possible that Braose

31

knew the truth of the matter and may in an unguarded moment have told his wife.

His growing power seems to have given the king pause for thought; in 1208 John determined to bring him to heel. One of his less attractive methods for disciplining his baronage was to demand their children as hostages. When the royal officers arrived to take the Braose children in charge, Matilda, his wife, 'with the sauciness of a woman' we are told by Roger Wendover the chronicler, refused to hand them over with the words: 'I will not deliver up my sons to your lord king John, for he basely murdered his nephew Arthur.'

Over the next two years the Braose lands in Wales were harried by John's new sheriff of Gloucester, Gerard d'Athée; the lands in Ireland were ravaged by an army led by John himself; and William's wife and eldest son, handed over to John by a Scottish laird when they fled north of the border, were in all probability starved to death. At any event they were incarcerated at Windsor and never emerged alive. By this time, William himself had fled to France where he died in exile in 1211. The given pretext for this appalling sequence of events was that William had defaulted on the payments on his 5000-mark debt for Limerick and that when the king's sheriff and other officers had reasonably attempted to distrain upon his lands for the debt he had forcibly resisted.

There is no direct evidence as to the death of Matilda de Braose and her son but the starvation story is found in every chronicle of the period and is probably true. To many barons the fate of de Braose himself must have seemed yet more worrying. Envious they may have been, yet he had been one of the most powerful of all the English baronage and high in royal favour. The terms of the Limerick loan had been repeated in many another case (one baron had been allowed to make repayments for a similar proffer on such generous terms that had they ever been completed the debt would have been discharged in 1917). If such a man could be destroyed by the will of the king, then who at all was safe?

The truth was that John only trusted men who were completely dependent on him. Patronized by his father and more or less openly despised by his brother, he never really grew up. He never learnt the self-assurance of dealing on equal terms with mature men whose personal interests might be at odds with his but who would expect to remain loyal to their king if he played his part within the terms of the mutual feudal bond. The mere fact that the reign was fifteen years old before the opposition united in open rebellion is proof not only of the power of the crown and the extent to which patronage could buy men's compliance but also of a genuine desire among the great families of England to live at peace with the king if at all possible.

According to the nineteenth-century historian J. R. Green, 'Hell itself was defiled by the fouler presence of King John'. His treatment of the de Braose family was vicious even by the standards of the day, and it was not the only well-authenticated example of the king's brutality. In addition he was a notorious womanizer, numbering among his mistresses the widowed Hawise, countess of Aumale, as well as women of low birth named in the records as Suzanne and Clementia. John is known to have had five bastards; a daughter, Joan (who married Llywelyn of Wales) and four sons, hardly remarkable for a medieval monarch and modest indeed when compared with the 21 sired by his great-grandfather Henry I. John's first marriage was contracted without the sanction of the church, while his second wife had to break a troth plighted to another man to marry him. But then King Philip of France had lived for years a bigamist in the eyes of the church. John was accused of debauching the wives of the nobility, yet even this charge has never been fully substantiated. More important to understanding his undeniably evil reputation was the way he mulcted their menfolk.

Money matters

When one reads through Magna Carta it can come as something of a surprise to discover how much of it is concerned with money. The ideals of liberty and freedom so resonant in the later history of the charter seem to have carried less weight with the framers of the document than the detailed, legalistic and now frankly arcane subtleties of 'scutage', 'wardship' and 'relief'. If we exclude the clauses dealing with the liberties of the church, the general principles governing the relation of king and barons and those relating to the interests of the barons' Scottish and Welsh allies, half of what remains have all the inspirational quality of an accountant's appeal against the Inland Revenue. For all its archaic phraseology, Magna Carta reveals itself in its basic concerns as a very modern document.

A major point at issue between the king and his barons concerned scutage, literally shield money, levied on barons in place of the military service owed by the terms of their land tenure.

Every baron held his land by military tenure based on contracts going back to the time of the conquest. By the terms of such a feudal 'lease' the landowner was bound to send a specified number of fully equipped mounted men-at-arms to serve in the royal army when required to do so by the king. The value of an estate or 'honour' was accounted in 'knights' fees' according to the number of such fighting men that it had been estimated its revenues could support at the time of the conquest. The knights raised were expected to serve for 40 days. The baron holding directly from the king, the 'tenant-in-chief', might sub-infeudate (i.e. sub-let) land to lesser men on condition that they would themselves answer the royal call-up or send a competent substitute.

From an early period it had been possible for a baron to make a cash payment equivalent to the cost to the king of raising fully equipped mercenaries, instead of sending some or all of his own tenants to the wars. He recovered the money from the rents of his estates or by levying his sub-tenants. Over the years various factors led to reassessments of service owed (Latin, *servitium debitum*), generally in the barons' favour. A tenant-in-chief made his own arrangements with the royal officers; some sent men-at-arms for part of the service owing and paid cash for the remainder. Gradually the fractional quota of knights sent came to be accepted as the actual full *servitium debitum*. Estates changed hands by marriage or their tenure changed with successive sub-infeudations, so the service owed changed again. With improvements in agriculture, the clearance of forest lands, whether authorized or not, and improved exploitation of land such as the pasturing of sheep on waste grazing-land, the value of properties increased. Knight service increasingly became a book-keeping anachronism relating neither to the original assessment nor to the real value of the land.

The king's problems were compounded by a decline in the value of money. Theoretically, scutage payments enabled the king to recruit mercenary knights to fill the quotas of the exempted landowner. This may have been possible in the early 1100s when the system was introduced, but while the value of money gradually declined, the scutage rate stayed fixed. King Richard made a small increase. John, to the ire of his barons, raised it still further, but he never managed to establish an economic rate. The daily wage for a knight was three times as high as it had been in his father's day, but his attempt in 1213-14 to levy a scutage at three times the traditional rate was met with blank refusals. John therefore resorted to various devices to increase the yield of the ageing tax. He levied it far more frequently than his predecessors, and on at least one occasion for a campaign which never took place. Since the barons made a profit by paying rather than serving, John followed Richard's example of imposing a fine or surcharge over and above the scutage rate.

No doubt John's demands were rapacious, and the policies they were to pay for unpopular, but the redress the barons aimed to impose at Runnymede was beyond reason. Clause 12, one of the most famous of the Charter, laid down that no scutage might be levied at all 'unless by the common consent of our kingdom'. This was clean contrary to feudal law and custom. The barons held their land in exchange for military service; scutage was merely its money equivalent. Carried to its logical conclusion, the clause meant that the baron held his land outright. The clause was omitted from reissues of the Charter.

Scutage was just one of numerous feudal levies allowed to the king. On the death of a tenant-in-chief holding by military tenure, his successor had to pay a 'relief'. £100 per barony was considered a reasonable rate but, needless to say, John generally charged more; indeed, according to one recent historian, 'there seems to be no doubt whatever that John charged exorbitant reliefs throughout his reign'. Then there were the aids – gifts of money which he could demand on three recognized occasions – to ransom himself if captured in war; for the expenses of knighting his eldest son; and on the marriage of his eldest daughter. Kings might ask for donations or aids on other occasions, but these, as even John recognized, depended on the concession of the barons.

In addition an unscrupulous king could make large profits from his rights of wardship and marriage. A juvenile heir, incapable of his feudal military service, had to yield the management of his estates to a royal agent and such agencies were cynically sold to the highest bidders, who squeezed all they could from the wardship during the heir's minority. An heiress or widow could marry only with the king's consent, on the theory that her lands might otherwise go to one of his enemies. Naturally, such consent had to be bought. Just as the Tory regime of 1980s Britain balanced its books by selling public utilities to private monopolies, the Angevin kings made ends meet as best they could by mulcting to the full those assets which the law and their control of public policy put into their power. None was more adept or ruthless in pursuing his rights than John. Much of Magna Carta was concerned with the bridling of these aspects of royal government. The fact that the system, even when stretched to its utmost, could not bridge the gap between expenditure and income led to the exploration of new modes of taxation.

CHURCHMEN, CHARTERS
AND POLITICS

Accoording to an earlier tradition of scholarship, Magna Carta might never have seen the light of day had it not been for the church. Historians had tended to accept a chronicle account that the idea of setting their grievances in the form of a charter had been suggested to the barons by the archbishop of Canterbury, Stephen Langton. The story occurs in the chronicle of Roger of Wendover and because it is both detailed and, nowadays, once again accorded a degree of respect, it is perhaps worth giving it at some length.

The antiquarian archbishop

The occasion was an assembly in London in August 1213 of a great concourse of lay and ecclesiastical magnates to discuss the state of the realm and the procedures to be observed in the situation created by the ending of the years of a papal interdict. The month before, at Winchester, Archbishop Langton had absolved King John from his personal excommunication. At that time, the king swore that he would love and defend the church; that he would abolish bad laws and restore good ones, 'such as those of King Edward'; that he would guarantee every man his rights, and that he would give every man justice according to the proper judgements of his own courts. Now, in London, the archbishop held a great service in St Paul's during the course of which he preached a sermon on the text: 'My heart hath trusted in God'.

In fact, the archbishop was too shrewd a man of affairs to rely entirely on simple faith. He had only been back in the country a few months and already he was proving a master of political reality tactics. By persuading John to swear to judge all men in accordance with the just judgements of his courts – the final promise made by the king to the archbishop at Winchester – Langton went to the heart of one of the chief grievances to be aired in Magna Carta. It was tantamount to a promise to abide by the rule of law and to abandon the ancient royal rights of *vis et voluntas*, a notable concession for any medieval monarch.

After the service, we are told, the archbishop took some of the great men aside for a private conference. He told them of his meeting with the king and then went on, 'a charter of King Henry I has now come to light with which, if you so wished, you could recover your long-lost liberties and your former condition'. Next, 'he had a document placed before them and had it read out', and when the reading was over and the document understood by the barons 'they rejoiced with exceeding great joy'. They thereupon took a formal oath in the archbishop's presence that when the time was ripe they would take up arms in defence of these liberties. For his part, the archbishop promised his loyal support to them 'as far as in him lay'.

Roger is the only source we have for believing that the episode ever took place, and this is the last we hear of Henry I's charter in the context of Magna Carta. A modern commentator has proposed to discount the whole story on the grounds that it is merely hearsay. It is also true that the public sermon Langton preached in St Paul's contains not even a hint that he was prepared to enter into a baronial conspiracy against the king. This too has been adduced to argue the improbability of the Wendover account.

But it would surely have been astonishing if the sermon had contained any such suggestion. The pope, through the person of the archbishop himself, had just formally welcomed the king back into the bosom of Holy Church; the kingdom of England was, by the king's own act, a feudal fief of the Holy See; and the service at St Paul's, held under the aegis of the pope's senior representative in the English church, was to some extent a celebration of the happy outcome, after years of hostility and hazard, of debates to reunite the king, his subjects and Mother Church. Not, one would have thought, precisely the best occasion for the head of that church in England to moot the possibility of a conspiracy against the Lord's anointed.

In these circumstances it may be thought improbable that Langton should even have gone so far as is reported. Such a meeting would certainly have had to have been secret and any report, by a chronicler for example, would have to be based on hearsay or a 'leak'.

Nevertheless, it seems to me that a close examination of the chronicle account reveals internal evidence to suggest that it was a true report of an actual event. The view that it may have been mere romancing by a clerical reporter anxious to enhance the reputation of his profession by claiming a central role for it in the heroic resistance to bad King John overlooks two small but to my mind significant points.

In his account of the secret conference, Roger of Wendover reports that the barons rejoiced 'when the document had been read and understood'. By this he does not mean to imply that the barons in question were slow-witted, muscle-bound backwoodsmen. Nor does he mean that they were simpletons. The charter in question was probably familiar to well-read academic lawyers, but there was no reason why a lay man of affairs should know of its existence. In any case, the medieval baronage, as a class, were quite used to dealing with legal technicalities in the administration of their often very large estates, and at the time of John were beginning to develop estate management offices modelled on the royal chancery and exchequer. There was nothing in the charter of Henry I beyond their mental capabilities to grasp, once it had been translated from its legal Latin into French. (See below pages 128, 156.)

With this in mind, a reading of Wendover's account of the scene in the vestry or perhaps the chapter-house of old St Paul's comes vividly to life. The archbishop first of all favours the select group of great men with a full account of his interview with the king at Winchester. Perhaps he affords them a certain grim amusement with the news that their slippery monarch had given his unsupported oath to reform his ways and that the great churchman had accepted the assurance.

They begin to be intrigued when he spreads out a copy of the ancient coronation charter from a hundred years back. Charters in legal Latin were long familiar to them in dealings with their tenants. No doubt the implications behind the archbishop's suggestion that they might be able to hold the king to similar legal commitments were beginning to spark a response. It all depended upon what this charter of Henry I actually said. When it had been read and the Latin terminology made explicitly clear the meeting was electrified – 'with exceeding great joy'.

39

Churchmen and politics

The second pointer that we may here be dealing with a report of an actual meeting is to be found in the description of the archbishop's reaction to the oath sworn by the barons. We are told that he 'promised them his loyal support as far as in him lay'. This is in marked contrast to the action of the churchmen at the time of the London commune in 1191, when barons, ecclesiastics and Prince John himself, as he then was, swore a communal oath against the tyranny of Richard I's justiciar William Longchamp. All were under a degree of duress from the incensed Londoners. Nevertheless all had sworn together (*conjuratio*) an oath of loyalty to the 'commune'; the idea and the events surrounding it seem to have been in the air at the time of Runnymede, and we may assume that the ceremony of the common oath in August 1213 awakened memories among some present of the events in London a generation back. The fact that the archbishop did not join the *conjuratio* but merely promised support suggests a schemer guarding his back, which chimes with at least one contemporary estimate of Langton's reputation.

Archbishop Langton had been an exile from England for some years before the meeting with the king at Winchester referred to above. It was only the ending of the interdict that made his return possible. It was a mixed blessing for King John, as Langton was to be at the centre of the events leading to Runnymede.

Modern politicians may inveigh against meddling clerics; their medieval predecessors had reason to. Bishops were something more than 'wet' moralists; many were officers of state. At the time of Langton's plotting in the precincts of St Paul's, the most influential man in the land was another churchman, Peter des Roches, the bishop of Winchester.

The historic seat of the old English kings, Winchester was throughout the middle ages the richest of England's bishoprics, and its holder was usually one of the most important men in the land. In the reign of Stephen, the king's brother, Henry of Blois, had shaped events from its cathedral and based his power on its revenues. Peter des Roches, born near Poitiers, had entered royal service under Richard I and rose to be justiciar under John. At the beginning of the reign the highest office in the land, that of chancellor, had been held by Hubert Walter, Langton's predecessor as archbishop of Canterbury. He held office as chancellor until his death in 1205. John's treasurer was a canon of St Paul's, his secretary, John de Gray, was bishop of Norwich and the word 'clerk' had the dual meaning of churchman and scrivener.

The world where that duality of meaning had sprung up was already passing during the reign of King John. More and more laymen were acquiring a smattering of learning, more than a few could read – John's father King Henry II was said to have read for pleasure, while a newly popular proverb held that an unlettered king was a crowned ass.

As the thirteenth century advanced a new sense of piety began to make itself felt as people heard the preaching of the new order of friars founded by St Francis of Assisi. But the days when the higher reaches of the civil service would no longer number churchmen among them were long in the future. During the reign of John and for generations to come, the church provided the natural career structure for men of talent outside the ranks of the land-owning baronage.

The system had drawbacks for the church and corresponding advantages for the lay administration. Chronically short of funds, as he usually was, the royal or baronial employer in need of clerical staff or estate managers, officers of state or humble clerks, could take them on at no expense by the simple expedient of appointing them rector of a prosperous parish, canon of a cathedral or even bishop. The office-holder received the revenues while a deputy or vicar (from the Latin *vicarius*) did the work, at a wage of suitably apostolic poverty. Observing the politics of ecclesiastical Europe one is sometimes tempted to think that the souls of the faithful were never less well served than at the height of the 'Ages of Faith'.

While many bishops were officers of state, all were great and powerful landowners, duty bound to send military contingents in time of war. Some still served on the battlefield in person – Peter des Roches was lampooned as *Wintoniensis armiger* – 'warrior of Winchester' – and the mace or cudgel was thought to be a typically episcopal weapon, as the clergy were not supposed to shed human blood. Given that the clergy, though but a small minority of the population, owned or controlled an estimated twenty-five per cent of the land, it is really not surprising that kings made use of these resources as best they could in the service of the crown.

Kings, electors and ecclesiastics

They also insisted on scrutinizing, approving and usually as good as controlling all the elections to the bishoprics and archbishoprics of their realm. When a see fell vacant by the death of the incumbent, convention allowed the administration of the revenues to pass to the sovereign. Inevitably they took advantage of such situations to divert a large proportion to their exchequer. Popes were willing to connive at any reasonable royal intervention, while kings, despite what one might suppose, were often reasonably God-fearing and also reasonable men. King John of England, of course, went too far. The result was a conflict which would, if dogma was to be believed, imperil the souls of all his subjects and put the king himself in jeopardy of eternal damnation. A dispute over the election to Canterbury began the trouble.

Considering that there is no mention of bishops in the New Testament it was, even to some people in the twelfth century, surprising that they existed in the church at all. (These people, called Waldenses after the merchant of Lyons, Peter Waldo, who founded them, believed in various impractical things such as apostolic poverty, and disapproved of other things like the excessive wealth of the princes of the church. Peter and his followers were properly condemned and persecuted as heretics – though their movement has survived into the twentieth century.

More surprising, perhaps, than the existence of bishops was the fact that there was a proper way to appoint them. As laid down in canon (i.e. church) law, a new bishop should be elected by the free vote of the staff, or chapter, of the cathedral and should then be installed, following the approval of the election and its procedure by the pope. However, it was also agreed that the election could only take place by authorization of the monarch, who, given the profits which accrued to his exchequer as long as the see lay vacant, might delay a long time and would, in any case, make it clear to the electors which man he favoured for the job, when at length he did give them permission to proceed with the election.

The appointment of bishops, then, followed a formula which everybody accepted and which usually ran smoothly. So long as the king chose men of decent life as well as administrative competence the pope could be expected to concur in their election. Since many of the clerks in a cathedral chapter were likely themselves to be royal placemen, i.e. clerics employed in the government service, they could be expected to vote for whomever the king nominated. It was a free election, of course, but people regularly spoke of the king giving a bishopric to someone; recording the succession of John de Gray, the king's secretary, to Norwich in the year 1200 the chronicler Roger of Howden said that he achieved the promotion 'by the gift of King John'.

De Gray was neither a saint nor a theologian, but he was a perfectly respectable Christian as well as a first-rate government servant. To King John he looked like ideal archbishop material. Accordingly, when Archbishop Hubert Walter of Canterbury died in July 1205 the king knew whom he wanted for successor and naturally hoped to have his way without undue difficulty.

However, a certain amount of finesse was needed. Ten of England's cathedrals were staffed by monks, not regular clergy, and Canterbury was one of them. Since monks lived apart from the world and were therefore not candidates for government employment, monastic chapters tended to be somewhat more independent at election time than canons and priests. Moreover, although it was only sixteen years since the appointment of Hubert Walter there was, or was claimed to be, some confusion over the correct procedure for appointing an archbishop.

The cathedral chapter found its supposedly exclusive right to conduct the election disputed by the bishops of the province. But the chapter had been in a long-drawn-out dispute with both Archbishop Walter and his predecessor and wanted the next incumbent to be one of their own number. The bishops were not in favour of such an outcome. Both sides appealed to Rome to settle the dispute over church government and the king properly postponed any further action in the matter until November.

He had not the slightest intention of allowing the premier appointment in the English church to be held by a monk out of his control. But he at least had the consolation that for the next five months the rich revenues of the province would flow to the royal coffers.

So far, in fact, the affairs of Canterbury were following the orderly and correct pattern. A clerical dispute was being referred to Rome with the royal blessing and the king was doing nothing to pressurize the electors – but it did seem to him a perfectly proper and reasonable precaution to let his wishes in the matter be known at the papal court. Royal agents were ordered to take advantage in the delay caused by the appeal to canvass the qualities of

Bishop Gray, the royal candidate, along the corridors of power in Rome.

The news of these manoeuvres in Rome soon reached England, where it provoked the Cathedral monks to the extraordinary expedient of a secret election at which their own prior, Reginald, emerged as archbishop designate. He still required papal approval, denoted by the conferral of the pallium, and was dispatched to Rome by his brothers with instructions to reveal his nomination only if this were unavoidable in thwarting John. Evidently the chapter recognized its own temerity and had promoted Reginald as a passed pawn to check the king by spurring the pope to nominate his own candidate.

The pawn, however, had aspirations. On arrival at Rome Prior Reginald proclaimed himself archbishop elect and sought full confirmation from the pope. When news of this reached England, King John flew down to Canterbury in a whirlwind rage; the monks promised on their honour that no election had taken place and, surprisingly, seem to have convinced the king. Under his direction they went on to the election of Gray, the bishops gave their blessing and a second delegation of monks turned up in Rome to ask Innocent III for his confirmation of their new choice. The English delegates already there – Prior Reginald, the bishops' proctor, and the king's agents – all contested the legitimacy of Gray's election.

Crisis, Canterbury and Rome

Pope Innocent ordered a re-run there and then. When the electors came out evenly balanced for Gray and Reginald he proposed a new candidate for their consideration – Stephen Langton, an English cardinal priest in Rome and a graduate master in the University of Paris. He received the unanimous voice of the wearied monks. The pope, bent on general reform of the church, was delighted to have 'taken' England's metropolitan see with so little effort. Langton was known across Europe for his lectures on the duties of a bishop and is remembered to this day in church circles as the man who divided the books of the Bible into the chapter divisions we still accept.

King John was neither impressed nor amused. He did not, he said, know Langton; he did not want him; and he would not accept him. The election to England's premier see had been conducted abroad and without his licence to elect having been granted. This and numerous other arguments were rehearsed in a fuming and petulant letter of the kind which a king by the grace of God ought never to have addressed to Christ's vicar on earth. The pope rejected them all, told the king he must accept the outcome of a perfectly canonical election, and went on to warn the king that as a loyal son of the church he must accept the consecration of Langton as archbishop of Canterbury.

The principles governing the election of bishops had been laid down at the Lateran Council barely thirty years before and Innocent, a renowned canon lawyer and, incidentally, one of the most dynamic in the history of the papacy ever to sit in the chair of St Peter, was not about to overturn a perfectly canonical procedure to suit the whim of a mere king. John expelled the monks of Canterbury, who went into exile in France, and refused an entry permit into England to the new archbishop.

It was all extremely distressing, but things were to get very much worse. While Innocent recognized that the issue was a matter of prestige for the king and was willing to give him time to accept the 'divine ordinance', he was not prepared to wait for ever. In June 1207, a year and more after the resounding events in Rome described above, the pope formally consecrated Cardinal Stephen Langton in the office of archbishop of Canterbury. In August the bishops of London, Worcester and Ely received instructions to order the king to accept the fact on pain of having his kingdom laid under a general interdict.

In November the pope himself wrote to the barons of England urging on them their loyalty to their king, but that they should also bear in mind their higher loyalty to God. To this end they should advise the king against his policy towards 'our venerable brother Stephen, archbishop of Canterbury' and the English church. They need have no fear of displeasing the king temporarily in the cause of justice, for in due course he would return to his sense and would then think them 'very dear friends for the sincerity of your counsel'. Pope Innocent is generally rated by admiring historians as one of the most brilliant men to have occupied the chair of St Peter, and he undoubtedly was a man of considerable talents: nonetheless, it is apparent that he would not have lasted long as a baron of King John of England if this letter represents his actual sentiments on opposing that monarch on a matter of morality and right behaviour. To no one's surprise, except possibly Innocent's, the king remained adamant. On 24 March 1208 the interdict came into force; on papal orders all the clergy came out on strike and the laity found themselves on the receiving end of a lockout.

Interdict

Similar action had been taken before, notably against the kingdom of France in 1199. Even so, the penalty was rarely imposed and even churchmen were far from clear just what was entailed. Their instructions were to refuse to carry out all ecclesiastical services except the baptism of infants and confession of the dying. The strength and weakness of this ecclesiastical bludgeon was that it stunned both the innocent and the guilty. The idea was that the king's subjects would urge him to refrain from 'walking in the counsel of the ungodly' and return to his senses, confident not only that he would consider them good friends but also that he would rectify his conduct and so enable the kingdom to return to the body of the church. But, of course, so long as he persisted in his stubbornness many good men would suffer.

Unfortunately for the pope, more or less everybody in England supported the king. Like him, few people outside church circles had heard of Langton; most people were incensed that an English king, even King John, should, as it appeared, have his choice of archbishop glibly overruled by papal whim; the barons wondered uneasily how safe were their own rights in presenting friends and relations to the livings under their control. By way of counter-attack John began by seizing church property. If the pope's men obeyed the pope, so did the king's men obey the king.

Anathemas and the age of faith

Few things are more tenacious than historical labels, and it would take more than this chapter to shift the stereotyped image of the middle ages as the 'Ages of Faith' imprinted on most people's imagination. A study of England during the interdict, however, might go some way to sharpening the focus.

46

The royal confiscation of church property was not an empty gesture. High government officials might be expected to be loyal, indeed John's officials would hardly be expected to be religious men. Directed by the king's sheriffs, lay administrators moved in on the great properties of the church and took over the running of the estate offices so that the revenues flowed to the crown. But even at parish level it was not difficult to find the men needed to make an accurate assessment of the lands and the fees owing and to assign a meagre living allowance to the priest, supposing the living was not held by a royal appointee.

This was only the first stage. The next was to make the clergy themselves administer their own confiscations. A week or two after the formal acts of seizure, the government announced that any churchman might recover control of his estates on payment of a fee which bore a striking resemblance to the farm paid by a sheriff for the administration of the revenues within his jurisdiction. The prior of Peterborough, for example, was allowed to regain the administration of the abbey's lands, with a known revenue of some £1000 p.a., for an annual payment to the crown of £600.

This was by no means the end of the king's exploitation of the golden windfalls blown down in the storm of papal anger. He entertained himself and the country by ordering a round-up of all clerical concubines, variously known as hearthmates, housekeepers or lady friends. When they were held to ransom most of them, be it said to the honour of a clearly uxurious if officially celibate clergy, were bought back by their reverend lovers.

All in all, the interdict relieved John of financial worries for a few years, nor does it seem to have deeply oppressed the citizenry. In fact, not to put too fine a point on it, we may say that the impact on the morale of the country in general was slight to minimal. Over the five years that the official ban of the church hung over the life of the nation we find little in the records to indicate its impact. Seven bishops soon went into exile, Archbishop Langton being of course already oversea. Four others died, leaving their sees vacant for the duration and at the mercy of the king's administrators. Bishop Gray of Norwich and Bishop des Roches of Winchester, of course, remained loyal to their king and patron. Yet although, after three years of the interdict, Winchester was the only English bishopric with a resident bishop (Gray was serving as the king's justiciar in Ireland) not one of the barons complained.

Nor does it appear that the clergy themselves were greatly worried about the spiritual aspect of the dreadful blight called down by the pope on the people of England. Even the chroniclers, also men of God and by profession concerned with the immortal souls of men and women, while willing to empty many an inkwell to blacken the name of the king, have next to nothing to say about the religious impact of it all. We are left to guess at the state of affairs. Week in, week out, men and women lived without the blessings of holy communion, married without the benefit of the church wedding, and were buried in unconsecrated ground, having died (before 1212) without receiving extreme unction. This we must assume to have been the state of affairs. Some, possibly many people, were fearful and depressed, and yet it has to be said that nowhere in the records of the time do we find mention of any form of unrest on the part of the populace at being denied the benefits of religion.

As to a general rising to force their sovereign to restore his kingdom to a state of grace, even the thought was not entertained. And yet, so we are required to believe, this was the theory behind the interdict. As we have seen, all but two of the bishops quit the royal service, either by the door of death or else via the less final exit afforded by the Channel ports. The lay barons made no move whatsoever – even when, in November 1209, Archbishop Langton, acting with the full authorization of Pope Innocent, excommuni-cated John by name, with all the elaborate terrors of the pronouncement anathema.

For an ordinary Christian this meant exclusion from the consolation and fellowship of the church in this world and the threat of eternal damnation in the world to come. For a king it meant that his subjects were freed from their allegiance. All this had long since been relegated, for many people, to the world of theory, since the church itself had devalued the coin of its own sanctions. Even as Pope Innocent thundered his anathemas and exhortations, northern French knights were, with the full blessing of Mother Church, preparing to plunder the lands of their Provençal cousins in the notorious brutalities of the Albigensian Crusade.

Many of John's Norman baronage must have been personally acquainted with the strange standards of religious orthodoxy, while their English peasantry had special reason to question Rome's honesty. Not one hundred and fifty years earlier, the last English king had been killed in battle by the ancestors of their Norman lords vaunting the name 'Crusader' under the papal aegis.

Yet while these things may explain a certain disillusionment with the church they do not account for the inertia of John's opponents during the years of the interdict. The sufferings of the ecclesiastics should have deeply concerned them. After all, bishops, whatever their faults, were great land-holders and representatives of the class most favoured and established in tradition; yet for five and more years they were harried and exiled, and their lands pillaged. Their fate must surely have been seen as a warning by the more thoughtful among the barons. And yet when presented by the pope with legitimate reason to disavow their allegiance, and, indeed prompted to rebellion for the sake of their immortal souls, the magnates of England still held aloof.

The big battalions are called in

As a weapon of international politics, the interdict had failed miserably. It was only when they saw a chance of dispatching their king with a stab in the back that the barons seemed willing to summon up the courage to attack. At about the same time rumour also whispered that Pope Innocent was planning to pronounce the formal deposition of the king and to call in the French king to enforce it. Events were conspiring to much better effect than ecclesiastical censures and thunderbolts.

In the year 1212 John was preparing to launch a crushing offensive against France. At the last moment he cancelled his invasion plans, intending to divert the vast armaments and resources in men that had been assembled to an attack against Wales. June had seen the beginning of an ugly little rebellion by the native prince Llywelyn against John, whom he recognized officially as overlord. In mid July the king had changed his plans once more. This time the news rumoured was of rebellions among his English magnates, and a well-based report that Philip of France was preparing for a major invasion, much more serious matters.

The plans against Wales were dropped. Leading English magnates were forced to surrender hostages to the king for their good behaviour and John marched into the northern parts of England, where it was said the seeds of rebellion were especially hardy. Two leading barons, Robert Fitzwalter and Eustace de Vesci, hurried abroad into exile. Even so, John was not going to trust to luck. Urged by the ever-loyal William Marshal, he determined to make his peace with the pope. It was as well he did. In view of the French king's initiative and the fact that the barons were at last, for reasons of their own, daring to consider rebellion, the pope really was preparing a final move against John. That Christmas Archbishop Langton was armed with letters declaring the king deposed and authorizing a crusade by Philip. They were never published.

Learning that John was ready to capitulate, Innocent first sent his legate Pandulf to England. Overtaking Langton on the road, he ordered him to hold back the letters of deposition and went on to astonishing negotiations with the ostensibly penitent King of England at Dover. There on 15 May King John of England proposed to surrender the kingdom of England and the lordship of Ireland as feudal fiefs of the Apostolic See. He made the proposal in the form of a Charter. The pope was enchanted. 'You now hold your kingdom by a more exalted and surer title than before, for the kingdom is become a priesthood' wrote Innocent, who would thenceforward prove a staunch ally to his favourite son in God.

4

THE ROAD
TO DISASTER

JOHN had bought the friendship of the pope, but his standing at home was still uncertain, while the situation overseas was positively dangerous. In the spring of 1213 the country was under imminent threat of invasion from Philip of France. The fact that John's desperate about-face in his own attitude to Rome had denied the French king the possibility of posing as a crusader had not deflected that monarch from his purpose.

King Philip had been at war with the Angevin family for some thirty years. During that time he had withstood John's father, outwitted his brother and roundly defeated John himself. The lands of Normandy, surrendered 300 years before to the Viking chief Rollo and for the past 150 years an immense and threatening beachhead of the English crown, were once more a full province of France. Philip was with reason confident that the recovery of full sovereignty in Aquitaine was only a matter of time: meanwhile he saw an opportunity to root out the devil's brood in its nest. Twice before he had been on the verge of an invasion across the Channel. Now, with opposition to John still seething below the surface of church-induced amity, the moment seemed entirely propitious.

At the very least, a French expedition would deter John's continuing designs for a campaign in Poitou. But much more was at stake than mere strategic diversion. The objective was nothing less than the overthrow and extirpation of the house of Anjou and the annexation of England as an appanage, i.e. a personal family estate, of the French crown, to be the fief of the eldest son of the monarch. In April 1213, the very month in which John must already have been at work with his advisers on the dramatic démarche which would surrender his realm as a feudal fiefdom to the pope, King Philip held a great council in the French city of Soissons to determine the legal relations between the two countries when his son Louis should be crowned king of England.

The defeat of the French Armada

All the parties to these high-sounding negotiations had apparently forgotten the rights of the emperor in the case, for had not King Richard, twenty years ago, surrendered the realm into the hands of Emperor Henry VI to receive it back as a fief from him? Some said the cession had ended with the death of Richard, others were not so sure. But Philip, surnamed 'Augustus' by admiring courtiers and likened by them to the Roman emperors of old, had little respect for the Germanic construct beyond the Rhine and grandiose ideas of his own which anticipated something of what later generations of Frenchmen have called '*la Gloire*'.

Meanwhile, with the English king harassed by his baronage and Otto of Brunswick fighting to assert his claims to be recognized as Emperor Otto IV, Philip could reasonably, it seemed, plan his schemes for the aggrandizement of his family and the enlargement of France. While the constitutional and legal experts in Soissons debated the details of Anglo-French relations following the conquest, shipwrights, quartermasters and chandlers were working on the final preparations for a vast fleet of ships assembling under the hands of skilled mariners and pilots in ports along the coasts of northern France and French Flanders.

The conquest of England seemed to be part of plans for a greater France already being realized on the continent of Europe. As he supervised the takeover of the great province of Normandy back in 1204-5, it must have been a matter of considerable irony to Philip that the little county of Boulogne, northwards along the coast, was still able to assert its autonomy from the French crown. In the year 1211 he trumped up a pretext for a quarrel with Count Renaud and expelled him from his lands, which were absorbed into France.

It will be remembered that King Stephen's wife had been the daughter of a count of Boulogne and, small though it was, the county was a vital piece of the political geography of north-western Europe. Bordering on Flanders and looking across the Channel for friends against the overmighty ambitions of the French, its counts were natural candidates for an English alliance. Count Renaud, aiming to recover his family inheritance, busied himself by recruiting support for England, in Flanders itself and further afield, and found the work light and agreeable.

Historically, the counts of Flanders, like the rulers of Holland and Brabant and other lordships in the Low Countries, owed technical homage either to the Emperor or the French king, according as they had been part of the territories of those old rivals, the eastern and western Frankish kingdoms. France had always claimed the suzerainty of Flanders, and now her king felt himself fully strong enough to exercise it.

At the time that Philip was expelling John from Normandy, the count of Flanders was campaigning with the Fourth Crusade. In due course he found himself a prisoner of war in the country of the Bulgars, where he died. His daughter Joanna and her husband inherited Flanders, with its rich but turbulent towns. The new count was glad of assistance from the powerful French king, though it was somewhat galling to have to stomach his assertions of suzerainty.

When, in the year 1213, Philip authorized his son Louis to seize the town of St Omer and ordered Flanders to join the invasion of England, the count's patience ran out. He refused any further collaboration until his town was returned. Contemptuously, Philip sent an army against him, laid siege to Ghent and brought his invasion fleet into the fine harbour of Damme, port to the great Flemish merchant city of Bruges. The count looked around for friends and found that Renaud of Boulogne and the lord of Holland were in alliance with King John. He sent messengers to England.

That country, despite the supposed unpopularity of the king, was in a strong state of preparedness. John was not short of capable and willing soldiers in a war against a French invader; but above all, thanks to the planning and investment of the earlier years of the reign, he had a navy of well-found ships and seasoned seamen. Morale was high, thanks to cross-Channel raids on Dieppe and Fécamp, and the crews were fully prepared for action when the messengers arrived from Flanders.

A council of war chaired by the king decided to answer the count's appeal for aid in handsome fashion. Seven hundred men-at-arms and a large body of mercenaries were embarked in some 500 ships and the whole flotilla set sail on 28 May, just three days after the call had come. With the earl of Salisbury in command the English reached the mouth of the River Zwyn in two days, despite contrary winds, heading for Damme and apparently unaware that it was crowded with a French armada. One contemporary put their number at 1700 ships.

The French commanders and military were on shore, leaving the ships in the charge of skeleton crews to manoeuvre them when tide or wind threatened. The bulk of the invasion fleet lay at anchor ready to sail on the next tide, as it seemed, supplies stowed and the personal impedimenta of the French knights lashed in place until they should be off-loaded at an English beach, ready to accompany their victorious owner to some castle or manor house in the home counties. Other boats were hauled up above the tide mark, undergoing last-minute repairs or cleaning.

The English commander ordered an immediate attack. A quarter of the French fleet was sent drifting out to sea or on to the sandbanks, looted or set ablaze, before sundown. The next day King Philip arrived at the head of his army, in time to send a rash English sortie scampering back to the safety of its ships, there to count the cost of their brief excursion across the North Sea.

The raiders got clean away, with scores of prizes and more booty than had been seen in England since 'the days of King Arthur'; they had brought away with them the count of Flanders. King Philip himself ordered the destruction of the beached transports and the scuttling of all the other vessels not already destroyed, for fear of a commando raid by the enemy; and his nobility were poorer by a ransom-worth of armour and luxury equipment. John's royal navy had more than paid for itself in its first engagement, and the most serious invasion England had confronted since the Conquest was over before it could begin.

The French undertaking

The Flanders enterprise had been just the kind of warfare John's baronage enjoyed: a quick jaunt into enemy territory, little danger, no casualties and immense booty. When he tried to mobilize forces for yet another attempt to recover his French inheritance, the reaction was sullen reluctance or outright refusal.

Part of the price for peace with the church had been pardons for the leaders of the plotted rebellion of the previous year. Even though both were probably implicated in the plans to murder the king during his proposed Welsh expedition, Robert Fitzwalter and Eustace de Vesci were allowed to return and readmitted to the king's 'goodwill'. In his few months of exile Fitzwalter had sought out the English bishops oversea and had protested his loathing for the service of an excommunicate. A year after his return he and de Vesci would be posing as Captains of the Army of God.

Exultant in his victory at long range over the French, John was anxious to take the fight into enemy territory. The barons demurred. He was excommunicate; they had served already by standing guard; and finally, as many and especially those from the north argued, the conditions of military service by which they held their lands did not carry the obligation to serve in Poitou, which was where, for reasons of strategy, John was proposing to launch his grand attack on France.

John stormed northwards, bent on a punitive expedition and infuriated by the resistance in the north to his demands for support, without a thought for his promise to Langton a month before to judge men only in accordance with the just judgements of his own court. The idea that the terms of military service might be open to interpretation by the courts had either not occurred to him or seemed simply outrageous. It was the basis of the whole system of landholding; the rebels had insolently presumed to question a matter beyond question for the king to decide. But he did, eventually, relent. No action should be taken until judgement had been given; the expedition, in any case, should be postponed to the spring of the following year, 1214. He marched north nevertheless, and months of uneasy tension followed as the king displayed his strength, his barons looked on apprehensively and churchmen did what they could to arrange a compromise.

These efforts may have included the document now called the Unknown Charter of Liberties, unnoticed by historians until its discovery in the French royal archives in the 1860s. One reason for proposing that the undated document was produced during the winter months of 1213-1214 is that Clause 7 specifically excuses the king's military tenants from any service oversea outside Normandy or Brittany. Perhaps the document was the first outcome of Archbishop Langton's suggestion to the barons to present their grievances to the king in charter form. Or perhaps – and there are aspects of the phrasing to suggest this – it was the memorandum of a meeting between the king and Langton, aimed at establishing a first royal reaction to the likely contents of any future baronial charter of grievances.

The first clause reiterates the fundamental promise given to Langton at Winchester in July 'that the king will not take men without justice'. The remaining ten items deal with matters raised in the Great Charter of 1215. There is no suggestion that King John gave his consent to any of the clauses – we cannot even be sure that he saw the document. But few historians doubt that the document is from the period immediately prior to the Great Charter itself, and it therefore constitutes a tantalizing side-light on the negotiations which lay behind it.

Be that as it may, as the new year of 1214 opened the king and his military advisers were readying themselves for one of the most momentous campaigns in the history of English arms and the recalcitrant baronage were loitering resentfully in the wings.

The king sailed for France in February. No judgement had been received on the question of service overseas and it is doubtful whether the issue had been submitted to any court of law. A significant number of the king's senior tenants had neither turned up nor sent knight service, nor compounded for scutage (shield money payable in lieu of the performance or rendering of military service).

William Marshal was among those absenting themselves, but he, honourable as always, could not attend in person because he also held land of King Philip and so would have been taking the field in person against his (other) liege lord. He did however send a contingent of knights and, remaining in England, was the king's doughty representative there. Otherwise the home government was in the capable if not very generous hands of Bishop Peter des Roches, justiciar following the death of Geoffrey Fitzpeter, an old-style royal servant from the reign of King Richard. Archbishop Langton, obliged by his office and the formal submission of the king to the pope, remained, as did William Briewer, notorious for his ruthless exploitation of the office of sheriff which he had held in many shires. The king left behind a band of able, tough but essentially loyal ministers, not one of them, unfortunately for him, from the aristocracy of the old Anglo-Norman blood.

Likewise, the royal army, professional and capable as it was, also presented contemporaries with an unedifying spectacle, comprising for the most part 'low class soldiers of fortune'. The king, always more concerned with results than with show, was, we may be sure, more at ease in the company of these hard-living, fast-riding professionals than that of his touchy self-absorbed barons concerned, as is the nature of aristocracies throughout the ages, only with family fortunes. But, of course, they were the men who ultimately counted in the kingdom he left behind, and in his absence they would have ample time to mull over their grievances and pray for a royal disaster. Their hopes would be met in full measure, pressed down and running over, but at the start of the great campaign this was by no means clear.

As John sailed west, heading to round Brittany en route for La Rochelle, still secure in English hands, his half-brother William earl of Salisbury, victor at Damme, sailed east heading once more for Flanders. He had a sizeable force of English and Flemish soldiers and, like his royal master, he had a large hoard of treasure. Where John needed to secure the loyalty of the malcontent Poitevin nobility, nominally his liegemen but actually bit players in their own eternal private feuds, William had the job of recruiting and securing allies to the Low Country/Rhenish confederacy begun the previous year with the forced defection from the French cause of the count of Boulogne.

It was an elaborate and, as it turned out, over-ambitious plan which the king had in mind. While he harried the French king from his lands in Poitou to the south-west, his nephew Otto of Brunswick, claimant to the Crown of the Empire, was to sweep down with the combined forces of his Rhineland allies and the lords of the Low Countries, all financed by the treasure chests of the earl of Salisbury and supported by his war veterans, to crush French resistance in the north-east. This was strategy on the grand scale to match Marlborough's march the length of Europe to link with Prinz Eugen on the battlefield of Blenheim, in August 1704. At the first attempt the alliance of England and the Empire was a disaster.

John and Otto had a common problem, namely to bring their allies to the starting-tape. Throughout the spring and early summer of 1214, the king was marching and counter-marching, involved in a seemingly endless series of sieges, sacks, raids and skirmishes to bring the Poitevin baronage to heel. At their head was the Lusignan family, still angered at John's seizure of Isabella of Angoulême from Hugh de Lusignan fifteen years before and unwilling to come to terms. All the time to the north John was aware of the large French army under its king and of his own need to force the issue. Early in May he launched one of his renowned lightning campaigns which by dint of hard fighting and quick responses to a changing situation was entirely successful. By the end of it Hugh was forced to contract for the marriage of his son to John's baby daughter. At last John was free to mobilize all his forces against Philip. Early in June we find him marching into Angers. Two weeks later he was in sight of the situation aimed for at the beginning of the campaign. The main French force in the area, now under the command of Prince Louis the Dauphin, was brought to bay.

John's run of successes was becoming so long as to seem threatening, and Louis at last prepared for a confrontation. Delighted, John prepared for the showdown. At the last moment the Poitevins deserted, unwilling, no doubt, to make open war against the heir to the French throne on French soil. For whatever reason, they put an end to the dreams of the English king. Once more reduced to the expeditionary force that he had brought with him, and knowing as he had at the start of the campaign that it was quite inadequate to take on the massive French force now facing him, John withdrew back to the port of La Rochelle. From there he wrote a ghastly-cheerful letter to the baronage of England, reporting all well – and begging for reinforcements. None came. This, of all moments, was the one chosen by his ally in the north to launch his great assault. But King Philip, after an apprehensive and indecisive five months, now saw his way clear to battle. His back secure and with the feudal levies and town bands marching alongside each other, he took the offensive. The armies clashed at Bouvines on 27 July. One of the decisive battles of Europe, it ended the hopes of Otto and guaranteed the future of the new monarchy which Philip Augustus had established in France. It also put an end to the plans of John of England. He delayed his return as long as he feasibly could, but as he lingered on in France it became obvious he could hope for no reinforcements from England. In October he put in at Dartmouth in the royal galley.

In fifteen years John had antagonized the leading members among his lay baronage in one way or another; he had ridden roughshod over the rights of the church. Adroit manoeuvring had brought him the support of Rome, but his own archbishop still distrusted him and, it seems, was even prepared to nudge the barons into dissidence. Yet John still retained the undisputed rights of his office; the sanctified charisma allowed to God's anointed; support from William Marshal, the most venerated lay figure in the kingdom; and a first-rate government machine.

The fatal flaw in John's armour was failure to win glory on the battlefield.

Victories and triumphs he had had, but nothing on the grand scale, nothing somehow that mattered. A king who won great victories could enforce loyalty no matter how extortionate he might be. Richard had demonstrated this. John's barons were now openly denying even the traditional obligations of war service. On his return from France, his military venture in ruins, he found an ugly mood of rebellion in the air once more.

During his absence, Peter des Roches had operated the full rigours of the well-hated Angevin system of government in his capacity as justiciar. Opposition was particularly strong in the north of England, and it was the northerners who seem to have headed the opposition. Talk about the Charter granted by Henry I would give place in the months ahead to talk of the customs of King Edward the Confessor. Both were rallying cries, both gave to rebellion the respectable gloss of principle. As a result, many undecided barons, who might have thrown their full weight behind the king had he faced outright military challenge, held back.

At the beginning of 1215 it seems that royalists and dissidents were almost equal in the support they could muster, and half the magnates of England remained aloof throughout the struggle that ensued. In this sense, as in so many others, the struggle for Magna Carta would have parallels with confrontation between opposition and government. The quarrel, or debate, is carried on by the committed of either side but the bulk of the population remain backbenchers, voting only when required and, for the most part, content to get on, so to speak, with constituency business.

The struggle over the Charter, of course, broke out more than once into civil war. Armed conflict was still part of the social reality of the time. Yet even the roughnecks were not looking to establish an anarchy in which they could exploit their own estates entirely untrammelled. Even they were looking for some principle, even if only of 'law and order'. In this sense, the appeal to the charters was always more than a mere battle cry. As the contest advanced it would come to benefit the community of the realm of England as a whole.

THE COMMUNITY OF ENGLAND

By the 1220s the Charter, as promulgated by the regency council of John's son Henry III, was being described as a charter for the 'Community of England'. In 1191 the Londoners had sought to establish their own 'commune' on the Continental model. In 1215 the barons at Runnymede proposed to enlist the 'community of the whole land' to coerce King John if he broke the terms of his undertaking. But behind such constitutional constructs, the maturing of the 'community of the realm' was a fact of real importance in the national history.

In theory, all Christians were members of the community of the faithful on earth called Christendom. In reality, the idea of even one of the peoples of Europe as a single community was slow to develop. England, for example, was a patchwork of towns and settlements, manors and villages, scattered over a landscape of forest and sparsely populated countryside and locked into their local identities by the clinging conventions of tradition.

In addition, the diverse orders of society each had their own sense of communal solidarity: the nobility with their knightly code acquiring ideas of chivalry, merchants with their guilds, priests with the mystic power, supposedly theirs, of converting the Host into the body of Christ, clergy in the lesser orders of the church with the shared interests of an intellectual élite. Even the despised Jews had their synagogues and officials. Because Magna Carta deals not only with the landowning élite and the church but also with merchants, Jews, women, forest dwellers and even the humble villein, to explore its meaning is to investigate the community of England itself.

5

THE COMMUNITY
OF BARONS

SINCE it was the barons who forced the Charter from the king the bulk of its provisions, naturally enough, concerned them, whether directly or indirectly. The Articles of the Barons give a clear indication of their priorities. Where the Great Charter piously and properly starts by securing the rights and liberties of the church, the Articles went straight for the chief grievance of the baronage – the king's arbitrary increase of the dues owing to him under various feudal obligations.

The chief ground for complaint was the rate at which John levied the payment known as 'relief' owing to the king before an heir could enjoy the revenues of his inheritance. No one contested that, as the ultimate owner of all the land in England since the division of the country by William the Conquerer, the king could reasonably demand such a payment. The question was, what was a reasonable amount?

With an appeal to the past characteristic of the Charter as a whole, Clause 2 lays down that payment shall be according to the 'old relief'. It then sets out a rate of charges which, remarkably enough, appear to have been observed during the following reign. When William Pantoll was charged £100 relief in the 1230s he protested that this was the charge for a full barony, the usual term for a large estate whose revenues might be large enough to finance twenty mounted men-at-arms or knights in the king's army. In fact, Pantoll protested, he only held land sufficient for five knights' fees; according to the Charter, a single knight's fee attracted a relief of only £5. The exchequer accepted the claim and he paid only £25; to the king, that is. An additional payment of two pounds and five shillings (9% of the relief) was owing to Queen Eleanor and had to be paid over to an official representing her private purse at the exchequer. (Among the protests against Henry III and his government in the rising of 1258, the barons rather unchivalrously included the matter of the 'queen's gold', and the practice was discontinued.)

Clause 3 continues the theme of relief, but in the special case where the king had enjoyed the wardship of the lands in question for an heir who was under age. In fact the rights of wards and heirs occupy this and the next three clauses. On the principle that all land was held in exchange for military service and that an heir who was under age could not discharge that service, the crown was entitled to take the estate into custody or wardship and administer its revenues until the boy came of age. In theory a reasonable sum had to be set aside to provide for the living expenses of the heir during this period, and the custodian, whether crown or other lord, was to take only reasonable charges and aids from the property. In fact, as we shall shortly see, John's administration of wardships was anything but reasonable and he was likely to top off his exploitation of the estate by demanding payment of a relief in addition. This practice is forbidden by the third clause of the Great Charter.

Rights of wardship were a valuable perquisite to the crown and presented classic opportunities for asset stripping. At the very least, the guardian could be expected to extort the last penny owing to him under the conventions. More probably he would appropriate all the revenues, leaving the heir the barest pittance and spending nothing on maintenance of the property. An heir to an estate unlucky enough to have been under the wardship of the king for any length of time could expect to find dilapidated houses and outbuildings, once profitable mills in bad need of repair, game running on neighbours' land because boundary fences had not been maintained, and ploughs or other farm implements sold off. Even worse, the estate's labour force might well have been seriously depleted ('the men wasted' in the expressive terminology of the Charter) because it was always easy to raise money by selling to villeins their freedom from traditional hereditary labour services owed to the heir's family.

From the rights of heirs, the Charter makes a natural transition to those of widows (Chapter 9). Next, having dealt with what we might term revenues from the family, it turns to the general question of debtors, whether to the crown or to Jewish moneylenders (Chapter 8), so important a part of the crown's revenue system. Not that one had to borrow from the king to be in debt to the crown. It has been said that if one took into account the various legitimate feudal incidents a baron might be liable to, the arbitrary fines or tallages which could be levied on towns or serfs, payments demanded in lieu of military service (*scutage*) and fines imposed merely 'to have the goodwill' of the king, 'a large proportion of Englishmen must have been permanently indebted to the crown'.

Following the remorseless logic of baronial interests, these matters are precisely the ones which come next under the scrutiny of the draftsmen of the Charter. 'No scutage nor aid,' reads Clause 12, 'shall be imposed . . . without the common counsel of the kingdom, except for the ransoming of our person, the knighting of our eldest son, or the first marriage of our eldest daughter.' The three 'aids' listed were standard feudal levies which no one contested. John's warlike brother had had to be ransomed barely twenty years before and while there were numerous complaints about the corruption and injustice of the collection, no one questioned King Richard's government's right to make it. Yet even these customary dues should be levied within reason, while for 'extraordinary aids' as they were called – effectively imposed voluntary grants – the Charter demanded that the king take counsel.

Later generations would invoke this clause as proof that the Charter had promulgated the principle of no taxation without the consent of parliament. The fact that it was set down some forty years before the first use of the word 'parliament' in any English text shows how prone later generations could be to romancing. But they were not alone in this. The barons' attempt to establish the principle that scutage could be levied only by consent was merely fantastical. Since all land was held in return for the guarantee to send armed men to the king's wars, the king had to be free to impose money payment in lieu on any unwilling to fulfil the obligation. This was one of the clauses dropped from the 1216 version of the Charter.

Having asserted the king's obligation to consult before imposing aids and even scutage, the Charter, after digressing briefly on the rights of London and the towns, cities and boroughs of the kingdom (see Chapter 6), went on to specify who should be summoned to the council and how the summonses were to be made out. Where the one clause was said to prove the Charter's commitment to parliamentary authority for taxation, this one supposedly spelt out the doctrine of parliamentary representation. In fact it seems clear that the council of consent was to comprise only the familiar personnel of the royal council – the great churchmen, the greater barons and, of lesser landholders, only those who held direct from the king, known as tenants-in-chief.

And of course, there were many landowners in England to whom this description did not apply, men who held not from the king but from some intermediary great lord, men who were termed '*mesne*' tenants. They were liable to the standard feudal aids – ransom, knighting the eldest son, marrying the eldest daughter. It was also true that, given the diversity of landowning, a tenant-in-chief might hold some of his land from another and thus, himself, be for that plot a *mesne* tenant. Either because they were altruists or to protect themselves all round, the barons of the Charter provided in Clause 15 that no tenant-in-chief could raise any extraordinary aid and that he should levy the standard aids only in reasonable amounts.

The section on feudal dues closes with a technicality about the 'performance of service for a knight's fee' before the Great Charter moves immediately to the important question as to where lawsuits should be held. The actual wording of Clause 17 reads 'The common pleas shall not follow our court but shall be held in some fixed place.' Justice was delivered, county by county, district by district, according to the law of that place or region. King Henry II had established the principle that by the payment of a fee, fixed for whoever paid it wherever it was paid, the royal justices would deliver justice according to what they conceived proper principles, no matter what local custom might claim or the local lord specify. It could release people from the arbitrary misinterpretation of local law as delivered by the local lord – the drawback was that this royal justice was to be had only where the royal judge happened to be.

In fact justice, like every other department of government at this time, followed the king's person. Nothing could be done outside the king's household and that household never lingered long in one place. The crown, in short, had introduced the idea that there was something which might be called absolute justice but then arranged that this should be available only at an undesignated place of its own choosing. If the king, let us say for example that inspired genius Henry II, decided he wished to move from Windsor to his hunting lodge at Woodstock and the home of his mistress the fair Rosamund, then to that destination travelled the royal court and with it the royal justices and with them the royal justice.

With Clause 20 the Charter reached an issue of general interest to all classes of society, the question of 'amercements', that is, payments levied by the courts for certain misdemeanours, mistakes in court procedure, failures by local communities to comply exactly with the requirements of the king's justices or inefficiency by local officials. (In passing one notes that life in King John's England cannot have been all bad if officials could be fined for inefficiency.)

As in various other clauses of the Charter, the complaint was not against the thing itself. A local law officer who failed to ensure that the finder of a dead child appeared for questioning would find himself amerced; failure to examine the body of a man who fell to his death in a quarry led to the penalization of a whole neighbourhood. It was a tribute to the thoroughness of royal justice that such little local details were taken note of and no one questioned that the guilty parties had put themselves outside the law, or in the king's mercy (*in misericordiam regis*), as the saying went. The objection was to the fact that amercements could be imposed for really petty offences but might be set for quite excessive amounts, or that they might be levied for purely notional offences. That, in short, fines supposedly meant to tighten up the administration of justice or keep local government running smoothly were being used simply as another source of government revenue.

There was no charge rate card, so to speak, and assessment was purely at the discretion of the king's justices. In the year 1210 the visit of the normal circuit judges was supplemented by a tour by special justices whose sole objective seems to have been to amerce all and sundry. Since in the normal run of things the average man could expect to be amerced at least once a year either directly or indirectly this further imposition was fiercely resented.

The wording of the clause deals precisely with the grievance; a man is not to be 'amerced for a slight offence, except in keeping with the degree of the offence'. But there were also two important additional provisos. No matter what the offence, no one was to be fined so heavily as to be left destitute. The freeholder should not be obliged to sell his land to clear the debt to the court, the merchant should not have to sell out his stock-in-trade, and even the villein should be spared his 'wainage'. Whether this means his agricultural implements or is in fact a corruption of the French word 'garnage' and therefore means 'tillage' is of little importance. The intention is clear. Villeins should not be amerced so heavily as to lose their means of livelihood.

This apparently touching concern for the well-being of the peasantry did not necessarily mean that the barons had a social conscience. The villeins were a vital element in estate economy, being bound to do labour services and liable to pay tallage at the whim of their lord. The clause is concerned with amercements by the king's court and seems to want to ensure that these will not so impoverish the villein that he can no longer meet his obligations to his lord's estate. Villeins, in short, were the property of the lords and the king was being obliged in this clause to respect the vested interests of his barons. The relevant clause in the version of the Charter issued by the young Henry III's government 1217 introduces a saving clause to protect the royal interest. The text now reads not 'a villein shall be amerced in the same way . . .' (i.e. reasonably) but 'a villein *other than our own* shall be amerced in the same way' (i.e. reasonably). The king was to retain his right to exploit the peasantry on his own estates even if he had to respect the livelihood of peasants on the estates of others. Obviously the king was to enjoy the same rights of exploitation over his own peasants as the barons had over theirs.

The barons were also determined to curb the arbitrary assessments handed down by the courts and stipulated that no amercements whatsoever could be imposed 'except by the oath of the honest men of the neighbourhood'. The following clause stipulated that 'earls and barons' should likewise be amerced only according to the degree of the offence and only by their peers. The clause after that applied it to the clergy who had a lay holding.

The bulk of the remaining clauses of special interest to the barons themselves were mostly concerned with money in one form or another. Since England was still in the process of becoming a fully-fledged money economy, cashflow was a chronic problem. Most of the barons on both sides of the dispute over the Charter were, we may assume, in debt for most of their lives and probably died in debt. The estate of a crown tenant would no doubt be encumbered at his death with arrears of unpaid scutage, outstanding instalments on aids or impossible commitments contracted to have the king's goodwill. The heir and family of the deceased would be harassed by visitations from the local sheriff and royal bailiffs intent on seizing whatever lay in their path, ostensibly to sell in the interests of their royal master.

As often as not far more was taken and sold than was needed to clear any outstanding debts. The surplus either stuck to the hands of the agent or was dispatched to the royal coffers as a welcome windfall for his royal master. Clause 26 aimed to stop all this by providing that the king's officer was empowered in the first instance merely to catalogue the goods and chattels and to sell nothing until the exact extent of the indebtedness to the crown had been established.

The next clause deals with intestacy. At least since the time of Henry II the goods of anyone who died without leaving a will were simply confiscated by the crown. Under the terms of the Charter the chattels were to be distributed by his kinsfolk and friends, presumably amongst themselves but under the supervision of the church. It was the custom among churchmen in the middle ages to encourage people to leave endowments for religion. Since they were in fact in a position to withhold extreme unction from the dying, or at least were perceived to have that power, it was not always difficult for them to persuade a man to perform his duty. If he died intestate the church, along with his relations, was deprived. One class of persons necessarily died intestate, namely felons, but they were a special case, one in which the interests of the king and his tenants-in-chief were liable to conflict, and are dealt with under Clause 32.

Like so many of the clauses it is short and to the point but conceals much more than it reveals. The crown promises to hold for no more than 'a year and a day the lands of those who have been convicted of felony', after which time the land was to be handed over to the lord of the fief. By ancient custom the land of a criminal formally indicted and sentenced for a felony went to his feudal lord while the chattels were the perquisite of the lord who had tried him.

In the course of time the crown encroached on both these customary rights. There was no problem when the felon was a tenant-in-chief, that is, held from the king as his immediate lord. When however he was the man of some other there was immediate conflict. It became recognized that if the felony in question was treason the mesne lords lost all rights in the land. Where however it was some lesser offence they had, in theory at least, the right to the property and chattels. Since the crown had established its usurped rights so strongly over the generations some compromise had to be arrived at; it was represented by Clause 32 of the Charter.

The king made good his claim to occupy the lands in question for a year and a day. During this time his officers were under instructions to seize whatever might be of profit to their royal master and to lay waste everything else. It is quite apparent from contemporary legal texts that the words were taken quite literally. Houses and outbuildings were thrown down, gardens destroyed, meadow land ploughed over, woods uprooted and livestock sold off. When the felon's lord did take up possession of the lands, he was likely to enter on a desert. The wording of Magna Carta is uncharacteristically loose on the subject. If by speaking of a year and a day rather than the more normal 'year, day and waste' it thought to abolish the practice of waste it failed in its intention. One of the most dramatic descriptions of waste is to be found in the pages of the thirteenth-century legal theorist known as Bracton.

A miscellany of clauses attempts to check abuses like demands for money in lieu of service on a castle garrison when the knight was willing to put in his time. No doubt the king preferred professional soldiers to rustic Sir Gawains, but it was the gentry's right to serve, and the week or two spent with the territorials, so to speak, could be a welcome break from the routine of life.

Always on the grab, the king even plundered the revenues of religious foundations endowed and hence 'owned' by mesne barons. The charters making such foundations, whether by the king or one of his lords, were careful to reserve various valuable property rights including that of wardship of the estate between the death of one abbot and the election of another. In Clause 46 of their Charter, for such Magna Carta must surely appear, the barons endeavoured to put a stop to this practice. Finally, in this summary of the baronial defence of their revenues, one can mention the vexed question of petty serjeanties.

Any estate of even modest size was liable to comprise a patchwork of properties large and small acquired over the generations by various means, from various lords and for various services. Those commonly grouped together as 'petty serjeanties' are among the most colourful. These could range from counting the lord's chess pieces after he had played and stowing them away in the box, to the annual render of a sheaf of arrows or a hunting knife – peppercorn rents, in fact, in the language of a later generation. On the principle, if that is the word, that a holding from the king must take precedence over any other, John had enforced where he could the right to wardship of a whole estate the bulk of which might owe knight service to one of his barons, but one or two parcels of land were held of the crown on some lesser tenure or even a petty serjeanty. Thus the true lord was deprived of the revenues accruing under any period of wardship. This abuse was legislated against in Clause 37.

If the baronial obsession with money and revenue of any kind seems somewhat mundane in the authors of what was once generally vaunted to be the foundation-stone of English liberties, this is surely as it should be. Money can make a fair claim to be the only truly international language and proves just as eloquent over time as it does over space. More than one historian has observed that the history of parliament is merely a story of rivalry over the control of the purse-strings. King John's repertoire of extortion was so wide and varied that what by medieval standards was a large charter was barely sufficient to do justice to it.

Schoolbook history customarily used to distinguish two phases in the history of the medieval nobility, from the earlier 'robber baron' to the chivalric knightly era. There is, it must be said, a grain of truth in the idea. The year 1200 may be seen as the watershed between the one and the other. The earliest recorded tournaments date from the mid eleventh century – they were, in fact, battles without a cause except the love of fighting and the ambition for plunder. The earliest code of rules, rudimentary though it no doubt was, is attributed to a French knight Godfrey de Preuilly who died in the year 1062, fittingly enough in the course of one of his own tournaments. Well into the next century tournaments continued to range over 'fields of play' several square miles in extent, with hundreds of participants organized into *ad hoc* war parties.

The sport was popular in sophisticated southern France, with its code of courtly love, as well as the north. The notion of the troubadours as exquisite if ineffectual lutenists is belied by verses from Bertrand de Born which, roughly translated, conclude: 'I love the gay time of Easter . . . the leaves and flowers . . . the joyous songs of birds . . . the knights and horses in the meadows in battle array. We are going to have a marvellous time. Trumpets and drums and horses . . . when men of good breeding think only of killing . . . nothing thrills me like the . . . sight of the last dead with the pennoned stumps of lances in their sides.' And if there was no war actually in progress a battle could quickly be set up. Honour played little part in these conflicts. It was not unknown for a combatant to stand aloof from the fray until well on into the day and then ride down some exhausted but well caparisoned young tournier, strip him of horse and armour and hold him hostage. Booty and ransom was the aim for most and fortunes could be made.

The most famous knight of his age was of course William Marshal who ended his days as England's revered elder statesman and champion of the boy king Henry III after John's death. But his beginnings had been obscure.

When he was about twenty-two he earned the admiration and gratitude of Eleanor of Aquitaine when fighting in her cause. Henry II appointed him tutor in chivalry to their eldest son Henry, 'the Young King'. In due course the once landless adventurer admitted the prince to the order of knighthood. Marshal was one of the last men to make a business out of the tourney field. Rich and noble families were increasingly loath to risk wealth and social status in such brawls. By the time Marshal retired the events were being codified. Europe's first organized sport was in the making. The robber barons, if not actually being transformed into Galahads, were learning to love King Arthur.

6

LONDON, CITIES, TOWNS AND COMMUNES

'AND THE CITY OF LONDON SHALL HAVE ALL ITS ANCIENT LIBERTIES AND FREE CUSTOMS, BY LAND AND WATER; FURTHERMORE, WE DECREE AND GRANT THAT ALL OTHER CITIES, BOROUGHS, TOWNS, AND PORTS SHALL HAVE ALL THEIR LIBERTIES AND FREE CUSTOMS.'

IN the year of Magna Carta London could already look back on more than a millennium of history. The name, with its Celtic associations, indicates that the settlement on the Thames antedated the Romans. At the height of the numerous rival Anglo-Saxon kingdoms known as the heptarchy (seventh-eighth centuries) it was a prize of dispute between Mercia and Wessex. By the time of the conquest, Winchester, as the treasury of the House of Wessex, could claim, if any town in England could be given that title, to be the capital. But London was undoubtedly the country's metropolis. Archaeological excavations in the later 1980s revealed that the place was considerably larger than had been supposed up to that time, with a population which may indeed have made it the largest city in northern Europe. As we have seen, the German noblemen who provided the escort to King Richard I on his return from captivity to the emperor were astonished by the wealth of the place and vowed that had their master been better informed he would have set the ransom at a much higher figure.

A decade before, the writer William FitzStephen wrote a eulogy of the city which has become legendary. The forest of ships congesting its port, the rich furs of its citizens, the splendour of its buildings, the number of its churches are all themes for obvious pride in being a citizen of the place. But the image that lives in the mind is of the young men wrestling and playing at pitch-the-stone and similar sports in Finsbury Fields, and the citizens going off on a spring morning to hunt in the woods of Middlesex.

One of the many anomalies of Great Britain today is that its capital is, technically speaking, not the seat of government – most departments of state being housed in offices in the City not of London but of Westminster. From the time of St Edward the Confessor Westminster was the coronation place of the English kings and London never became a royal city in the sense that Paris was.

To this day, visitors at all familiar with London observe the way in which, outside the City proper, it has the feeling of a cluster of villages rather than of a single metropolitan area. To some extent, of course, this is and must be true of any very large conurbation, but of London it has been true at least since the eleventh century when, it has been said, the city was 'a bundle of communities, townships, parishes and lordships', each of which had its own constitution. By the twelfth century, there were two institutions which expressed its corporate identity – the folkmoot and the 'hustings' (held indoors and, from its name, apparently going back to the time of the ninth-century Danish invasions). The city could field its own militia. Ancestor of the famous London trained bands, this was a force to be reckoned with – in 1145 Robert of Gloucester retreated from his new castle at Faringdon before the '*Londonensium terribiliem et numerosum exercitum*', 'the large and fearsome army of London', which by this campaign quite probably ensured King Stephen's final success in the civil war. In fact he began his reign indebted to the Londoners.

The acclamation of the populace, a vital part in the coronation ceremony of the English kings, in practice generally meant the leading men and the citizenry of London. At the coronation of William I on Christmas Day 1066, the shout of acclaim within the church was so loud that William's Norman guards at the doors rushed to set fire to the nearby buildings, mistakenly supposing that their duke-king had been killed and the English were about to burst out of the building to begin a counter-conquest. It was of course merely a loyal salute, no doubt led by carefully chosen establishment figures, Norman and English, many of the latter being leading men of the city.

Perhaps a few remembered a similar scene half a century before. Then, another foreign invader had the kingdom by the throat. Cnut of Denmark and his army controlled the greater part of the country when King Aethelred II 'the Unready' died, early in the year 1016. He left a handsome and warlike young son, Edmund Ironside, the natural candidate, it would seem, for loyal Englishmen. At that time, however, the eastern half of England was Danish by allegiance and Cnut, young like Edmund, seems to have had the larger forces to draw on as well as the hardier soldiers. But London held firm for Edmund and we are told that those members of the Witan (the council of the realm) who were there together with the '*burhwaru*' of London, i.e. the chief citizens, chose him to be king. To complete the formalities the populace as a whole acclaimed him.

For constitutional historians the chief interest of the story is the light it throws on the element of 'election' in the English coronation rituals. But for generations of Londoners it may have been these events which lay behind the extraordinary claim, made in the year 1135, that it belonged to them as of right to choose the king of England. On 1 December that year King Henry I died at Lyons la Forêt in southern Normandy, after days of a lingering death following a hunting accident. Barely three weeks later Stephen of Blois, count of Boulogne, was crowned his successor and acclaimed by the men of London, just like Edmund Ironside, as Stephen's biographer rather oddly pointed out. At the coronation of Richard I, as we have seen, the city rioted when it appeared that its leading citizens had been rebuffed. London's claim to choose England's king was no doubt arrant nonsense: equally clear is the fact that the city had more than once played a prominent role in king-makings and that without its backing no king could hope to be secure.

For if the claims of the chief citizens sounded bombastic – they particularly vaunted the title of 'barons of London' when, following the Conquest, the word came into vogue for the chief nobility of the realm – they were not empty. Some two years before the historic events that marked the accession and coronation of Stephen, his predecessor King Henry I had made some notable concessions to the capital city in the form of a charter. The revenues franchised or farmed for the crown by the sheriff of London were valued at an annual farm at the very low figure of £300. Secondly the citizens acquired the right to appoint the sheriff of London and also the sheriff of the surrounding county of Middlesex – which meant that the king agreed to the exclusion of his own tax gatherers (for revenue collection was then the sheriff's principal job) from the richest city in northern Europe. The third major concession was that the Londoners should appoint their own justiciar (i.e. law administrator).

The arrangements so highly flattering to London did not survive unscathed for long. In February 1141 King Stephen, the Londoners' favourite, was defeated and captured at the battle of Lincoln. His rival, the Empress Matilda, was in the ascendant and at Winchester his own brother Henry the bishop, proclaiming the capture to be the judgement of God, claimed for the clergy the priority in election to the crown and declared in favour of Matilda. London's representatives arriving in Winchester to take their part in the 'election' can hardly have been best pleased by any of this. Only six years before they had asserted their claim to elect the monarch as of right and had acclaimed Stephen. Now they gathered their dignity about them as best they could and merely demanded that he be released.

Everyone in England except Matilda, who had spent her formative years in Germany as the wife of the Emperor Henry V and revelled in exacting the honour and obeisances due an empress, knew that now was the time to woo the Londoners. Matilda entered the city like a conqueror in triumph, wore the insignia of an empress, required the leading members of the city's militia to do homage as was customary to an empress by kissing her stirrup, and then ordered a tax to be levied on the very city her own father had granted should be free of royal revenue officials. Her forces were not sufficient to maintain such arrogance. The citizens first swore to establish a 'commune', an early use of the word even by the standards of the continent, where the north Italian cities were flexing their muscles against imperial power, and then expelled Matilda. She next fell out with the bishop of Winchester and proceeded to besiege him in his own city. Need one say, she never became queen of England.

The charter granted by Henry II did not mention the right to elect the sheriff or the justiciar, and did not confirm the reduction of the farm to £300 (hardly surprising 20 years on – even in the twelfth century there was inflation, though it was somewhat less severe than today).

During the reign of Richard I the city took advantage of the dispute between Chancellor William Longchamp and Prince John to trade their support for the prince in exchange for royal recognition of their formation of a 'commune'. The word, which was well known on the continent, was still something of an oddity in the English political vocabulary. But then the role of London itself in the early history of England is still something of an enigma.

It would appear that in the eleventh and twelfth centuries the bulk of London's citizenry were English rather than Norman. In their important work, *Medieval Kingship*, Henry A. Myers and Herwig Wolfram comment that whereas French kings used *baillis* (town officials) to counterbalance the nobility, 'even Henry II generally took men from the lower feudal ranks of his service rather than from the middle class. Possibly Saxon preeminence in the merchant interest inclined him to this.'

Be that as it may, it was in London that the issue was joined between William Longchamp, first nominated by Richard as his representative, and Prince John, recognized by Richard as rector of the realm. And it was in London that Longchamp was charged with being a foreigner – with having 'insulted the English nation and being ignorant of the English language' – as well as with being corrupt and incompetent. As a result, in October 1191 the administration found itself paralysed by the conflict and London found itself the stage for the resolution of the drama. In the words of J. H. Round, 'The chronicles of the day allow us to picture the scene for ourselves, as the excited citizens, who had poured forth overnight, with lanterns and torches, to welcome John to the capital, streamed together on the morning of the eventful 8th October at the well-known sound of the great bell, swinging from its campanile in St Paul's Churchyard. There they heard John take the oath to the "Commune"'.

Longchamp was removed from, or at least obliged to leave, office by two meetings of the citizenry, those present preening themselves no doubt as members of the London commune. One of the meetings was held in the chapter house of St Paul's, the second on open ground near the Tower.

The use of the word 'English' in the indictment of Longchamp is interesting on a number of counts. It seems out of kilter with the conventional view of the middle ages as a period when national concepts did not exist. In fact the modern word 'nation' derives from the medieval usage of the Latin word '*natio*' to mean a person's origin by birth. At least since the treaty of Verdun in 843 between the eastern and western successor states to the Carolingian empire had had to be written in French and German as well as Latin versions, people had been well aware of the differences between the various '*natios*' of Europe, as we might call them. The nation state might lie in the future but most of the sentiments of nationalism and chauvinism were thriving well before the twelfth century.

More surprising is to find a Norman official being pilloried for 'insulting' the English nation in a land where even yet the death of a Norman meant the indictment of the community where it happened on a 'presentment of Englishry', on the assumption that the killing was by a patriot Englishman against the occupying power. At this time the term English, besides meaning people of English race, could also designate those who lived in England, whatever their race. Thus a Norman baron whose estates lay in England, while he might be insulted were it suggested he had English blood in his veins, would consider himself an English man by contrast to a cousin who held the family lands in Normandy. But the allusion to Longchamp's ignorance of the language not only indicates that its use was much more widespread than might have been expected but must also indicate that the term 'English' is being used in its first sense.

So what was Prince John, an Angevin prince with Norman pretensions and only a part of a great-grandmother by way of English antecedents, doing in acceding to such rhetoric? And if the answer is that he would seize any opportunity to further his own ambitions, surely it was taking opportunism too far to meddle in the politics of a commune. Like the other magnates and the bishops in London at that time who also took the common oath, John can have had little choice between discretion and valour, even had he wished for one. The city was roused, the tocsin had sounded and the populace were ready to stand to arms if needed.

They were stirring times. M. T. Clanchy sees the 'removal of Longchamp by an association which claimed to speak for the English people and the Londoners in particular' as a 'significant step towards the articulation of public opinion as a political force'. But surely we can go further in assessing the contribution of the events surrounding the London commune of 1191 to the still more dramatic dénouement at Runnymede a generation later. The oath taken by the barons before their fateful encounters with the king is reminiscent of the proceedings of the London commune and may have been prompted by memories of it.

There is still debate among historians about the precise nature of communes in medieval Europe, and still greater uncertainty as to the commune of London – England's lone example. Speaking with cynical detachment, the ecclesiastical chronicler Richard of Devizes, present during the stirring days of '91, observed: 'A commune is an unnatural growth on the people, a cause of fear to the realm and a matter of indifference to the clergy (*tepor sacerdotii*)'. Less emotively we can say that a commune was an urban community, with an elective council and elected head. To establish such an institution in the world of feudal Europe, which recognized only force or the claims of birth or descent, required a novel procedure by townsmen: the taking of a common oath. This procedure was the '*conjuratio*' (literally, 'swearing together'), a term loosely translated by modern historians as 'conspiracy'. On the continent communes were, to all intents and purposes, revolutionary associations, and the part played by John, the magnates and the bishops in the oath-taking of 1191 must have struck contemporaries forcibly.

It was certainly a landmark for London, for with the establishment of the commune the citizens also established the right to elect a mayor as its head. The city further strengthened its position when John succeeded to the crown. In exchange for 3000 marks he granted a series of charters which confirmed the charter of Henry I in all points except the liberty to appoint its own justiciar.

As the thirteenth century opens the outlines of the familiar pattern of medieval London's business community and municipal government are beginning to emerge. The structure of guilds and companies is in place; principal among them the weavers, bakers, pepperers, butchers, goldsmiths and cloth dressers and also the enigmatic 'guilds of the bridge'. How long the city's 'revolution', if we may use the term, lasted is less clear. There is a reference to the 'mayor and commune of London' as late as 1221, from which it has been assumed that 'liberties and free customs' guaranteed to the city in Clause 13 of John's Charter included the confirmation of the commune.

A charter dated 9 May 1215, clearly intended as a bait to woo the city from the baronial cause, confirmed all existing liberties; gave guarantees to foreign merchants that they would be tolled only once by the king's chamberlain selecting items from their stock for the royal household; and also conceded the right to appoint a mayor annually and to replace him with another at the end of the term if required (by the terms of 1191 the mayor of the commune had been elected for life). With this provision, London's maturity as a self-governing municipality is fully validated.

Some of these provisions were listed in a document known as the 'Nine Articles' which appears to be the headings of a petition prepared by a committee of Londoners and generally supposed to have been intended for submission to the king. The main points are exemption from arbitrary tallage, control of the Thames, the annual election of the mayor in the folkmoot, the right to distrain for debt against the property and persons of debtors, and freedom of access for foreign traders. Some of these feature in the articles and some in the Great Charter itself.

The point about foreign merchants is an interesting one. It had always been one of the most valued privileges of borough status to levy exactions on and raise toll barriers against foreign merchants or those not members of one's own guild. It was however a different matter when the royal government added harassments of its own. At first glance, then, it may seem inconsistent that the Londoners are protecting the interests of alien merchants but, as McKechnie drily remarked: 'The inconsistency . . . is perhaps greater in appearance than reality, since the . . . chapter aimed at abolition of "evil customs" inflicted by the king, not those inflicted by the boroughs.'

From the moment they occupied the city the opposition barons found firm friends and allies among London's leading men. The articles of the barons contained important clauses aimed to protect London interests, and most of these are to be found in the Great Charter, if in modified form. But there were omissions, the most serious concerning the Londoners' liability to tallage. This was the purest form of protection money, levied at will and without appeal by king or lord from townsman or serf, village or city. It was particularly loathed because it was arbitrary, could be extortionate, and above all because it was not levied on the barons. To be subject to tallage was a badge of inferior status. But whereas the articles of the barons contain explicit exemption for London from aids *and* tallage, the relevant clause in the Great Charter deals only with the question of the feudal aids.

The contrast between the two types of levy was marked. Whereas, in theory at least, one could name the sum one proposed to pay by way of aid, with the prospect that a sensibly generous offer would be accepted, the level of a tallage was fixed by a king's officials. Whereas the aid was paid in a lump sum from the citizens as a body and they were responsible for raising it from amongst their membership, tallage was assessed by the royal revenue officials on the wealth of each citizen individually and levied from them directly. Aid was at least in theory voluntary; tallage was forced and had a striking resemblance to modern income tax, and was equally hated.

Despite the Great Charter, and for all its power and wealth, London found that it was still humiliatingly subject to occasional arbitrary taxation. The city continued the struggle to gain exemption but to no avail. In 1255, the government of Henry III demanded a tallage of 3000 marks. The city's first response was to offer an aid of 2000 marks, and when this was rejected they denied outright that they were liable for tallage. The mayor and leading citizens were thereupon ordered to present themselves at the exchequer, where they were confronted with the entries in the exchequer and chancery roll which demonstrated quite clearly that the city had paid tallage on numerous occasions in the past. The following day they turned up with the cash.

It is hardly surprising that of all the towns and cities in England London should be the only one mentioned by name. Not only was it incomparably the largest, it was also a steady ally of the baronial party, and its mayor was named as one of the Twenty-five charged with supervising the king's adherence to the terms of Runnymede. In fact one important source for our knowledge concerning the selection and resources of the Twenty-five occurs in a manuscript compiled by a Londoner, most likely employed in the chamber at Guildhall, over a period of about 10 years from 1206. Among other things it contains the supposed 'Laws of Edward the Confessor', the customs of London and a group of historical documents. Clearly interested in politics, the compiler may well have been close in the councils of the opposition to John in the days immediately before Runnymede.

Known as the Lambeth manuscript, it not only lists the names of the Twenty-five – though excluding the mayor of London – it also adds after each name a quota of knights. Since these quotas correspond neither to the known power nor the knight service owed by the barons in question, it is assumed that the figures indicate the number of retainers each of the names could call on in the London-Runnymede region at the time the list was drawn up. Presumably the information contained in the memorandum came from a baronial source; it seems equally likely that the scribe was a Londoner.

No doubt to many a hard-headed London merchant the guarantee of free customs by land as well as by water was as important as constitutional liberties. Control of river traffic on the Thames and Medway was much valued as a means of restraining the rivalry of smaller towns. Yet outside the circuit of the metropolis town life was beginning to grow apace. Though no English town outside London could match a Florence or a Nuremberg, many were thriving and more were being founded. John himself founded the new town of Liverpool, while his father had granted a monopoly of Irish trade to Bristol, which now begins its rise to the status of the country's second city. Soon it, like London, would be able to claim full county status, while centres such as York and Norwich were rising to new prominence as the wool trade of England grew ever more prosperous.

So much depends on the evidence which has survived. The archaeological reassessment of London's size and importance might tempt us to up-rate various other centres where they were subjects of comparison with the capital. Work during the 1970s on the archaeology of standing buildings in Chester led to a reassessment of the age of the structures in the famous 'Rows', dating some of the shops back to the thirteenth century. Such revisions would fit the fragmentary literary evidence, for Chester was the subject of a panegyric similar to FitzStephen's on London and written only a little later, round about 1200, by a monk of the nearby monastery of St Werburgha.

A further example from the south may show how townsmen all over England had reason to applaud the work of the barons and the Londoners that day in Runnymede when they forced King John to agree that 'all other cities, boroughs, towns and ports' should have their 'liberties and free customs'.

In 1191, the year of London's commune, the royal exchequer held its accounting sessions in Oxford and the town proudly issued its own charter under its own seal. At this time, Oxford was a flourishing commercial centre with a population estimated at some 5000. It had emerged from a prolonged struggle over market rights with nearby Abingdon and Wallingford, and besides trade had a sizeable weaving industry. This was regulated by its own guild under royal charter, handsomely paid for, and had a monopoly of cloth production within a radius of five leagues from the town centre.

By 1200 Oxford was growing in reputation as an academic centre. During the twelfth century numerous towns, among them Exeter, Northampton and Lincoln, had notable schools and attracted masters in various faculties. But law was then as today the academic discipline for the ambitious, and outside London there were few places more suited than Oxford for the study of this passport to royal service. With the court continually on the move and Oxford but a day's march from Windsor, the town was often on the itinerary. Nearby, the royal hunting lodge of Woodstock was a favourite with both Henry I and Henry II. King Stephen had held his first council at Oxford and the empress had made it her capital when she lost London. Henry II held two great councils there and his sons John and Richard were born at Beaumont Palace, just outside the town's west gate.

'King John and the Barons at Runnymede'. This mural done by Ernest Normande for the Royal Exchange, London, perfectly captures the classic myth of Magna Carta. A shifty King John, seated in all the panoply of state, is confronted by the wise and freedom-loving leaders of the barons. In the right foreground the 'spignel' (official of the seal) operates the press to produce the wax seal ready for its attachment to the document. In fact this was almost certainly done elsewhere.

Sealed writ of Edward the Confessor in favour of Westminster Abbey, written in Anglo-Saxon and issued shortly before the king's death in January 1066.

Below: William I's charter, guaranteeing their pre-Conquest liberties to the bishop, portreeve and citizens of London. The language is still Anglo-Saxon, though the Norman regime would shortly go over to Latin.

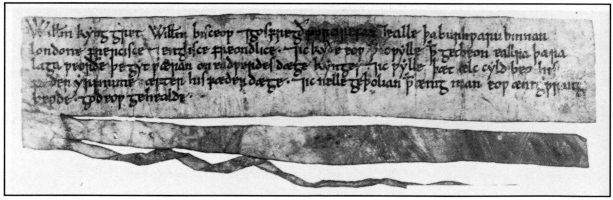

Writs and charters had been tools of the English government since Anglo-Saxon times. Brief, business-like, often in beautiful calligraphy and authenticated by the royal seal, they were treasured by their recipients as proofs of often valuable rights and liberties.

The figure seated in the upper lobe of this capital 'E' initial may be intended for King Edward I. However it is the little windmill above the royal head which gives the manuscript its name as 'The Windmill Psalter'.

A passage in the Exchequer memorandum roll for the year 1300 depicts King Edward I pointing solemnly at the words 'Magna Carta' in a request that the Exchequer henceforward observe the clauses of the Charters, confirmed that year. Five years later the king received a papal absolution from his oath.

Magna Carta 1225. The version issued by Henry III which entered the statute book. This authorized copy (or 'exemplification') has the young king's seal attached.

The full majesty of the court of the king's bench in the fourteenth century, complete with shackled criminals at the bar. Notice that behind the judges hang, from right to left, the royal arms of England, the king's arms of France and England and the (fictional) arms of the House of Wessex, for Edward the Confessor, who before Magna Carta was considered the fount of English justice and liberties.

The 'Dorchester Crusader'. This fine tomb carving in the thirteenth-century abbey church of Dorchester on Thames, Oxfordshire, depicts the figure of a recumbent knight, his legs crossed in symbol of service on the Crusade.

This famous illumination of Sir Geoffrey Luttrell is the classic English image of the knight in the Age of Chivalry. By the 1340s the unruly tournaments of the days of King John had given way to more regulated jousts, while ring mail had been replaced by plate armour. Sir Geoffrey proudly flaunts his family arms on surcoat, shield and the caparisons of his horse.

The stone coffin made in the fourteenth century to receive the body of Joan, the illegitimate daughter of King John who became the wife of Prince Llywelyn ap Iorworth ('the Great') of Gwynedd. Beaumaris Church, Anglesey. It was Joan who warned her father of the conspiracy against his life in 1212.

Among the cluster of royal camp-followers and hopeful courtiers were ambitious clerks looking for permanent employment and in need of the increasingly vital qualifications in civil or canon law, the keys to promotion in church and state. More and more distinguished lawyers, graduates of Paris or Bologna, found Oxford a profitable base to set up teaching practice. Masters in other faculties followed, and by the early 1200s the place was recognized as a *studium generale*, or university.

Oxford had its moment of glory in the year 1258 as focus in the historic conflict between King Henry III and the rebels among the baronage led by Simon de Montfort, Earl of Leicester. On 12 April Simon and six other magnates swore on oath of common purpose, reminiscent of those *conjuratios* made at the time of the London commune and the Articles of the Barons all those years before. Others joined them and some three weeks later, at a confrontation in Westminster Hall, they forced King Henry and his son the Lord Edward (later king as Edward I) to take an oath on the Gospel to follow their rulings.

The king now issued letters announcing that he had agreed to a reform of the realm and convening a general meeting at Oxford for early June. By now this great centre of learning with its numerous law teachers was a natural venue for such a debate. Simon had been a friend of the great Bishop Robert Grosseteste, first chancellor of the university, and the Oxford canon lawyer Thomas Cantilupe, one of his successors in the post, became an adviser to the baronial opposition.

Assembling on 9 June 1258 many of them armed, the delegates to this constitutional assembly, as we would call it today, the king and his son and leading advisers among them, all swore oaths of common loyalty in the name of *le commun de Engleterre*. Oaths were the cement of medieval society, the most common being the oath of homage sworn by a man to his lord. The bond thus established was one of dependency and subordination in exchange for protection and favours granted. The oath to a commune, by contrast, was one in which members, considered equal for the purposes of the oath, swore to work together for the common good. Magna Carta Clause 61 provides for action by *communa tocius terre* to distrain against the king if he should fail to observe its terms.

The meeting at Oxford continued with the framing of the conditions for the reorganization of the government of the kingdom, known to history as the Provisions of Oxford. Like the Great Charter, they were careful to lay down a monitoring body, in this case numbering twenty-four, with twelve from the king's side and twelve from the opposition. The daily business of government was to be conducted by the king in consultation with a council of fifteen; and there were to be discussions or 'parlemenz' (the first record of the word 'parliament') three times a year between the council and twelve appointees of the 'commune'.

Altogether, the Provisions appear to have been much more stringent and carefully thought out than the arrangements of Magna Carta. Had Henry III died the year after signing them, as his father mistakenly had done, England could have been set fair to becoming a republic on the model of the Italian city states. As it was, he worked unremittingly to free himself of these intolerable limitations on royal power. The 'commune of England', like the commune of London, is now barely a memory among the might-have-beens of history.

7

COMMUNITIES
OF THE FOREST

Today the word conjures up images of leafy glades, animal sounds, bird calls, the idea of nature sanctuary, tales of Robin Hood and the greenwood stories of poachers and gamekeepers. These were part of the medieval experience, but more important were the utilitarian connotations associated in the modern mind with the forestry commission, for the wastes and forests of medieval Europe were a prime source of food and raw materials.

The word forest derives from the Latin *foris*, 'outside', and was used to designate any area, wooded or not, which was barred to common use and reserved for the king, and above all for the royal hunt. The forests resembled the sacred groves of the Germanic ancestors of the Anglo-Saxon kings; the royal hunt had once had religious and mythical associations and the woodlands had their own ceremonies and services. Echoes of these ancient traditions, and possibly still older ones dating back to Celtic times, linger in the services and dues recorded in the Domesday Book. Legends of wood spirits and mystic huntsmen survived long into Elizabethan times, so that 'Herne the Huntsman', a spirit of Windsor Forest, could terrorize Falstaff at the end of Shakespeare's *Merry Wives of Windsor*. But such folk memories played little part in the calculations of the royal foresters of the Angevin kings, who saw the lands under their control exclusively in terms of exploitation and profit.

Modern commercial woodlands are mainly managed by monoculture, for timber. The medieval forest was a diverse ecosystem whose animals and fruits were all carefully husbanded. In his book *La Forêt au Moyen Age* the

French scholar Roland Bechmann gives a vivid account of the diverse nature of forest resources. Berries and mushrooms provided foods, and in addition there were medicinal plants and poisons; bee products such as honey and candle wax; oil, from walnuts and beechnuts; forage, such as the salt-rich compost of fallen leaves, for farm and draught animals; wood resins for torches, pitch and glue; leaves for mattress stuffing for humble households (beech leaves were called 'wood feathers'); bark for tiles and shingles, boats and baskets; wood ash for fertilizer and washing lye; leather and furs from the wild animals; horn for drinking-vessels, hunting-horns and knife-handles. Nevertheless, the principal forest resource, then as now, was wood.

Timber was a prime material in the building industry. All but the grandest town houses were built of wood, while churches and cathedrals consumed vast quantities in scaffolding and centring for the masonry vaults and arches. The thirteenth century was a time of expanding trade and developments in England's naval establishment, and John's royal shipyards consumed great quantities of timber. Then there was the increasing range of industrial users, such as glass-makers (who preferred beechwood) and ironmasters (50 cubic metres of wood fuel to make 100 kgm of iron). There were osiers for basket-weaving; coppiced rods for hurdle-making and charcoal-burning; hardwood for spades and hoes (given the expense of metal working, only the cutting edge was iron shod, if at all) or softwood saplings which could be bent and tied to grow to shape for scythe handles and other such specialized applications. And in the troubled times of the civil war timber was in heavy demand for war machines and castles. Clause 31 of the Charter pledged that in future royal officers would not take 'other people's timber for castles or other works' except by agreement.

The law of the forest

Behind the busy pageant of forest life loomed the sinister presence of the forest laws, absolute and binding on all who lived or owned land within the forest boundary. A juridical rather than a topographical concept, this was widely drawn and could embrace not only woodland but heaths and upland wastes which on their lower margins might include cultivated lands, villages and even towns. Nor was it confined to royal properties, as the game runs might cross into neighbouring estates. Twelfth-century kings had afforested land at their will and pleasure, without deigning to consult barons or people.

Since the days of Henry I in the early twelfth century forest law had been at the unfettered will of the king. It rested on the twin principles of 'venison' and 'vert'. The one prohibited not only the killing but even the disturbing of game animals, the second forbade the cutting of timber or the cultivation of further land, since this would damage the habitat. Not content with robbing private landowners of the profitable exploitation of their forest land, the crown insisted that owners of private woodland within the forest boundary maintain at their own expense full-time wood-wards with the duty of protecting the king's interests within their masters' lands. Their principal job was to prevent damage to trees, as these formed shelter for the game.

The pre-Conquest kings had guarded the hunting rights in their own domains. Cnut forbade trespassing on the royal hunting 'wherever I wish to have it preserved' – but the Normans afforested vast areas which before had been free of restrictions. The very name of the most famous, the New Forest, proclaims the change brought in by the Conquest settlement.

Royal prerogatives in the forest lands were infringed during the civil wars under Stephen; Henry II more than restored the status quo. He reinforced royal rights in the forest and appointed itinerant forest justices, less to do justice than to investigate former practice and restore rights which had lapsed. Henry not only re-established forest boundaries but, it was claimed, brought large new tracts of land under forest regulations. By the end of his reign a third of the country, including the entire county of Essex, was forest in the legal sense – one acre in every three, whether waste, arable, or tree-covered, came under a jurisdiction which, to quote the words of Henry II's treasurer Richard FitzNeal, rested 'not on the common law of the realm but on the will of the ruler'. As the modern historian W. L. Warren wrote: 'To live under forest laws was not to be excluded from the normal law as administered in the shires but to be subjected to an additional law of a harshly restrictive and punitive kind administered in special courts.'

Law officers, courts and penalties

The law of the forest was administered by its own officers. In each forest county twelve knights were appointed as 'regarders' to make tours of inspection every third year to report on encroachments on forest lands and to ensure that the prohibitions against carrying arms, particularly bows and arrows, were strictly enforced. It was their duty to see that any hunting-dog, mastiff or greyhound, kept by a forest dweller was 'lawed', that is, had three claws cut from the paws of each front foot. Four other knights called 'agistors' had the duty of protecting the king's interest in matters pertaining to the pasturage of swine or cattle. The landowner was not allowed to turn his own livestock loose in the forest, or rent out the grazing ('pannage') until thirty days after Michaelmas, when the best season for acorns and beech-mast was over.

At the head of the forest administration stood the forest justiciar, or chief forester (after 1238 the country was divided between two chief justiciars, one north, the other south of the River Trent). Next under him came the wardens, men of great power in the land, each having one or more forests under his control. Directly answerable to them an army of foresters and under-foresters effectively combined the functions of game-keeper with the powers of magistrate. If a man were charged with an offence under the forest laws the evidence was laid before the verderers, men of knightly status elected in the shire court. It was for them to assess whether there was a case to answer and, if so, to produce the culprit for trial in due course. In fact many a minor offender found himself at the mercy of the foresters.

The warden, in many cases constable of the principal royal castle in his district, was answerable only to the king. Instead of a salary he derived his income from the exercise of rights and perquisites large enough to ensure him a handsome living and to enable him to pay his foresters, who in theory were thus salaried officials. The system ensured corruption and extortion. Wardens paid handsomely for their appointments in anticipation of the immense private fortunes their powers would enable them to accumulate. They began to recoup the outlay the moment they were installed in office, selling off under-foresters' appointments to the highest bidders (no warden actually paid his underlings, who in their turn, to use the expressive phrase of the time, 'lived upon the country'). For the average forest dweller the result was often little better than a reign of terror.

The hierarchy of officials was matched by a hierarchy of courts. At the lowest level investigatory tribunals held every six weeks took evidence for cases to be tried usually before the itinerant forest justices. Since these higher courts were held at wide intervals offenders might have the prospect of conviction hanging over them for years. The multifarious offences under forest law were a rich source of profit to the crown but could reduce the forest-dwellers to abject poverty. If they failed to serve on a court inquisition, or if serving failed to produce a culprit, they were liable to a fine. If they gave or were judged to have given false information they were fined. If they sold or gave away timber; if a bow and arrow were found in their keeping; if they kept greyhounds or mastiffs which had not been lawed they paid a fine.

The penalties were draconian. By the terms of the 1217 Forest Charter possession of an unlawed dog carried a fine of 3 shillings – the best part of a month's pay for a skilled master huntsman. And yet this was regarded as a reform. Up to that time, a peasant caught with a hunt-ready dog in the king's forest was required to hand over an ox, without which he could hardly hope to plough his land.

Penalties were also often arbitrary, especially in the event of a 'serious trespass'. If one of the royal 'beasts' of the chase was found dead in the forest, an extraordinary 'Court of Inquisition' was convened which all the men of the nearest settlements were liable to attend. In the summer of 1209, the town of Maidford in Northamptonshire – the profits of its traders, the proceeds of its farms, the wealth of its inhabitants, the value of its livestock, in short 'the whole of the aforesaid town of Maidford' – was 'seized into the king's hand', as retribution for the death of a hart in the wood of Henry Dawney. The king's foresters had discovered the severed head of the animal on Dawney's land. His forester had recently died, while Dawney himself disclaimed all knowledge of the matter. When the townsmen refused to finger a culprit they were summarily dealt with.

The term 'serious trespass' was elastic. In the Pleas of the Forest we read how men representing four townships in the Forest of Somerton sat in solemn judgement on the corpse of a hare, deemed by the forester to be a beast of the chase. They found that 'the said hare died of a murrain'. Since the deposition contains no reference to any trap, and since it is clear that a poacher would have removed his booty from the scene of the crime, it is fairly obvious that the creature met its end by misadventure. Notwithstanding, the authorities proceeded to fine all four townships on the pretext that they had not sent a sufficient number of representatives.

Attendance at the court was an onerous duty. Travel, which meant by foot for most of the jurors, and the day or two of the session itself, could mean the best part of the week knocked out of one's schedule without, of course, either expenses or attendance allowance. When the king's justices of the forest made their appearance in a district the entire population, whether inside the forest boundaries or in adjacent outlying districts, was due to attend, according to the laws of Henry II. This duty was bitterly resented by those who lived beyond the boundaries, who reckoned their duty to the county court onerous enough. Clause 44 of the Great Charter at last freed them of the duty.

Even freeholders within the forest were restricted in the exercise of their proprietary rights. A list of things which a man might not do on his own land if it fell within the forest makes impressive reading. He might not uproot trees and clear land for cultivation, for that was to commit an assart which robbed the game animals of cover; the lopping or pruning of branches without due permission attracted its own fine. Outside the coverts he was forbidden to put waste or pasture land under the plough, to exploit natural deposits of marl or lime, to enclose any area by hedge or paling, to dig fishponds or to build water-mills and channel rivers into millstreams, for all these constituted purprestures, i.e. encroachments on the king's rights. Such restrictions on land development meant that any land within the legal forest tended to scrub and woodland cover. Thus the word 'forest' developed the meaning we understand by it today.

Hunting, the sport of barons and kings

Sport, the king's determination to have good hunting wherever he might be in the kingdom, lay at the root of the system. The beasts of the chase – the red deer, fallow deer, roe deer and wild boar – could be taken only by the king and his men or by the authorization of an express royal warrant. Anyone else might hunt only small animals such as hares, foxes, badgers, wolves or wild cats. Even these might not be taken without formal notification to the royal forester. Peter of Liddington was held in chains for 48 hours in a flooded subterranean cell on the suspicion of having taken a rabbit in Eastwood, Leicestershire. Many a prosperous peasant found himself arrested on such pretexts and put to the torture until he bought his release.

Hunting was not only the prime sport of the baronial class, it was also exceedingly popular with all ranks of society. At the lowest level a rabbit in the pot was a valuable addition to the daily diet. Higher up the social scale, the citizens of London claimed the ancient right to hunt the woodlands of Middlesex. But the most coveted of all game were the 'royal beasts', and these remained in the gift of the king.

A concession was made to the baronial love of the hunt by Clause 11 of the Forest Charter. It provided that a magnate passing through a forest might take two 'royal beasts' if he first notified the royal forester or, if the forester could not be found, signalled his presence with a horn blast. It was a modest enough allowance. In the June of 1252, Henry III's brother Richard, Earl of Cornwall, hunted for nine days over the forest of Rockingham and took more than thirty buck. Twelve years later, when civil war had reduced royal authority to a low ebb, the young earl of Derby and his companions invaded the royal forest of the Peak in Derbyshire and made a bag of fifty deer of various types.

A baron could win rights in the forest. Grants of vert and venison on one's own land could be bought, and specially favoured or powerful nobles might be given the franchise to hunt over a tract of royal forest. While such land, technically known as a 'chase', was not formally disafforested, within its boundaries the forest law was administered, generally in a modified form, by officials appointed by the franchisee.

But the king made grants very selectively, and to be sure of his hunting a baron was wise to create his own deer park by enclosing land outside the forest. This was then stocked by purchase or, if he was favoured, by gift from the king. Statute law required him to fence it round securely so that there might be no confusion with the beasts of the neighbouring royal forest. The newly enclosed hunting-ground, its livestock and the maintenance of the boundary fence were the responsibility of a parker. Barred appeal to royal forest law, he had to rely instead on strong boundary fencing and the common law of theft and trespass which soon acquired a specialist branch. By the nineteenth century this had evolved into a code of game laws almost as vicious as the medieval law of the forest.

Deer parks were to be found all over the country, some a modest 70 acres, others, like Wiscomb Park in the parish of Southleigh in East Devon, very extensive indeed. First made about the year 1200, it had a 4-mile boundary fence enclosing 640 acres of well-watered pastures and woodlands, rich in wild fruits in season such as strawberries and raspberries, well-stocked trout streams and, of course, game.

The typical park enclosure was an earth bank with an inside ditch and topped with a paling fence or quickset hedge. Despite the huge extent of the forests, royal beasts did stray from time to time and the construction of concealed deer leaps – inviting to jump but impossible to recross – was an art all its own. Outside the forest meant outside the forest law and the beast could be taken legitimately.

But the same principle also applied in reverse. One autumn day in 1251 the 29-year-old Richard de Clare, Earl of Gloucester, took his dinner guests on a stroll through his chase at Micklewood. The earl's dogs started a hart and finally brought it down in a covert in the neighbouring royal forest. As an earl, Richard was answerable only to the king; his friends were summoned to appear before the justices of the forest.

The officers of the forest law were no respecters of persons. Some years after the incident at Micklewood Chase Prince Llywelyn of Wales was hunting along the River Dyfi in Meirionydd when a stag ran out of a brake in front of his party and plunged across the river to the king's forest. The Welshmen followed and ran it down. Then 'the king's officers of those parts and others came to the huntsmen with horns and cries just as is done in times of war.' The prince looked on outraged as the English foresters took charge of the animal and, 'a thing almost unheard of', jostled and ill-treated his huntsmen.

Given the tensions of the border territories, the comparison with war was telling. Passions could run high in the hunting-field at the best of times. The mysteries of the hunt were served by a large establishment of skilled men to tend the horses, train and care for the dogs and draw the coverts. Among this band of professionals incompetence or any breach of the code was not to be tolerated. Early in the fourteenth century William Twici, chief huntsman to King Edward II, summed up the state of the art in his 'L'art de vénerie'. His salary matched what Edward's father had paid the architect mason of Caernarvon Castle. The repertoire of horn calls still heard today in the hunting-field was already well developed and must have been the most familiar music in the ears of many a nobleman and his lady.

The Forest Charter

Restrictions on the freedom of the chase were irksome, but it was the restrictions imposed on their rights as landowners which the baronial draughters of Magna Carta had in mind when they had the king swear to institute committees of enquiry and to abolish all 'evil customs' within 40 days of the completion of the enquiries.

By an order of June 1209 John had ordered that hedges should be burned and ditches levelled 'so that while men starved, the beasts might fatten upon the crops and fruits'. But such 'evil customs' had been part of the standard conduct of public life in England since the time of the Conquest. Even when not abused by royal forest officials, they constituted gross limitations on the freedom of landowners. Anyone in breach of them 'had no protection from the common law of England any more than from the law of a foreign land'. The few short clauses of the Charter which dealt with forest law were of lively interest to the barons.

With the Forest Charter of November 1217 the barons embarked on 'a massive intrusion' into what had been accepted as traditional, if resented, powers of the crown. 'Now the community was intervening to regulate [the forest] boundaries, to investigate its officials and to amend its regulations'.

The first clause of the charter formally rescinded all new afforestations made by King Henry II, and the third clause rescinded similar provisions by 'King Richard our uncle' and 'King John our father'. The framers of the Charter went on to make comprehensive provisions over a wide range of grievances which had been building up for generations against the autocratic exercise of royal power in the forest. For centuries to come the Forest Charter would be regarded as on a par with the Great Charter as one of the sureties of the Liberties of England.

The reason is not far to seek, for if it did not bring the forest code into line with the common law, it secured some amelioration of life for the average forest dweller and made some valuable concessions to landowners within the forest boundary. From now on it was legal to build mills on one's property, to develop fishponds, to dig drainage ditches and bring land into cultivation, so long as one did not damage the coverts for the royal game or infringe on neighbours' rights. The landowner could even harvest wild honey from hives in his own trees. A third of the land area of England had been brought an important step nearer to the property rights which landowners, at least, considered proper.

The common people were less well served by the Forest Charter. Chapter 16 banned the former practice whereby the wardens, generally those who brought the cases before the forest courts, actually held the pleas of the forest, and were in effect judges in their own cause. But the conventions of the forests sternly curtailed the interests of the poor in three primary needs: food, firewood and building timber. No commoner could hope for the right to take game in the forest and even the gathering of firewood was subject to stringent rules and payment to the forester.

Not all such fees were considered unreasonable. The 1217 Charter confirmed to certain foresters the right to levy 'chiminage' (from the French *chemin*, 'way'), a toll on wagons and sumpter horses using forest roads and trails. Yet abuses specifically banned by the charter continued well into the century, such was the power of forest officials in their districts and the ineffectiveness, if not the corruption, of central government itself.

A complaint from Somerset in the 1270s charged that at harvest time the foresters 'come with horses and collect sheaves of every kind of corn within the bounds of the forest and outside near the forest and make their ale from that collection'. Plundered of their barley, the peasants now had to drink and pay for the ale or lose their rights to winter firewood from the forest. Sixty years after Clause 7 of the Forest Charter had specifically banned the practice of the foresters' 'scotale' (i.e. 'tax'-ale), the celebrations of harvest were still soured by abuse and extortion, 'for none dare brew when the foresters brew, nor sell ale so long as the foresters have any kind of ale to sell'.

All over the country, forests sheltered and resourced a wide variety of activities and were home for a variety of forest dwellers and communities quite distinct from the manor economy of the arable lands or the companies and guilds of the towns.

Foresters and miners

The royal Forest of Dean in Gloucestershire, running northwards from the rivers Severn and Wye, rich in coal and iron ore, and a centre for iron-working, was the classic instance. Its self-contained isolated woodland community retained much of its private and withdrawn character down to the twentieth century.

In addition to the actual iron-workers, every forge made work for a given number of charcoal-burners and miners. In most other areas of the country these workers, like the coalminers, ranked as ordinary labourers. In the Forest of Dean, however, partly because of its remote location, in the unstable border country between England and Wales, partly because of the extreme wealth of the lodes, the mining community enjoyed a status rare outside the feudal hierarchy or the town guilds.

The aristocrats of this forest community were the iron-ore miners, but they accepted into their association the coalminers, charcoal-burners and forge-hands as associate members of the organization of 'free miners', whose privileges, rooted in ancient tradition, were officially recognized in royal prescripts by the government of Henry III and confirmed by Edward I. The value of the extractive industries to the growing tradition of medieval technology is amply demonstrated by the wide terms of the privileges, which are in marked contrast to the habitat/vert regulations governing ordinary forest dwellers elsewhere in the country.

First, the customs assured the miners of their monopoly. The right to mine in the region was restricted to men resident within the bounds of the forest and members of the 'free miners'. They controlled not only extraction of the ore but also its export out of the region along the River Severn; carriers were bound to pay dues to the miners on penalty of having their boats confiscated.

By contrast with the stringent limitations on land development elsewhere in forest law, the free miners of Dean were permitted to prospect and dig anywhere in the royal forest, except in gardens and orchards. Prospecting teams or partnerships comprised four 'verns' or partners. In addition to this *carte blanche* to open mines as and where they would prove profitable, the verns were entitled to free access to the pit-head from the highway and to timber necessary for shoring. In return the miners were required to incorporate the lord of the soil, whether king or private landowner, as one of the verns, with a partner's share in the proceeds; while each miner raising more than three loads of ore per week paid a penny-levy to the gaveller, every Tuesday morning. From these and other records it seems that during the late thirteenth century the forest was exporting about 10,000 loads of ore annually. Miners' skills were both recognized and respected. When King Henry V was laying siege to the French city of Meaux in his post-Agincourt campaigns of 1420, the cream of his sapper corps was provided by miners from the Forest of Dean.

Rights in a mine could be bequeathed by will. To prevent trespass on a neighbour's claim and lessen disputes, it was stipulated that no man could start a working near another miner's adit 'within so much space that the miner may stand and cast ridding and stones so far from him with a bale, as the manner is'. Disputes were settled at the miners' court every three weeks at St Briavels under the presidency of the constable by a jury of twelve miners – appeals were possible to a jury of twenty-four or of forty-eight miners. Penalty for perjury was that 'all the working tooles and habitt he burned before his face' – his cap, his leather breeches 'tied below the knee', wooden mine-hod, mattock and the candlestick held between the teeth to light him at work.

The court of the free miners was held at St Briavels under the aegis of the Warden of the Forest, as often as not the constable of the royal castle there. He also presided over the administration of the forest law proper, for, despite their privileged status in many respects, the denizens of Dean were exempt neither from its provisions nor its draconian penalties.

Rebels, outlaws and Robin Hood

Yet for all the harshness of its law, forest land provided a haven for criminals, vagrants and vagabonds of all kinds. It was in this context that the legends of Robin Hood were born. The oral tradition was well established by the fourteenth century and the rhymes of the outlaw yeoman Robin rivalled in popularity those of the noble ruffian Earl Ranulf of Chester (d.1232). They may recall an actual person who, like Ranulf, was active in the north and north midlands in the 1220s; or, it has been suggested, another outlaw from somewhat later in the century.

The Yorkshire pipe roll for 1226 records a charge on the chattels of 'Robert Hod, fugitive'. He may have been a common debtor on the run from his creditors. It is equally possible that he was a victim of corrupt forest officials who, rather than submit to extortion, had voluntarily gone outlaw. Two royal officials of the period are possible candidates for the 'Sheriff of Nottingham' role: Philip Marc, sheriff of Nottinghamshire and Derbyshire, with custody of Sherwood Forest; and Brian de Lisle, chief forester of Nottinghamshire and Derbyshire, chief justice of the forest in the early 1220s and sheriff of Yorkshire in the 1230s. A third candidate has also been suggested, Reginald de Grey, the sheriff of Nottingham in 1266-7.

Whether or not Hod was the original inspiration for the Robin Hood ballads and stories, the period immediately following the royalist victory in the baronial wars of Henry III's reign would have provided fertile soil for such stories to proliferate in. After the defeat and death of Simon de Montfort, Earl of Leicester and champion of the rebel cause at the battle of Evesham in August 1265, the forests of England seem to have become almost congested with a distinctly better class of outlaw as the disinherited rebels sought refuge in the greenwood. Chief among them were David of Uffington, whose company roamed the Forest of Epping, and Adam Gurdon, flushed out from the woods around Alton in Hampshire in the spring of 1266 by Henry's son and heir the Lord Edward (later King Edward I). Gurdon was very much gamekeeper turned poacher, having been a royal forester before the civil wars, and an aroma of the chivalry of the greenwood lingers round his name. According to one tradition, when the royal troopers caught up with Gurdon's band, Prince Edward himself took on the outlaw captain in hand-to-hand combat and was so impressed by his courage that he spared his life.

Simon de Montfort had died excommunicated by the church, but soon enjoyed popular veneration as a saint. Stories of his miracles were spread on every side, 'vain and fatuous marvels which should not soil the lips'. Dead, the earl of Leicester was almost as potent in the anti-monarchist cause as he had been living. Men like Uffington and Gurdon kept the cause alive; Sherwood Forest, with its royal hunting-lodge at Clipstone, was one of the notorious places of refuge of the rebels, while a certain Robert Godberd, pardoned in a general amnesty the year after Evesham, returned to the outlaw life and led a band of outlaws who terrorized the shires of Leicester, Derby and Nottingham for another six years. He was finally captured in the early weeks of 1272 by Reginald de Grey who, as sheriff of Nottingham, had been hunting rebels in Sherwood at the time of Godberd's amnesty.

By the time of his first mention in literature, in Will Langland's allegorical poem *Piers Plowman* in the 1370s, Robin Hood had featured in popular tradition for at least a century. Langland, something of a moralist, did not greatly approve of the greenwood hero. Castigating the vices of his time, he personifies Sloth as a lazy priest who knew no Latin but was fully versed in the rhymes of Ranulf of Chester and Robin.

And, truth to tell, the Robin Hood of those days was no Douglas Fairbanks. One rhyme tells how he hacked off the head of an enemy and speared it on the end of his bowstave, the better to carve its features, like some Halloween pumpkin, with his woodsman's knife. The figure of the benign, sporting, Hollywood Robin seems to have emerged in the broadsheet ballads of a later age, while his supposed associations with Richard the Lionheart were thought up by the eighteenth-century antiquarian William Stukeley.

Nor is there any hint in the original rhymes of Robin as the English champion against Norman oppression. Two centuries after the Conquest the concept of Englishry certainly survived, while the court of Henry III was imbued with the king's cult of Saint Edward, the last of the old English kings, in whose honour he embarked on the rebuilding of the saint's great church at Westminster. The abbey as we know it today is largely the work of Henry, and a lasting memorial to the cult of the English past, of which the barons' devotion to the *legi Edwardi* was a somewhat quaint political expression. While the bulk of the country's peasant population was of English descent, and although it would be their language which resurfaced as the language of the country, the English theme in thirteenth-century society was an essentially nostalgic construct, and it was not the nostalgia of the greenwood where later ages were to locate Robin Hood.

To many the outlaw was not a glamorous figure but a threatening one whom they viewed much as the average citizen today views the urban terrorist. Yet there was an underlying appeal which ensured the survival of the legends. In one perspective we can see Robin Hood as the first in a line of English criminal heroes stretching through Dick Turpin and the eighteenth-century highwayman to the great train robbers of the 1960s. The lower orders of medieval England may well have seen Robin as an embattled hero against the brutal establishment represented by the forest law, and he had an appeal to the lower gentry and to a latent mood of anticlericalism.

For not only did Robin wage his campaigns against prosperous landowners, he was particularly the enemy of rich church landowners.

The transformation of Robin the bandit into Robin the merry outlaw mirrors the contracting role of the forest in English life over the centuries. For a hundred years after Magna Carta the struggle over forest matters was focused on the question of boundaries. Clause 47 of Magna Carta provided that all new forests made in John's reign to the disadvantage of private landowners should be disafforested forthwith and the Forest Charter of 1217 extended the same summary treatment to forests similarly made by Henry II and Richard.

In fact the boundary issue was bitterly fought between crown and barons for the rest of the century. Periodically, attempts were made to define the proper limits by perambulations and enquiries along the boundaries. Despite repeated findings against the crown Edward I, the strongest of all England's medieval kings, resisted all demands for change. Even after the baronial opposition had forced him to reduce boundaries at the parliament of Lincoln (1301) he got a special bull from Pope Clement V which revoked the concessions because they had been granted under duress.

This was the last royal victory in the great struggle. Edward's son Edward II was forced to restore the Lincoln settlement and it was never reversed. Two hundred years later, when Henry VIII took a fancy to enlarge the forest land around Hampton Court, he not only made sure of parliament's consent but paid compensation to all the landowners affected.

In the seventeenth century King Charles I, always on the lookout for ways of raising money without recourse to parliament, did for a time restore certain long-forgotten levies of medieval forest law and extended the bounds of the royal forest. When he was forced to recall parliament it passed a statute ordaining that the forest should be 'as in the time of King Edward I'. Thus, for a moment, the liberties of the forest featured along with the liberties of the community of England as the country girded itself for the historic struggle of the Civil War.

Today the acres of forest still remaining to the crown are administered by the Forestry Commission. But in the 1980s as more and more of Britain's woodlands were turned over to the private sector, oak and ash, beech and hornbeam found themselves outnumbered by mercenary regiments of monotonous conifer. The cruel regime of the forest law is long past, but so is the colourful tapestry of forest life and lore. While Robin Hood leads his

97

merry men across the film and television screen, the villains of the piece out there in the greenwood seem to have an uncanny resemblance to city accountants and their clients.

The dawning of the 1990s brought hopes that England might once more boast woodlands of beauty and ecological diversity with the news that the Countryside Commission was planning to develop a new national forest in the Midlands. The realization that exploitative monocultures practised at the scale and intensity demanding modern technology must be damaging as well as monotonous may lead to policy decisions which will restore sizeable tracts of Britain's landscape to an appearance and condition they have not known since the middle ages. Whether all the changes will be welcomed given the pressure for building land and leisure facilities is doubtful: change of any kind provokes reaction and often hostility. The forest clauses of the great Charter meant commissions of investigation which, in turn, disturbed developing customs rights. Indeed they provoked outbreaks of lawlessness which undermined the forest administration and settled nothing. In fact, the upheaval was one reason for the framing of the Forest Charter.

8

THE COMMUNITY
OF JEWRY

'LIKE THE OTHER COMMUNITIES OF MEDIEVAL ENGLAND,
THE CLERGY FOR EXAMPLE, OR ENGLISH CITIES AND
BOROUGHS — THE JEWRY WAS LARGELY SELF GOVERN-
ING.'

BEHIND the official and legal documents which provide the bulk of our knowledge of medieval Europe, it is not always too easy to glimpse the everyday life of any given period, and in the case of Jewish society this is especially difficult. Most of the sources are Christian and therefore indifferent when they are not positively hostile. For the draughtsmen of the Great Charter the Jews are interesting only in relation to their business as money men, and in this capacity they often seemed to be little better than agents of the royal exchequer.

10) If anyone who has borrowed from the Jews any sum, great or small, dies before it is repaid, the debt shall not bear interest while the heir is under age, whosoever tenant he may be; and if the debt falls into our hands we will not take anything except the principal mentioned in the bond.
11) And if anyone die indebted to the Jews, his wife shall have her dower and pay nothing of that debt; and if any children of the deceased are left under age, necessaries shall be provided for them in keeping with the holding of the deceased.

The two clauses in the Charter of 1215 which mention Jews are concerned with the plight of heirs and widows encumbered by debts to Jewish moneylenders at the death of the head of the family. As they stand they seem particularly hard on the moneylenders. Given the relation between the crown and English Jewry, they in fact represented damaging financial consequences for the royal government. They were dropped from the 1216 reissue and never reappear in any subsequent version of the Charter. Later in this chapter we shall examine the financial technicalities, naturally the principal concern of most commentators on these clauses. But since the Charter was for 'the community of the whole realm of England', itself made up of numerous independent 'communities' ('minorities' or 'special interest groups' are presumably the nearest modern equivalents) let us look first at the medieval Jewish community of England, a late developer in the European context.

Cultural traditions: cultural divides

Throughout Europe, Jews were subject to severe legal discrimination. As early as the sixth century the Byzantine emperor Justinian had prohibited the study of the Talmud and Midrash. In the long term it had little effect, as the great series of medieval commentaries on these texts was to show. In the short run it had a positively beneficial effect for the worship of the synagogues, since the immediate response of the Jews in Mediterranean territories ruled from the Greek-Roman imperial city of Constantinople was the development of metrical hymns of *piyyutim* (derived from the Greek *poietes*, poet) as vehicles of popular instruction in the teachings of the faith.

By the year 650, less than a century after the death of Justinian, most Mediterranean synagogues appear to have had their own *chazzan*, a professional singer and poet supported by the community, to maintain the sung liturgy which had arisen from the *piyyutim*. Early in the eighth century, when in some sections of Judaism the *piyyutim* themselves were under attack, Rabbi Yehudai Gaom, apparently himself skilled in the arts of the *chazzan*, introduced the singing of the *Kol nidre* into his synagogue.

Frowned on by the more austere representatives of the strict tradition, melodic embellishments of the liturgy, which are found in northern Europe as well as in the Mediterranean area, seem to have been popular with their own congregations and even to have attracted Christians. In the mid ninth century we find a bishop complaining that people wanted to learn Jewish religious melodies. Yet more dramatic evidence of Christian interest in Jewish ways comes from the fact that the earliest surviving *piyyutim* melodies survive in a manuscript written by an Italian Norman nobleman who converted to Judaism about the year 1100.

Just eighteen years before Runnymede we find an episcopal prohibition on Christian clergy attempting to study Jewish doctrine or melodies. A generation later orthodox Jews in Germany were forbidding the teaching of synagogue melodies to Christian clergy. Both the interests of these wayward clergy and the fact that they were able to find willing teachers confirms what we know from other sources – that contacts between Jewish and Christian communities could be both close and friendly. Just how the Christians came to know of the Jewish melodies is nevertheless intriguing and implies visits to the synagogue after interest had been aroused, perhaps, by hearing Jewish *joculatores* (the medieval term for travelling musicians).

The fact that on the Christian side the prohibition was against learning and on the Jewish side the authorities had to rule against teaching makes it clear who were the explorers in the exchange and is an interesting early example of the extrovert bent which has for centuries been the characteristic of western civilization. Yet in truth the official attitude of both church and state to the Jews was, almost necessarily, ambivalent.

Following the Gospel account of the Crucifixion which attributes blame for Christ's death to the Jerusalem mob primed by the chief priests, the church held all Jews guilty – had not the mob shouted, 'His blood be upon us and on our children'? Equally, of course, the church could not, nor did it wish to, deny the origins of Christianity in Judaism – Christ and his disciples were Jews, the books of the Jewish 'Old' Testament were almost as important in the theology of the church as the New Testament of Christ's teaching. A common image of 'synagogue', the emblem of 'Jewry', was a beautiful woman blindfolded, to symbolize a tradition rich in the beauty of truth which had wilfully closed its eyes to the fulfilment of that truth. For the state the ambivalence was much more, so to speak, straightforward. The enemies of Christ were for most kings a necessary part of economic management.

History had to be adjusted to accommodate the embarrassing fact that not only was the Christian faith itself an offshoot of the despised Judaism, but

Jewish culture, represented by Jerusalem, was much more ancient. An early tradition concerning the Roman persecution of the Christians in Britain rather surprisingly gives one of the most revered martyrs, a native of Carlisle, the name of Aaron – a 'classic' Jewish name during the middle ages. Carlisle itself, according to the *History of the Kings of Britain* by Geoffrey of Monmouth, was built by 'King Leil . . . at the time when Solomon began to build the kingdom of Jerusalem and when the Queen of Sheba came to listen to his wisdom.' Such ideas, quaint though they may be in the context of a modern secular society, made some attempt, however clumsy, to accommodate the enemies of Christ into the world of Christendom.

Pride and prejudice

Suspicion and dislike were, of course, more general sentiments across the religious divide. During the boyhood of King John, the people of Arles in southern France commissioned a handsome stone bridge across the River Rhône at their city. Throughout the middle ages bridge-building was considered a work of piety. In fact there is a mystery surrounding bridges which reaches back into classical times. The chief priest of the Roman empire was the '*pontifex maximus*', literally 'principal bridge-builder' – a title which was adopted by the popes. In very ancient times, it would appear, the function of the 'bridge priest' was to placate the naiads – the *genii loci* ('spirits of the place') or local nature spirits of rivers – when the bridge-builders desecrated their domain.

Things were not always quite so mystical, of course. In early medieval England, even before the Norman conquest, all freemen were subject to the ancient tripartite obligation known as the *trinoda necessitas* which comprised: attendance at the summons to the fyrd, or national militia; the making of roads; and the repair of bridges and fortifications. Overland communications were not only of service to travellers but also to the king's government, being the sole means of communication between him and the districts of the realm and also, in an age when the royal court travelled from manor to manor to consume its rents in kind, vital to the royal household economy. And finally, in the sport of hawking and falconry to which King

John was addicted, well-maintained bridges (if not roads) were needed for a free run across country following the birds of prey. It was a special grievance that he and his immediate predecessors had enforced the obligation to bridge repair upon men and communities who had no traditional obligation. The subject, accordingly, finds special mention under Clause 23 of the Great Charter, where the king promises not to impose such work in future.

In Christian Europe, the expensive, expert and laborious work of bridge-building was also considered a work of charity to travellers – many bridges had little chapels in which wayfarers were invited to pray for the soul of the builders. But in cases where a single private patron was not forthcoming to pay the whole cost of the work, a community had to raise funds as best it could. The Jews of Arles, being among the richest groups in the city, were natural 'volunteers' for the fund. Equally, it seems apparent that their money was considered tainted for the purposes of this semi-sacred public enterprise. A nasty little arrangement was reached whereby the Christian authorities got the cash without accepting charity from the 'enemies of Christ'. The Jews of Arles, to avert the hostility and retain the custom of their Christian fellow citizens, agreed to a document which bound them for 100 years of forced building labour to be done on the Sabbath. They then bought themselves out of this impossible obligation with a suitable immediate down payment and agreement to an annual levy.

By such fictions, historical, legal, and financial, and at the cost of sporadic victimization in outbreaks of bloody and murderous violence, the Jews of medieval Europe were bitterly accustomed to collaborating in their status as second-class citizens. In times of unrest the underlying context of humiliation was punctuated by mortal terror, but in 'normal' times they could be reasonably assured of the practice of their religion and customs within their own closely-knit communities.

A story from Rouen at the time of William Rufus, recorded in his 'New History' by the church chronicler Eadmer not less than fifteen years after the king's death in 1100 and still no doubt current in ecclesiastical circles when the clauses concerning the Jews were being framed at Runnymede, neatly illustrates the point, though in fact it is recounted to demonstrate a different moral.

William spent long periods in the Norman capital during the later years of his reign (his brother Robert, the duke, was on crusade and both William and his other brother Henry harboured designs on the ducal inheritance). At the time in question a number of Jews had recently been converted to Christianity. Dismayed, a group of their pious coreligionists approached the king to use his influence to persuade the apostates to return to the faith. According to Eadmer they offered handsome bribes. In the writer's view, such behaviour was fully in keeping with the nature of both the rapacity of the king and the venality of the Jews.

One of the petitioners was seeking the king's help in the case of his son, converted by a vision of St Stephen, the first martyr. The father offered no less than 60 marks, the pay of 50 fully armed mercenaries for a month, if the king would intervene. What followed bordered on farce, if we are to believe the chronicler. Having called the recalcitrant youth into the royal presence, William admonished him to obey his father and renounce Christianity. 'You must be joking,' came the reply. 'Would I joke with you, son of the dung? Do as I say and look sharp about it or by the Face of Lucca (a relic believed to be imprinted with the image of the face of the Blessed Virgin Mary) I'll have your eyes put out.' Looking forward perhaps to a martyrdom of his own, the young Jewish convert not only continued to refuse but went on to rebuke the Christian king for his unChristian sentiments. No doubt to his surprise, possibly to his disappointment, he was merely dismissed from the court. The king for his part, we may suppose, was not unduly disappointed, since the boy's father tactfully paid half the agreed fee in any case.

Since the chronicler's intention was to blacken the name of the king with examples of his irreligion and blasphemies we may assume that the setting of the tale was quite credible to contemporaries. In the last years of the eleventh century (Rufus died in the year 1100), some of the Jewish communities in Europe were threatened by outbursts of fanaticism amongst the Christian population prompted by the preaching of the crusade. Some of the Rouenais converts may have been timorous time-servers, others may have been genuine converts, but clearly their community had standing in the town and its leading members felt free to speak on terms amounting to familiarity with at least one Christian ruler.

The Jews in England

It seems that the first Jewish contact with the Anglo-Norman world was the Jewish community at Rouen. There had been Jews in Gaul in the late Roman period and the Rouenais may have been a continuous settlement from that time. Rouen merchants were occasional visitors to Anglo-Saxon London and some of them no doubt were Jews. However, the first Jewish settlement in England came after the conquest when, according to the chronicler William of Malmesbury, William I brought the Jews to London from Rouen.

Our first written notice of the condition of the Jews in England comes in the document known as the *Laws of Edward the Confessor*, written probably towards the end of the reign of King Henry I in the 1130s. Incidentally, its reference to the Jews is one of the clearest indications that the document itself has nothing to do with the king whose laws it purports to record since, as we have seen, the first Jews were introduced to England under his successor William the Conqueror. There is no evidence that King Henry himself granted a charter to the Jews (nor is there any mention of them in Henry's famous coronation charter which played so important a part in the run up to Magna Carta). So far as we can tell, all that Henry did was to extend to the Jews of England the conventions governing the relations between the dukes of Normandy and the Jewish community which had grown up in Rouen and which almost certainly provided the context for the first Jewish settlers in England.

London was naturally home to the largest group of Jews in England, but as the twelfth century advanced we find Jewish businessmen listed in most of the main towns of the kingdom from Bristol in the west to Norwich in the east. Even the troubled reign of Stephen seems to have offered opportunities. The unsettled nature of the times and the competition for the favours of King Stephen and his rival for the crown the Empress Matilda meant that money was in demand as never before.

But whatever the opportunities, the Jewish communities like the rest of the kingdom benefited from the restoration of order under Stephen's successor, King Henry II. Within two years, one chronicler tells us, anarchy had been reduced to order. 'Merchants travelled in safety beyond town and castle wall and the Jews to their eager clients.'

The Jews and the Charter

Be that as it may, the Jews feature in the 'Laws of King Edward' and so, like all the other petitioners represented in Magna Carta, were able to claim customary status dating back to the time of the sainted monarch. The broad principles recorded in the 'Laws' provided the framework of Jewish life in England down to the expulsion by King Edward I. First, they and all their possessions belonged to the king; second, they might put themselves under the protection of a local lord, but only with the king's permission; third, the king could at any time demand the return of such Jews and their money; and fourth, the king's Christian lieges throughout the country were duty bound to guard and protect all Jews in their districts.

Although it has not survived, we know that Henry II granted a special charter to the Jews which among other things authorized the terms on which they might trade and provided for sons to succeed to their fathers' estates on payment of an estate levy, usually a swingeing 33%. The principle was obviously the same as that of the relief paid by the heir to a barony, but whereas the baron had the absolute right to succeed to his father's estate, the Jew might be refused permission, since at law the king was heir of every Jew in the kingdom. When the famous merchant and financier Aaron of Lincoln died in 1186 not only did the exchequer have to set up a special department to handle his vast estate, but neither his sons Vives and Elias, nor his nephew Benedict were granted leave to succeed.

Although Henry and his sons Richard and John all granted them charters, the Jewish community was in the last resort at the king's mercy, liable to punitive and arbitrary levies, confiscations or fines. In fact, John was so hated by the church chroniclers that they even troubled to pillory him for persecuting the Jews – a class considered fair, almost proper, victims for most Christian oppressors. His favourite pastime in this regard was, apparently, torturing rich Jewish moneylenders to learn the whereabouts of their cash. Indeed, the frequency with which the charge was made led one modern historian to remark that King John seemed always to be pulling out teeth with the celerity and industry of a piecework dentist. Not only their estates but they themselves ranked effectively as the property of the king.

The king was also their protector against all other men. In litigation between a Jew and a Christian, oaths and the evidence of witnesses of both religions were to be taken according to Jewish custom. It seemed to Christian plaintiffs that crown officials under John favoured Jews. Whereas a Christian wishing to clear himself on oath might, as the law then stood, have to find eleven 'oath helpers' to swear with him, a Jewish defendant was allowed to make his oath 'single-handed' on the book of the Jewish Law.

But there was always the possibility of course that a man might forswear himself, i.e. commit perjury, whether Christian or Jew. The courts seem to have grasped that it was more likely if the litigant was taking an oath which he did not consider binding; the Christian plaintiff by contrast merely observed that a man whom he probably regarded as an alien and an enemy of Christ was allowed to clear his name with a simple oath on a strange book, whereas he had to recruit a body of neighbours.

Such were the proceedings in civil cases and many a Christian plaintiff considered the Jews were permitted to defend themselves 'contrary to the custom of the realm'. In cases brought by the crown the situation was a little more complicated. Moreover, by the terms of John's charter to the Jews of 1201, if a Christian brought a charge against a Jew it was to be adjudged by '*pares Judei*', which whether it means men of their own race or, as was once argued, justices or custodians of Jewish affairs is clearly a reasonable provision bordering on what today might be called 'positive discrimination'. Not that human rights were the issue, but rather the efficient administration of the king's business and concern for some of the king's most valuable subjects.

The phrase is a fascinating pre-echo of the historic words '*per judicium parium*' ('by judgement of peers', i.e. 'equals') of Clause 39 of the 1215 Charter which in turn recalls 'judgement of his peers' ('*per pares suos judicandus*') found in the Laws of Henry I which it was claimed had been abrogated by John. In addition to the special procedures he had access to in the law courts the Jew was also under the special protection of the royal sheriffs and castellans, who were held responsible for the well-being of Jews within their jurisdictions.

Up to the end of the twelfth century any case involving Jews, whether as plaintiffs or defendants, involved men of both religions – any jury must include Jews as well as Christians. But in the 1190s Jewish affairs were handed over to specialist officials of the exchequer headed by the 'keepers of the Jews', or more correctly 'the king's justices at London assigned to have custody of the Jews'. One of the earliest was Hugh of Nunant, bishop of Coventry.

'Bishops' and cantors

From the Jewish point of view, it appears, these royal officials were far less important than their opposite number elected by the Jewish community itself and known as the 'priest' or 'archpriest of the commune of the Jews of England'. One such archpriest not only admitted but boasted his responsibility for the 'great' debts of the English Jewry, the small debts such as individual fines being recorded by his clerk subject to the control of the steward of one of the king's justices of the Jews. The origin of the term *archipresbyter Iudeorum* i.e. 'archpriest of the Jews' is unclear.

Ecclesiastical-sounding titles such as 'bishop' and even 'archbishop' were accorded to other Jewish functionaries. Despite its churchy sound, the archpriest seems to have been concerned exclusively with secular duties. In the Christian church hierarchy the 'archpriest' discharged some of the administrative functions today associated with the title rural dean and in the middle ages with the president of the local ecclesiastical court or rural chapter. The term 'priest' was also applied by the Jews themselves to officers of their own synagogue or community (they were most likely the *chazzanim* or cantors). The terms were no doubt first coined for use in an attempt to explain functionaries of their society to Christian officials and neighbours in terms which they would understand. We find Jewish 'bishops' at Exeter, Hereford, London, York and elsewhere: occasionally they discharge the functions of bailiffs.

The term *episcopus* was, it is true, sometimes used as an equivalent of 'Cohen'. Whatever the precise signification, it seems clear that these ecclesiastical designations implied that the man involved held public office in his community. These officers were not domestic officers of the Jewish communities but were chosen in ways of which we are ignorant, to act as intermediaries between the crown and the local Jewries: if a bishop was to be chosen to be a bailiff, this was on personal grounds and not ex officio.

The Jewish community suffered heavily from John's exactions and many appear to have emigrated; the turbulent period of the Barons' War, precipitated by the struggle over Magna Carta, accelerated the trend. As the situation in England began to normalize after John's death many of the refugees returned. But conditions had changed, and the self-governing communities of the old days had given way to direct rule by the royal sheriffs and castle constables. Jews had always been vulnerable to prejudice and sudden outbursts of violence, but as the thirteenth century advanced conditions of life became increasingly hostile since the royal government, less dependent on the financial services of the Jews with the rapid development of Christian banking, became less concerned with protecting 'the king's Jews'.

While it is true that moneylending was the principal business of the Jewish community, it was by no means the only one. Aaron of Lincoln, probably the wealthiest commoner of his time, dealt extensively in corn and probably in wool too. Other Jews are known to have been physicians, soldiers, vintners, fishmongers, cheesemongers and goldsmiths. Pawnbroking, the most widespread trade among Jews, called for the skills of jeweller and metal worker in the repair and refurbishing of plate, armour and jewellery, to make unredeemed pledges saleable. However, Jews were automatically excluded from membership of the craft guilds which were both religious and monopolistic, so that it was virtually impossible for them to make a full career in the major urban trades and crafts.

From occasional references in government records it is clear that there was a steady trickle of converts to Christianity. The pressure on the small Jewish communities which had spread outwards from London during the course of the twelfth century to most of the major towns was constant, even during the long intervals of comparative peace between the outbursts of violent anti-semitism. Suspicion and hatred and the sense of ostracism from the normal concourse of human society were hard enough to bear. When to these we add the standing discrimination against Jews in all fields of skilled or professional employment it is clear that many must have been sorely tempted to abandon the faith.

But there were pressures working the other way. Since at law a Jew's property was reckoned to belong to the king, any wealthy Jew who converted was liable to surrender all his wealth to the king. One thirteenth-century churchman preached against the provision, not out of sympathy with the Jews but because, in his view, it was the principal obstacle to widespread conversions. It seems likely, indeed, that most of the converts were poor men, of little use to the king and so liable to expulsion from the kingdom.

If the general attitude towards the Jews was dislike and suspicion of the alien, violent hostilities, such as the atrocious events of 1190 sparked off at Richard I's coronation in London and prompted by crusading fanaticism, came from the mob. In the upper orders of society, both religious and lay, individuals and institutions were perfectly prepared to do business with 'the enemies of Christ' if profit beckoned. In the 1180s, for example, five prosperous London merchants combined in a property development in Old Jewry near the site of Mansion House, financed by loans from Aaron of Lincoln, whose London house was nearby.

Rather unexpectedly, in England at least, Jewish financiers often played a crucial role in the pious benefactions by which many a wealthy religious house extended its landed possessions. Although a Jew was outside the feudal network of obligation and homage, land was often pledged to Jewish moneylenders as security for a loan. If the debtor was unable to meet his debt the Jew would not enter into possession of the land but he did obtain seisin of the gage and could arrange for conveyance of the land to a purchaser willing to discharge the debt. Many debt-encumbered properties passed to religious houses in this way. Monastery charter collections or 'cartularies' conceal many an outright land purchase in records which purport to record pious benefactions.

Councils and troubles

As the thirteenth century advanced even the modicum of 'integration' which Jews had enjoyed in northern Europe seemed increasingly in jeopardy. (In the Spanish kingdoms their standing as scholars and physicians was much respected and brought prestige to the whole Jewish community which probably reached its peak during the reign [1252-84] of Alfonso X 'the Wise'.) Crucial in the deterioration of the Jewish position was the Fourth Lateran Council held only a few months later than Magna Carta, in November 1215. It marked the culmination of the reign of Pope Innocent III, the most dynamic and powerful of all the later medieval popes, and in something under three weeks passed 70 canons. Only four concerned the Jews, but they were ominous. It was the first time that the papacy had intervened directly.

The Council was held against the darkening backdrop of religious passions swirling up from the campaigns against the Albigensian, 'Cathar' heretics of Provence. The next decade would see the founding of the Inquisition. Meanwhile the Lateran council decreed that converts should break entirely with their old religion. Although not aimed specifically at Jewish converts it must have heightened popular awareness where many a Sunday Christian would have preferred to keep a low profile. But it was tolerable. So, too, one imagines, were the injunctions requiring Jews to pay tithes and other ecclesiastical dues: no doubt technically unjust impositions on non-believers, they were, after all, merely taxes, and taxes moreover already paid by their Christian neighbours. In like manner the ban on intermarriage with Christians was hardly arduous – orthodox Jewish law, then as now, was also opposed to mixed marriages. Far more objectionable and potentially very dangerous were the two measures of outright discrimination: the order which confined Jews to their houses on Passion Sunday and during Holy Week; and, most hostile of all, the order that all Jews should wear a badge or some distinguishing item of dress.

The decrees of the council presumably reached England in the early weeks of 1216. King John, who had cheerfully endured four years of interdict against his kingdom and excommunication against himself, may have noticed the opportunity for money-raising which the decree on dress presented, but was preoccupied with the more pressing business of bringing his rebellious baronage to heel. After his death and the departure of Louis of France in September 1217 the civil administration of the country began to return to its normal rhythms and the Council of Regency regulated, among other things, the position of England's Jews.

Actually, their chief concern was to reassure the Jews who had remained in England during the past few troubled years and to encourage those who had emigrated to return. Late in 1217 they issued instructions that those who returned need only register with the Justice of the Jews and that the local authorities were to ensure their protection, especially against crusaders who had taken the cross in accordance with another decree of the Lateran council.

To ensure these orders were enforced, William Marshal, the regent, personally saw to it that committees of burgesses were set up in various towns – Lincoln, Bristol and Oxford among them – early in 1218. Memories of 1190 were still vivid and a government wishing to woo the return of valued money-men had no desire to see them slaughtered by self-styled soldiers of God.

Given that this was the political environment, a papal order requiring these valued citizens to be publicly humiliated and marked out by unmistakable recognition signs must have been distinctly unwelcome. However, since the regency council numbered among its members no less a person than the pope's personal representative, Legate Guala, something had to be done. Accordingly, in March 1218, we find a decree ordering that all Jews in England should wear a white 'tabula' or badge.

At first it does not appear to have been rigorously enforced, but the regulation tightened. A series of statutes of 1253 include one concerning the wearing of the tabula. In other respects these interesting enactments reveal a pattern of society in which Jews, however despised by their Christian neighbours, clearly had a part. There are laws to govern the construction of new synagogues, intermarriage between Christians and Jews, and also the employment of Jewish servants by Christians, including Jewish nurses. As a matter of interest, Jewish authorities were equally solicitous in matters of child care: about this time *The Book of the Pious* issued for the guidance of Rhineland Jewry deplored the singing of Gentile melodies to Jewish babies.

But if they were concerned with the rights of heirs in debt to the Jews, the barons at Runnymede had little or no interest in lullabies. And it is now time to look rather more closely at the aspects of Jewish affairs which did concern the draughtsmen of the Charter.

There were many ways a baron could get into debt to the king. The crown was of course the fountain of honour; more important, in the middle ages it was the principal source of revenues, land and, to use a modern term, 'income' of every kind. Ambitious and successful men of the early thirteenth century were no different in essence from their modern counterparts. Wealth and power were the objectives – merely that they came differently packaged. Money was to be had by marrying one's son to an heiress, and if she was a royal ward the king had to be paid; rich profits could be creamed off the administration of a minor's estate – if a royal wardship the king again had to be paid. To win the grant of a fief in the king's gift, the constableship of a castle, the wardenship of a forest, even to have justice, and above all the king's goodwill, all demanded money. And in an economy based on land money was short, cashflow was the problem and it was necessarily a sellers' market for moneylenders. Payment of reliefs to enter into one's inheritance was a special harassment ... 'there is no fixed amount which the heir must pay to the king, he must make what terms he can', a treasury expert had written in the previous century.

To be in debt to the king was to be in the king's power – debts were paid on the instalment plan, terms and payments fixed by the king. John enjoyed the power he held over his debtors and made the point explicit by demanding they put their lands in pledge, which of course opened them to the threat of forfeiture. (The vast estates of the earldom of Leicester were impounded between 1207 and 1215.) One way out of the king's debt was to borrow from a Jew. But, as W. L. Warren has pointed out, not only was interest heavy but a debt to a Jew was an indirect debt to the king, who regularly raided Jews' profits by taking arbitrary tallages. The king was every Jew's heir – at his death the king could take not only the man's chattels and cash but also his credit notes. 'Thus the baron after years of paying heavy interest to the Jew might find himself still the king's debtor for the principal.'

It is perhaps not to be wondered at if rich and powerful Jews sometimes attracted hostility from the great of the land. Inexhaustibly rich, it seemed, in the one thing the barons were perennially short of – money; spared the strictures of moralizing priests; favourites of the king's laws, and at the same time heirs to the murderers of Christ; they did not seem ideally placed to win friends and influence people.

As the thirteenth century advanced the position of England's medieval Jewry worsened. Increasingly irrelevant to the requirements of royal finance as other sources of revenue became available, the Jews found themselves without royal protection when they needed it more desperately, perhaps, than ever before. In the middle decades of the century a group of sensational child-murder trials were laid at their door; the Jews supposedly killed Christian children in ritual murders for their blood. Such charges were still being seriously brought in nineteenth-century France, so we should not perhaps be too superior about 'medieval' superstition.

For the authorities the public outcry surrounding the cases suited what seemed to amount in all but name to an anti-Jewish policy. In 1290 Edward I ordered the expulsion of all the Jews in England, and so impoverished the national life by reducing the diversity of the communities of the realm. In the 1650s Lord Protector Cromwell opened England once more to Jewish immigrants. Thus the community of Jewry, part of the community of England in the year of Magna Carta, was welcomed back to the realm in the century which had seen the greatest triumphs of the Charter and to which the parliamentarians, who approved their return, owed so much.

9

THE COMMUNITY
OF WOMEN

THE position of women in the middle ages was, in theory, one of subjection. The Old Testament, that part of their faith which the dominant Christian culture shared with the despised and oppressed minority the Jews, taught that God had created man in his own image, that woman had been created from Adam's rib, and that by yielding to the temptation of the serpent she had been the cause of sin in the world. But for Christians the New Testament introduced a new liberalizing possibility which gave a potently ambivalent colouration to the old mythology of Genesis. For while Eve, made from Adam's body, caused his fall from God's Grace, the Blessed Virgin Mary, by giving birth to Christ, the second Adam, had brought into the world the possibility of redemption from that original sin.

During the twelfth century two important new ideas were added to the view of women's place in society: the cult of the Virgin Mary herself, which first becomes a popular movement in this period, and the cult of courtly love which, emerging from the poetry of the troubadours, developed from a sophisticated high-society game in the courts of Provence and became an ideology or philosophy of living among its more ardent devotees. Both accorded elements of respect for the female principle which would initiate an evolution on the concepts of women's rights pioneered by western civilization. At the height of her fame, John's own mother the fabulous Eleanor of Aquitaine virtually embodied one aspect, presiding over the most brilliant manifestation of the courtly love cult in her court at Poitiers.

The generation which had known Eleanor must have found it more difficult than most to subscribe to the fustian dogma of the church on the subject of women. A lifetime before Magna Carta she had mesmerized Europe by the reports of her Amazonian entourage at the time of the Second Crusade (1147). Travelling the coasts of Palestine with ladies tricked out in armour and one knew not what else, flirting – and many said worse – with her uncle the crusade leader Count Raymond of Toulouse, she delightfully scandalized the court gossips from Antioch to Paris. Exotically, it was even claimed she had born children to the hero of Islam, the chivalrous Saladin. A legend this certainly was, since Saladin was but eleven at the time of Eleanor's visit to the Holy Land; even so it is telling evidence of the kind of culture shock the southern and fiery beauty of Eleanor of Aquitaine represented.

The French king Louis VI, to whom she was married at the time, was both scandalized by her reputation and worried by her inability to bear sons. With papal cooperation he found reasons for having the marriage declared null. While he sought a more compliant and fecund partner, Eleanor wedded the dashing young Henry Plantagenet (soon to be Henry II of England), for whom almost at once she began to breed sons, and with whom she lived in turbulent disharmony for the rest of his life. As much at home in the saddle as in the boudoir, a schemer and a revenger, Eleanor recruited her sons in the quarrel with her husband and was imprisoned by him for her pains. Released by her eldest surviving son Richard I when he became king, she outlived her husband by a dozen years.

For her admirers, Eleanor of Aquitaine ranks ahead of Helen of Troy, after whom she was no doubt named. She was surely as beautiful – the troubadour Bertrand de Born sighed to have the queen of England in his arms – and whereas Helen was content to play the part of *femme fatale* in besieged Troy, Eleanor would no doubt have taken charge of the city's defences and driven the Greeks back to their ships.

Eleanor's century had had its share of warrior women. King Stephen of England had probably owed his throne to his soldier-like queen, Matilda of Boulogne. Their rival, the Empress Matilda, though not so good a strategist, was no less familiar with the campaigning life. The career of Nicolaa de la Haye, castellan of Lincoln, spanned the turn of the century to the benefit of the royal cause. A favourite image of medieval secular art is women playing at chess. Today a quiet intellectual game, in the middle ages the board was a place for betting and a metaphor of battle. The demure ladies we see depicted in the miniatures could play the role of silken dalliance but could, when occasion demanded, ride to the wars or direct a garrison's defence.

For a society lady, whatever the social theory, life could be full and exciting, though it must be admitted that campaigning was not commonplace. For women not inclined for marriage or not placed on the marriage market, the life of religion offered what in today's terms were distinct career opportunities. The running of a large religious community was a complex administrative business, and in a world which rated the life of religion extremely high, it was a prestigious one too. As the life of Eloise showed, women could pursue the intellectual life, while the *Ancrene Wisse* (*c.*1200), written in Old English as a spiritual guide for women, reminds us of the cohorts of sisters engaged in the day-to-day campaign of the most important army in medieval life – the army of God.

Even in her most characteristic role, that of housewife, the woman of the early thirteenth century had important responsibilities. The running of a large household was a large undertaking. But the peasant's wife was as important a member of the family team as her husband, for poverty recruited all able-bodied hands to the common enterprise. Church teaching buttressed the social convention and the natural physical superiority of men with a doctrine that sanctioned their mastery, often brutal and loutish. Yet the women worked along with their menfolk, and whatever the sanctions of society or theology, affection, together with the qualities of intelligence and strength of character, shaped relationships within the home then as they do now.

The draughters of the Charter were not concerned with such matters, but they did address the legal position of society women in marriage and widowhood, both matters where property rights and obligations were of vital interest. They were also topics of vital financial concern to the great men of the land, and as such were dealt with among the first of the Charter's clauses. The relevant text can be paraphrased as follows:

6) Heirs are to be married without loss of status; but their next of kin are to be informed before the marriage contract is made.
8) No widow shall be compelled to marry, so long as she guarantees not to marry without consent of the king if she holds (her land) of him, or . . . of the lord from whom she does hold.

In a society where land and the ownership of land were the bases of wealth and power, marriages between families of great landowners were naturally arranged. To this day the arranged marriage remains the norm in societies which are structured on relations between kin-groups rather than individuals, and for them, as in feudal Europe, it is closely tied up with the division and exchange of wealth. Even so, it comes as something of a surprise to find the subject cropping up in the Great Charter of Liberties. It is obvious from the wording that the clause is not concerned with anything we would recognize as human rights.

The death of a landowner before his heir had come of age meant, in the case of a male heir, problems over the discharge of the land's military dues. If the heir was a woman there was the possibility that the land could be lost to another overlord by her marriage out of her own lord's domain; worse still, the land might go to an enemy. To use the language of anthropology, in a society where men and land provided the basis of society, women and kinship posed the problem.

From very early times lords therefore claimed the right to forbid an heiress to marry any man whom they reckoned a personal enemy, on the grounds that by the marriage the husband would become a tenant. Long before Magna Carta the rights of wardship over a female heir had been expanded into an absolute right to dispose not only of the lands but also of the person of the young woman. She had become, in the words of one commentator, 'a mere adjunct to her own estates'.

She had also become a very valuable property. A lord with a rich heiress at his disposal had valuable patronage in his gift. The affections of the girl did not enter into the case. Technically, of course, she could not be married without giving her own consent. Very occasionally a girl might be determined or courageous enough to withhold it. In that case the church was obliged to support her. But examples were rare indeed. The whole weight of social convention was against such a stand by women in a society dominated by the assumptions of male superiority, quite apart from the fact that the idea of marriage for love was still as alien to feudal Europe as it is to fundamentalist Islam today. And if a girl did hold out for whatever reason, she ran the risk of being a pauper for life.

The records of John are as rich in detail as any in Europe for the period. It has been said that the papal chancery itself could not match the royal chancery of England in the ordering of its archives, but even they do not hint at the personal drama which must have lain behind the decision of Alice Bertram to refuse to marry at the summons of the king. They record merely the fact that all her chattels were sold.

There were two other options open to those determined to avoid forced marriage: either they could take the life of religion, in other words enter a nunnery and thus become dead in the eyes of the law, or they could attempt to outbid objectionable suitors for their own hand. When Godfrey of Louvain set his mark at the wealthy widow of Ralph of Cornhill, he made an offer to the king of 400 marks to have the lady's hand, should she be unable to show any just cause or impediment against his suit. Perhaps the king took pity, perhaps the lady was pretty, perhaps her counter-offer capped his in value. At any rate, she fought off the suit with a bid of just 200 marks along with three palfreys (pedigree walking horses) and two hawks. When all provisos have been made and all human exceptions considered, the fact is that the past was a different place. To all intents and purposes, an heiress could be married at the wish of her feudal overlord to any man willing to pay the going rate. At the time of King John the term 'the marriage market' could be taken quite literally.

And not only were the heiresses up for sale, so too were the rights of their wardship, in that a man could pay for the right to sell a woman in marriage. Three years after the case of Godfrey of Louvain it is recorded that one Bartholomew of Muleton received the 'marriage' of the Widow Lambert together with wardship of her heir and his lands for another 400 marks. De Muleton was required to swear to marry off his widow *absque disparagacione* (literally 'without disparagement').

Few of the king's barons can have objected to the principle of wardships and the sale of marriage: they too found them a valuable source of revenue in their own domains. They did object however to the fact that the crown courts had limited the extortions they were permitted while doing nothing against the king's levies on his own wards and the widows of tenants holding directly from him. Above all, they objected to John's penchant for marrying off ladies of great families to low-born adventurers or even his mercenary captains, either because they had the money to pay or as a reward for their military services. Twelve years after the de Muleton case, Magna Carta uses exactly the same turn of phrase, *absque disparagacione*, in the clause aiming to impose on the king the kind of limitations his courts had long been enforcing against them.

The term is almost impossible to translate because the context of life has changed so much. Indeed it was beginning to change in the generation after the Charter itself which, be it noted, made no attempt to define its own term.

In the 1230s the Statute of Merton gave marriage to a villein or a burgess as examples of disparagement. Still later a commentator on the law specified marriage to anyone of no matter what social status who was maimed or deformed. In 1215 it seems likely that the chief objection was to marriage to people either of lower social status or foreign, especially if he was one of the king's hated mercenary captains. In a petition of 1258 the barons gave as their opinion that an heiress was 'disparaged' if married to anyone not English born. Perhaps 'without loss of status' is the nearest we can get to the meaning in modern colloquial English, though it cannot convey the sense of outrage felt for the fate of women like Margaret Redvers, widow of Baldwin de Redvers, Earl of Devon.

The arguments which made heiresses wards applied with equal force to widows, who could make a second marriage only with permission or under direction, and were required to have permission of their overlord should they seek a second marriage.

It might be more true to say that the baronial indignation was provoked more often by the dishonour done to venerated families by unsuitable marriage alliances than by any outrage, real or imagined, done to the women. Margaret de Redvers certainly seems to have awoken little sympathy. Her first husband, the young and sickly Baldwin de Redvers, had died after barely three years of marriage. The sole child of an officer of the king's household and heiress to large estates in Devon and the Isle of Wight, the widowed Margaret was a considerable catch. She came into the king's power during the winter following Runnymede.

The large estates of which she was now the lady needed the control and protection of a man in the unsettled times; she, a young woman, needed a husband for the sake of social propriety. So at least it could have been argued. In fact, the king was desperately short of resources and had loyal servants long overdue their rewards. Margaret was married off to Fawkes de Bréauté, an outstanding soldier of obscure origins – possibly the son of a Norman squire – but unswervingly loyal to the king. Fawkes was one of the witnesses of the king's will and a major factor in the survival of the royalist cause after John's death. But he was a mercenary, and as such heartily despised by the magnates. When the defeated French had been safely bought off, Fawkes was stripped of his honours and forced to leave England. Margaret took the opportunity to abandon her husband, claiming that she had married him under duress.

Yet while that was her right, it does not seem to have convinced even the baronage. Women, and especially widows, could buy their way out of unwanted unions. In the very year of the Charter another Margaret, the widow of Robert fitzRoger, had paid the immense sum of £1000 for the crown's rights in her marriageability. Lesser women bargained smaller sums – offered hawks or hunting-dogs or what they could if 'they preferred to live without a husband'. Margaret had married Fawkes when he was in the king's favour and deserted him when the king was dead and he disgraced. That at least is how it might have seemed to contemporaries. In any event she ended her life in a convent, apparently friendless.

If at this distance in time it is impossible to know for sure what personal dramas shaped the life of ladies like Margaret de Redvers, we know a good deal about the system under which they had to live. Before 1215 heiresses and widows had to make such deals as they could with king or lord – for, be it noted, the wording of the Charter's clauses in these matters makes it quite clear that the king was not the only offender. It is merely that, thanks to the superior thoroughness of the royal records and their survival in quantity, we are able to expose the dealings of King John in the marriage market. Deals could be struck in this as in any other market, and charters bought which confirmed the terms in writing. By the time of John, the charter had become a standard tool of business administration, both royal and baronial. That the greater magnates already had officers matching the chancellor of the king and were increasingly used to attesting charters for their own tenants is no doubt yet another cause of the impact which the great charter made on the public mind. In this context, too, charters like that granted to Alice Countess of Warwick in January 1205 take on an additional significance. She paid handsomely, but in return she received certification that she would not be forced to marry; that she should retain sole guardianship of her sons; that she should enjoy a third of her late husband's lands dower and that she should be free of the duty of attending the local shire and hundred courts and of paying certain dues to the sheriff – so long as she remained unmarried. Private negotiations like this were the order of the day before 1215, and not all ladies made such successful bargains. Magna Carta introduced the rule of law into a field where it had been noticeably absent. True, the topic had been touched on generations before by the coronation of Henry I, but in this, as in so many other matters, that venerable document had long been a dead letter. The Great Charter made only one stipulation – that the lady give a guarantee (*securitatem*, i.e. 'security') that if she did decide to marry she would not do so without the consent of her feudal lord. A relaxation in the human aspects of the great lady's life did not alter the fact that landholding meant legal obligations.

Even before the question of any second marriage could come up for consideration, a widow could well find herself in difficulties, depending on the settlements her husband had made for her. She might find herself a prosperous dowager, or she might find herself a poor relation to her sons and daughters. Her first concern was where she would sleep the night of the funeral, for she had no automatic right of residence in the 'marital home', which in all probability was the ancestral home of her husband's family. Things could sometimes be as bad as this brief summary makes them sound, and here again Magna Carta did good work in the cause of English widows.

7) A widow shall have her marriage portion and her [full] inheritance immediately following the death of her husband . . . ; she shall be obliged to pay nothing for her dower or for the marriage portion, nor for the inheritance which she and her husband held at the day of his death. She shall be permitted to remain in the house of her dead husband for up to forty days, during which time the settlement as to her dower shall be agreed.

The very vocabulary of the clause presents problems, though not perhaps to a British aristocrat or a Nuer tribesman in the Sudan, both of them fully at home with the arcana of kinship systems and marriage systems that leave the sophisticated city dweller or impoverished intellectual bemused. So we had best begin with some definitions.

By 'dower' is here meant that portion of a husband's lands which was set aside at the time of the marriage to support his wife should he die first. 'At the time of the marriage' more often than not meant on the very day of the wedding and the act of transfer was often performed in a colourful ceremony at the church door. Although the husband presented and the wife merely accepted the *dos*, as it was called, the ceremony was considered a form of contract and was in any case so well established a part of tradition that if it was omitted and the husband left her a widow, the law fixed the dower at one-third of the man's lands. The Charter's simple guarantee that the 'widow shall have her dower' is made in the context of this convention. The issue of 1217 was to go further.

If a man chose to endow his widow with less than one-third of his estate, his actual endowment rather than the supposed 'legal minimum' would be awarded to her. It is this state of affairs that the 1217 Charter makes explicit. 'The widow shall have for her dower the third part of all her husband's land . . . unless a smaller share had been assigned her at the church door'. Many a calculating husband must have been tempted to protect the integrity of his family's holding against partition to an incomer from another kin in this way. The church door ceremony, it would appear, could easily lose its attributes of 'colourful' traditionalism to become a fraudulent sham. Yet one assurance she did have: thanks to the Charter (Clause 11), whatever the size of her dower lands they could not be attached by her husband's creditors.

Where the dower came from the husband, the marriage portion *maritagium* was land set aside by a girl's father from his own land to be hers when she married. This marriage portion she 'took' to her husband, and so long as he lived he was treated as the virtual owner. Should he die his widow resumed her absolute and indisputable title. Exactly what was intended by the third term, the '*hereditas*', has been a matter of dispute among scholars. Was it simply another name for the *dos* or *maritagium*? This seems improbable given the tight professional wording which is a general characteristic of the Charter. Perhaps it denoted lands which had fallen to the widow during the course of the marriage, such as bequests from her own family and so forth, lands which could be described as being jointly held by the husband during his lifetime but which, as now provided, reverted to the wife on his death.

Brief though they are, the clauses in Magna Carta which deal with marriage law reflect a number of important points. For some fifty years past it had become increasingly common for interested parties to bid for the wardship or marriage of heiress or widow. Such 'proffers' often came from her family, anxious if at all possible, given the bounds of consanguinity laid down by the church, to keep the lands within the territory of the kin or at least use her lands in the dynastic policies of interest to the family rather than those of the king. By the time we get to the reign of John this objective of excluding the king was quite often stated explicitly. In fact one historian has suggested that 'the crown was coming to accept so many proffers concerned with the marriage of heiresses and the remarriage of widows that the principles laid down in 1215 did little more than confirm existing trends and ideas'. This may be overstating the case somewhat, but it is certainly true that in this matter, as in so many others with which it concerned itself, the Charter stated no new principles. The innovation consisted in stating and recording them at all.

A tailpiece to the story of Magna Carta and women's rights is provided by a sad story from the fifteenth century concerning Eleanor Cobham, Duchess of Gloucester, reported in the rolls of parliament for 1442. Charged along with Thomas Southwell and Roger Balingbroke, graduates of Oxford and her supposed accomplices, with planning to compass the death of King Henry VI by witchcraft, she was given the final sentence for treason by the king, though without trial by a duly constituted secular court of law. At the next parliament, 'a petition introduced into the Commons House, appealed to Magna Carta on behalf of such defenceless women [i.e. women charged with witchcraft in the ecclesiastical courts]'; it also ensured that in future peeresses in their own right, or as the wives of their husbands, should be guaranteed the same trial 'by their peerage', for charges of felony, 'as was enjoyed by their husbands'. Thus in at least one respect, and for them a very important one, women won equality at law with men.

Should we try to assess the place of the Charter's specific clauses on women as a stage in the history of the emancipation of women we at once confront a difficulty inherent in the problem. The modern idea of female emancipation originated exclusively in western Christian society. The patterns of male domination in medieval England were so oppressive in comparison with modern practice and expectations that to discuss conditions then with a view to identifying possible signs of hope must seem naively optimistic. Nevertheless in comparison with other societies medieval western Europe seems to have been extravagantly enlightened.

Writing in the 1160s, the Arab gentleman Prince Usamah of Shaizar recounts with unconcealed amazement the freedom the Franks of the cru-sader kingdom of Jerusalem allowed their womenfolk. Not only were they permitted to walk openly in the streets with their husbands, but if one happened to meet a friend, man or woman, the husband would stand patiently by while the friends had their chat. If the conversation dragged on, the Frank thought nothing of leaving his wife with the man while he went about his business.

At that time, of course, western women were not free to marry the man of their choice as a matter of right – had *that* been permitted them as well, Usamah, who refers the extraordinary behaviour of Franks to the mysterious ways of Allah whom no man may question, might have found even his faith in the divine providence tested beyond endurance. A commentator on Magna Carta had said that 'one of the great stages in the emancipation of women is to be traced in the emergence of the proffer that they should not be distrained to marry for a second time without their consent'. It seems little enough for a woman to ask. And yet compared to the treatment accorded to women in other cultures as revealed by anthropology one can accept that it was indeed a step forward.

Slow though the process may have been, the emancipation of the individual, whether male or female, has been the theme in western civilization which distinguishes it from all others. Inevitably the process started at the top. The rights or disabilities of rich heiresses in early thirteenth-century society had little bearing on the lot of their peasant contemporaries. Yet the fact that women of any rank could gain at law the right to marry at will, in no matter how circumscribed circumstances, was a notable victory of principle of interest to all women.

CRISIS CHARTER TO LEGAL CHARTER

By the beginning of 1215 the whole community of England, from the Scottish border country to the king's shipyards on the Solent, had learnt to recognize the firm hand of Angevin government, which to many smacked of tyranny. Nowhere was resentment stronger than in the north where, until King John became more or less resident in England after 1204, the reach of the administration had been less effective. No one was more enthusiastic in the agitation for a charter of liberties than the baronial group dubbed by chronicler and royal clerk alike 'the Northerners'. A natural focus for the malcontents was Eustace de Vesci, the lord of Alnwick in Northumberland, long time enemy of the king.

But if the coordinated movement which took the last lap on the road to Runnymede began with the northerners, the leadership was soon taken up by greater men from southern and Eastern counties – chief among them Robert Fitzwalter, lord of Dunmow in Essex. Back in 1212 he and Vesci had fled into exile after being denounced by John's illegitimate daughter Joan, wife of the Welsh prince Llewelyn ap Iorworth, for conspiring 'to drive the king and his family from the kingdom and choose someone else as king in his place'. Reunited they headed a far more formidable combination.

10

TIMETABLE
OF A CRISIS

As the month of July 1214 drew to its close, a visitor to Paris would have found the city *en fête;* when news of the French king's victory at Bouvines reached the capital the student quarter broke into a seven-day spree of singing and dancing. The threat to France between the armies of the empire to the north and John of England in the south-west was over.

The French triumph not only shattered John's ambitions to recover his lost lands in France, it undermined his credibility at home. Deserted by his Poitevin barons, John had failed to rally reinforcements from England. Philip August of France, the hero of the hour, made no move against the English army at La Rochelle, correctly calculating that there was nothing to fear from that quarter, at least for the time being. A papal emissary mediated a six-year truce between France and England and on 15 October the royal galley put into harbour at Dartmouth.

John faced a rebellious baronage with his prestige critically weakened. Back in May a group of northern barons had refused not only to join the royal expedition in Poitou but even to pay scutage money, on the quite illegal pretext that their terms of service did not include campaigning out of the kingdom. Now, they brazened out royal recriminations while opposition hardened elsewhere in the country.

Shortly after the king's return, it appears that magnates from East Anglia and the eastern midlands assembled at Bury St Edmunds to pledge mutual support. Roger of Wendover, indeed, writing more than a decade after the event, recorded in his chronicle at St Albans that the entire baronage of

England had assembled, to 'confer secretly' about a charter granted more than a century before by King Henry I. The numbers must be exaggerated. Even at the height of the civil war which broke out the following year, the opposition party only slightly outnumbered the loyalist barons. But late in 1214 malcontents were looking to coordinate action and the Bury meeting may have provided a lead, for there insurgency approached respectability under the veneer of the archaic yet undoubtedly royal charter, issued by Henry at his coronation in the year 1100 and laid before the barons in the August meeting in St Paul's London in 1213 (described page 37). It had never been implemented. The youngest of William the Conqueror's three sons, Henry had seized the throne on the death of his brother William Rufus under suspicious circumstances and despite the claims of his eldest brother, Robert Duke of Normandy. The charter was designed to win friends and influence barons. It was shelved once Henry was firmly on the throne.

By 1213 it was ancient history of little interest to anyone, apart, perhaps, from professional lawyers. We do not know who suggested its relevance to the current situation. Archbishop Langton is the most likely candidate, though a partisan of the northern barons gave them the credit. It was an inspired bit of antiquarianism, whoever was responsible. Henry's charter had nothing to say on the matter of scutage but it covered a number of other very topical issues – the rate of reliefs, rights of wardship and marriage and debts to the crown. Moreover, it promised to abolish abuses introduced in the reign of Henry's brother, William Rufus, and to restore the laws of King Edward the Confessor. Such an appeal to past customs chimed perfectly with the mood of John's critics, who dreamed of a return to the good old days before the advent of the Angevin brood in England, and an end to the entire system of government introduced by Henry II and developed by John and his brother Richard. A royal charter, no matter how ancient, indeed the more ancient the better, which coupled repudiation of a brother with an appeal to the age of old England's saint king offered the ideal format to legitimate protests which bordered on rebellion.

At the Christmas court John was confronted by a group of dissidents demanding confirmation of the laws of Edward the Confessor and of the laws and charter of Henry I. His first reaction was to promise an enquiry into any abuses that might have developed over the past twenty-five years, that is, during the reigns of himself and his brother. Today, a royal commission with carefully restricted terms of reference is Whitehall's routine response to calls for reforms to which it is opposed, but John's barons were less easily side-tracked than modern parliamentarians. Their claim that the abuses were far more deeply rooted, and their production of a charter to prove it, forced the king and his advisers to rethink their strategy. Playing for time, they proposed a postponement of full negotiations to a London conference set for 6 January.

The baronial dissidents had achieved the basic preconditions for successful opposition – a common purpose, a common loyalty almost certainly based on oaths of solidarity, and a common programme. From now on general discontent and vague if vehement protest gave place to a campaign for a charter of liberties. Discussions within and between the rival groups of court and barons must have kept many a clerk busy noting memoranda of the points agreed or debated. Two documents survive as evidence to this activity, though it is hard to date them precisely.

The first, called the 'Unknown Charter' (because it was not published until the 1860s), may represent the first form of the settlement from which Magna Carta itself derived. It consists of a version of Henry I's charter with a number of concessions said to be granted by John. Most of them were featured in Magna Carta. The second document, described in detail below, is known as the 'Articles of the Barons'.

The 6 January meeting ended in deadlock. The king might be obliged to enter into formal negotiations with his opponents, but he had no intention of meeting their demands. Having dismissed their representatives with letters of safe conduct for a further meeting on 26 April at which, he promised, their demands would be answered, he briefed envoys to Rome to lobby for legal support at the papal curia. On 13 January another delegation was dispatched with a copy of the charter which John had granted to the church in England the previous November. The barons too dispatched agents to the curia. In the coming months negotiations would be divided between the English and papal courts. Given that the round trip could take anything up to two months there were obvious problems of communication – there might also be advantages if papal threats drafted to meet conditions that were in fact out of date could be brandished to cow opponents.

Meanwhile, the aim of both parties was to curry favour with influential members of the curia and to establish their legal credentials. The baronial opposition based their claims on the legally imprecise 'customs of the realm', but it was a no-win position. Reforms would come only with the agreement of the king, and since the reforms meant curbs on royal powers this would never be given voluntarily. Only by force or by the threat of force could they get John to the bargaining table. But an oath given under duress was worthless and could be repudiated at any time on appeal to the pope. So long as the king lived, the lives and property of his opponents were in pawn.

In an apparently conciliatory gesture on 19 February, John issued letters of safe conduct to a group of the northerners for a meeting with Archbishop Langton and William Marshal at Oxford three days later. The barons did not turn up, either because the notice was unreasonably short or because they distrusted the impartiality of the king's proposed mediators. John kept the initiative with a further offer to redress the more 'burdensome grievances' arising from excesses committed during his reign or that of his brother Richard. But his master-step in the diplomatic minuet came on 4 March when he took the vows of a crusader.

Ever since the débâcle of the Fourth Crusade of 1204, when the army of the cross had sacked the Christian city of Constantinople and left the infidel unscathed, Pope Innocent had had the project of a new crusade very close to his heart. John's pious and public gesture was certain to score impressively. It also yielded the 'crusaders' respite', valuable legal immunities until the warrior of God should return from the Holy War. The glow of virtue which now surrounded John can hardly have concealed the grin of the cat who had got the cream. Two years before, he had pledged his kingdom to the Holy See, now he was pledged to the Holy War; yet here was this most Christian of kings being harassed by subjects who had already refused dues legally demanded of them. The study of Roman and church law revived in Italy fifty years before and now being taught at the *studium generale* of Oxford was fashionable in intellectual and government circles and legally there was no question who was in the right. John could afford to wait.

He was now so confident that he felt able to economize on his military precautions. Letters dated 13 March order a detachment of mercenaries recruited in Poitou to disperse to their homes 'as the business for which they had been required had been settled'. Although he could not know it, events in Rome were developing still further to the king's advantage. On 19 March the pope drew up a group of letters which he regarded as a threefold form of peace but which, to the baronial agents who were present, must have seemed tantamount to an ultimatum answerable only by war.

The letters, known to historians as the '*triplex forma pacis*', were addressed: to the king, who was asked to hear all just petitions of the barons and to treat them kindly; to the archbishop, ordering him to bring the parties into agreement; and finally to the barons. After condemning all leagues and conspiracies Innocent ordered them to renounce armed resistance under pain of excommunication and to petition the king with all the reverence due to his honour. Quite simply they were ordered to approach the king as suppliants, which, when the king in question was John of England, was as good as to say to abandon their petition.

The pope was simply spelling out the law, and as John was his liege vassal this was perhaps to be expected. But since the king would never voluntarily abandon one jot of the authority enjoyed by the crown of England it meant that the barons could not act within the law at all. The letters carried a bombshell. It would not reach England for another five or six weeks. When it arrived the explosion would be almost instantaneous.

On 1 April Innocent carried the logic of his case a step further and issued orders that the barons should pay the long-disputed Poitevin scutage, 'lest they hinder the king's good design'. This can only refer to John's crusading vow and reveals the king at his Machiavellian best as a political wheeler-dealer. Perhaps the pope knew merely that John was contemplating crusader vows – the delegation that left England on 8 January may have been briefed to this effect. But news of the king's intended vows could have reached Rome by 29 or 30 March, even if the decision to make them had been taken only a day or two before the public declaration on 4 March. In the summer of 1316 King Edward II received news in York of a papal election in Avignon just ten days after the event. Allowing for the Channel crossing, the distance of some 905 miles was covered at an average of more than 90 miles per day. Road conditions were probably somewhat worse in March than in August but in 1215 there would have been time for royal couriers travelling at just 50 miles a day to have made the 1200-mile journey from London to Rome by the end of March. As to the Poitevin scutage, the pope's argument was legally impeccable. The barons' refusal had been arbitrary and unreasonable. How could they ask the king to restore what they considered their rights when they had deprived him of what were undoubtedly his rights? The scutage controversy was two years old, the argument between the king and barons older still. If the pope believed that negotiations were impossible until the barons capitulated he might have law on his side, but such legality made war and reform inseparable.

Relationships between the two sides were already worsening before the papal letters reached England. As Easter week approached, with its meeting scheduled for 26 April, the eastern and northern counties saw increasing activity as great men rallied their retainers and fortified their castles. The meeting of king and barons was fixed for Northampton. The 'northerners' mustered at Stamford in Lincolnshire; on their way southwards they were joined by contingents from East Anglia, Robert Fitzwalter, lord of Dunmow and Geoffrey de Mandeville.

On the appointed day the little township below the castle at Northampton was thronging with armed men but the king and the royalists were away to the south, moving between the capital, the castle of Wallingford and the great abbey at Reading. The opposition barons adjourned from Northampton to nearby Brackley where one of their leaders, Saer de Quenci, Earl of Winchester, was lord of the manor. The king reached Wallingford on the last day of April and offered letters of safe conduct up to 28 May for any who wished to discuss matters with his mediators, Archbishop Langton and William Marshal.

If he hoped thereby to divide the opposition the ruse failed. At Wallingford he was presented with a schedule of chapters or capitula on behalf of the united barons at Brackley (this may have been the document called today the 'Unknown Charter'), which when it was read out 'provoked the king to fury'. This display of the famous Angevin wrath may have been provoked not so much by the concessions demanded as by the remarkable request that John guarantee his agreement by having his seal attached to the document. It was neither a true charter, a grant conceded by the crown, nor even a record of agreements already reached in negotiations; it was, in effect, merely a baronial 'shopping list'. No doubt the assembly at Brackley stipulated the royal seal to forestall the possibility of the king's disclaiming the agreement. It was an unprecedented demand from subjects to their sovereign and dire comment on the respect accorded the royal word of honour.

In the first week of May the situation developed alarmingly and fast, important events occurring almost daily. It seems the pope's letters exploded on the scene shortly after the Wallingford confrontation. His instruction to the barons to petition the king with due reverence to his honour made their demand for the royal seal seem the more outrageous. To them it was obvious that to observe the papal conditions would rule out meaningful negotiation.

On 5 May they made their feudal renunciation of the king in a formal act of *diffidatio*, published at Reading.

The pace of events, which has left a confused record in the chronicles, may even have taken the king by surprise. On 6 May he proposed as a compromise to reform any evil customs of his own and his brother's reign. The gesture was too late, and in any case entirely unconvincing. It merely repeated, after all, the very formula rejected by the barons at Christmas. John's closest advisers knew with certainty that he was acting in bad faith, since just two days later he required Langton to excommunicate his enemies and, when the archbishop refused, wrote to the pope to enforce the request.

The country was now technically in a state of civil war, though the king's opponents represented only a minority of the baronage, his active supporters were hardly more numerous, and the remainder of England's magnates held themselves aloof as best they could. Continuing his diplomatic manoeuvres John now issued a charter, dated 9 May, which proposed that the 'issues and articles' in dispute be submitted to eight barons, four chosen by himself, four by his opponents, sitting under the pope as arbiter. He can hardly have been serious. Quite apart from the fact that to convene such an arbitration court at Rome would have taken months, who could suppose that the opposition would accept as arbiter a potentate who apparently expected them to negotiate on their knees?

The following day (10 May) royal letters patent affirmed that the king 'would not arrest or disseise his opponents or their men except by the law of the land and by the judgement of their peers in his court'. Judgement by peers was a familiar concept to feudal law. It featured in the Ancient Customs of Normandy, recorded in written form shortly after John became duke, had been the subject of a German edict as long ago as 1037, and in England was guaranteed by the laws of Henry I. No doubt John regarded this promise to return to feudal propriety as the final flourish in his diplomatic offensive.

So far as he was concerned, the 10 May letters patent marked the end of the phoney war. Nottingham and its castle, the strategic key to the Midlands, had been systematically reinforced and provisioned since October and for the past several weeks John had been securing strongpoints throughout the kingdom. New orders had been sent out for Poitevin mercenaries; key northern garrisons such as Scarborough, Doncaster and Skipton were increased; and huge financial inducements were offered to secure the loyalty of doubtful castellans like Robert de Ros at Carlisle and John de Lacy at

Chester. On 12 May writs were dispatched to the sheriffs to seize the lands and chattels of the king's enemies and two days later John was assigning rebel territories among his supporters.

Hostilities broke out across the country. Rebel forces laid ineffectual siege to Northampton but seized Bedford. Llywelyn ap Iorworth of Wales, opposed in his Marcher territories by royalist lords such as Walter de Lacy and William Marshal, seized the opportunity of an alliance with Giles de Braose, bishop of Hereford, burning with revenge for his brother and sister-in-law, to sack Shrewsbury on 15-16 May. Always looking to buy time, John, headquartered at Windsor, ordered agents in various parts of the country to accept truce terms, if offered. The following day, 17 May, time ran out.

After their success at Bedford, the baronial army heading south for London had been met at Ware in Hertfordshire by a deputation offering to arrange the capital's surrender. On Sunday the 17th, when the bulk of the citizenry were at church, the rebel forces marched through the gates virtually unopposed. Messengers were dispatched throughout England 'to those earls and barons and knights, who appeared to be still faithful to the king (though they only pretended to be so), exhorting them with threats, as they valued their castles and possessions, warrens, parks and orchards to abandon the king and to form a united front in a fight for liberties and peace'. 'Capital of the crown and realm', no English town could approach London in size or wealth, while in the northern European rankings it came second only to Paris. With this prize in their hands, the opposition barons could force the king to the conference table and expect to rally support among the undecided. To the king's dismay the deserters included John de Lacy and Robert de Ros.

In the words of J. C. Holt, 'if Bouvines brought on a political crisis and the pope's intervention a war, the baronial seizure of London led directly to Runnymede.' So it seems in the perspective of history. To contemporaries the inevitability of events was less obvious. Many maintained full loyalty to the king, others sent their sons to London so as to have a foot in both camps, while many, particularly those in remoter parts of the kingdom, continued to watch developments from the safe neutrality of their estates. Of England's 197 baronies, it has been estimated that 39 were active for the barons and 39 for the king. On these figures well over half the chief landowners held aloof from the struggle.

Nevertheless the opposition, led by Fitzwalter under the grandiose title of

'Marshal of the Army of God', was formidable. A week after the fall of London the king issued letters of safe conduct to Saer de Quenci, Earl of Winchester, to come to his court to discuss terms on the barons' behalf, and two days later to Archbishop Langton and others to attend him at Staines 'to treat concerning peace'. Four royal agents were informed by letter that a truce had been arranged. The times were ripe for 'jaw jaw' rather than 'war war'.

On 28 May John received delivery of royal regalia from the custody of the master of the Temple. Generally impatient of ceremonial, the king knew the trappings of monarchy had their uses. At Odiham the following day, in the presence of Saer de Quenci, he gave an audience to a messenger recently arrived from Rome at which he repeated his willingness to submit the dispute to the pope. The baronial representative was no more inclined to accept now than before and the same day John dictated a letter for the pope. Giving a selective account of the past three months, it portrayed John as a paragon of reasonableness and concluded: 'So, whereas they have refused to humble themselves to us as they should, we have, for the service of God and the relief of the Holy Land, humbled ourselves . . . before them . . . and even offered them full justice by the judgement of their peers.'

Having prepared as best he could for papal reactions a month ahead, John moved to Windsor, from where he could be kept informed of the discussions and drafting sessions between his and the barons' advisers at Staines. On 5 June, to sound opinion among his supporters perhaps, he made a rapid progress through friendly territory to Winchester. Returning via Merton, where he issued further safe conducts, he was back in Windsor by the 9th. Days of 'shuttle diplomacy' were beginning to yield tangible results. Whereas on 25 May Saer de Quenci and Langton were invited to 'treat concerning peace', the Merton safe-conducts are for a baronial deputation which is to 'make and secure' peace. Furthermore, the safe-conducts are for a limited period – from 9 June to midnight on the 11th. Events were evidently moving to a climax.

On the evening of 9 June Hugh, the newly elected abbot of Bury St Edmunds, arrived at Windsor to petition royal approval of his election. There he found Archbishop Langton in conference with the king. Even in these stirring times the lordship of East Anglia's richest religious foundation claimed due deliberation and Hugh was told to present himself the following morning in 'the meadow of Staines', known to posterity as Runnymede. John was not accustomed to settle ecclesiastical business by appointment in the open fields. An encounter with a hostile, suspicious and well-armed deputation of barons was another matter. Clearly a meeting of high importance had been set for the morning of 10 June and the place of destiny had been chosen.

Conveniently situated between London and Windsor, Runnymede was a recognized point of assembly. In June 1215 it met a third requirement, being south of the river from the barons' base at Staines. Lying between marshy ground to the east and south and a stream flowing into the Thames from the west, it was virtually an island with only two easy lines of access, one from the Windsor direction, the other from the Staines direction. Of all the romantic images surrounding Magna Carta, that of two wary and hostile deputations cautiously moving towards one another into a meadow of pavilions and fluttering pennants surely pictures the actual scene in those distant June days. The exact sequence and nature of the events which unfolded is more difficult to determine. Most scholars now assume a timetable of meetings culminating in a ceremonial oath-pledging on Saturday the 19th.

The sequence opens on the morning of 10 June. Among the observers was Abbot Hugh, awaiting his audience with the king. John's first business that morning appears to have been to dictate letters to his military agents in the southern and midland counties informing them that the truce had been extended to the 15th. He and his advisers now turned to the main proceedings of the day.

For the first time since Easter he was face to face with his opponents, represented by the leaders of the baronial force at Staines (a contingent remained in London as a garrison force). Negotiations over the previous two weeks, in which Archbishop Langton had been closely involved, had reached a stage where the points under discussion needed to be consolidated and confirmed. As at Wallingford six weeks before, the barons were determined to get something in writing, as a hostage for the king's good faith. 'The Articles of the Barons' was, we may assume, the outcome. Drawn up in a royal clerk's hand under the heading 'These are the clauses which the barons seek and the lord king concedes', it lists in non-technical language a number of points mostly confirmed by Magna Carta, and it carries the royal seal. It was neither a true charter nor a royal letter patent, it had no legal force, it conveyed and granted nothing, and yet the dramatic break with protocol refused so angrily just six weeks before has now been conceded. We can assume that the seal was to reassure the baronial garrison in London and that their presence in the capital was the sole reason why the king had agreed to append it to such a document.

Everything indicates that the 10th was scheduled as a make-or-break day. Either the basis of a settlement would be agreed or hostilities would resume in full force. The day's business would not have been possible had the principal points for debate not already been decided in previous discussions. The baronial envoys left the meadow at Staines with proof that the king was at last in earnest. When they had gone John could give his attention to the Abbot of Bury St Edmunds. Letters in chancery dated the 11th confirmed him in the revenues of the abbey.

But if the king was in earnest, neither he nor his opponents were fully committed. The negotiating teams were agreed on the terms of the settlement and a truce was set to run to the early morning of the 15th. But over the next four days the baronial delegates would have conferred with their colleagues at Staines and in London. The outcome of these deliberations would decide whether the 10 June document would become the basis of a full charter in the form of a legal grant. 15 June is the date actually on the Great Charter. On this day, it seems, the long, tortuous and nervous negotiating process reached a conclusion with the confirmation by all interested parties of the terms agreed. Four more days of work by the technical advisers and lawyers prepared the ground for the solemn and ceremonial exchange of oaths, apparently held on 19 June, which would give legal force to the clauses agreed between king and barons.

Elaborate and unprecedented conditions were laid down in an attempt to ensure they were honoured. The barons were to choose twenty-five of their number 'who with all their might are to observe, maintain and cause to be observed the peace and liberties which we have granted and confirmed to them by this our present charter'. To ensure compliance, they were authorized to distrain royal property to make good any breach of the charter by the king or his officers. In the last resort, of course, the sanction relied on force, and it has been called a right to legalized rebellion. But the feudal system already provided for this in the *diffidatio* by which the barons had barely a month before defied the king. The charter's '*forma securitatis*' adopted the legal sanctions applied by the courts against common defaulters; it was extraordinary in so far as it proposed to levy them against a king, but it was not technically a threat of duress of the kind which would invalidate his oath.

The real sanction was a naked piece of such duress carefully insulated from the grant of liberties in the shape of a treaty, also agreed on the 19th, which laid down that the baronial garrison should remain in control of London until 15 August, Archbishop Langton having custody of the Tower. During the intervening weeks the oaths to the Twenty-five were to be administered throughout the kingdom, and the king was to meet all the claims against him and restore rights and properties. Should he fail to comply London would still be held against him. This was duress indeed.

'At length they met at Runnymede' wrote the Dunstable annalist, 'and on 19 June peace was made between the king and barons. And the king received homage, which the barons had withdrawn at the beginning of the civil war.' Only with the renewal of homage was the state of war at an end, only now could the contracting parties pledge their oaths to the confirmation of the terms. Neither the writing of the charter nor the affixing of the king's seal by the royal official known as the spignel carried the charisma of authority conferred by the oath-taking. The impression which the great ceremony made on contemporaries echoes from the pages of the chronicler Ralph of Coggeshall: 'Peace of a kind ("*quasi*") was made between the king and the barons and all, even the king, swore on holy relics to observe it inviolate.' According to the Dunstable chronicler John 'then restored to many of them their castles and other rights, and charters were completed there concerning the liberties of the realm of England.' Each of these copy charters, Coggeshall tells us, had the royal seal attached. Four of them survive, but it is unlikely that there ever was one 'original' charter to which the king himself witnessed the affixing of his seal. It was the oath-taking which secured the 'liberties of England'; only later did they become identified with the physical documents.

In June 1215 the important documents were the writs, many dated 19 June, drawn up for the enforcement of the various clauses of the agreement. They deal with such matters as the release of prisoners and hostages, the return of mercenaries from Dover to the continent, and the surrender of castles and other matters. Above all, there are the letters patent providing for administering of the oaths to the committee of Twenty-five.

It was with good reason that Coggeshall described the arrangement as a 'quasi peace' for, as Dunstable observed, it 'lasted only for a little time'. The writs enforcing the charter sparked local conflicts between those who claimed the restoration of lands and those in possession. The whole interpretation of the charter, the question of who should arbitrate on the king's fulfilment of his obligations and of when London should be returned to him opened new problems. Their hold on the capital was the barons' strongest card, and they were unlikely to relinquish it voluntarily. The terms of the 'quasi peace' held the seeds of a new war and by September it would be in full swing.

Timetable of principal events from October 1214 to June 1215

October 14	John finally returns to England
	Barons conferring at Bury St Edmunds on Henry I's Charter
Christmas	Baronial demand that John confirm Henry's Charter
January 6	London meeting with opposition barons deadlocked
8	John sends legal representatives to Rome
February 19	Letters of safe conduct for Northerners to come to Oxford conference with William Marshal and Langton
March 4	John takes crusading vows
13	He sends letters cancelling Poitevin mercenaries
19	In Rome Pope Innocent draws up '*triplex forma pacis*'
April 26	Opposition barons gather at Northampton
30	John at Wallingford receives 'capitula', possibly the 'Unknown Charter', and angrily rejects it
May 5	Opposition barons make formal *diffidatio* at Reading
6	John offers compromise settlement
8	. . . asks Langton to excommunicate barons and then writes to the pope when Langton refuses
10	Royal letters patent offer 'judgement of peers'
12–14	Royal sheriffs seize rebel lands and king begins distribution among his supporters
17	REBEL BARONS TAKE LONDON
28	John receives regalia from Master of Temple
June 9	John in conference with Langton at Windsor
10	. . . faces baronial deputation in Runnymede when draft heads of agreement presumably drawn up
15	Date on the Charter, presumed of actual agreement
19	Ceremony of 'peace between the king and barons . . .'

11

THE MAKING
OF A CHARTER

'JOHN, BY THE GRACE OF GOD, KING OF ENGLAND, LORD
OF IRELAND, DUKE OF NORMANDY AND AQUITAINE, AND
COUNT OF ANJOU, TO THE ARCHBISHOPS, BISHOPS, AB-
BOTS, EARLS, BARONS, JUSTICIARS, FORESTERS, SHERIFFS,
STEWARDS, SERVANTS, AND TO ALL HIS BAILIFFS AND
LIEGE SUBJECTS, GREETINGS . . .'

So begins the most famous document in English history. It follows a
formula used in scores of others drawn up in the reign of King John,
naming first the grantor of the charter and then those to whom it was
addressed, for Magna Carta was a bureaucratic document.

The terms of this particular charter were so wide that it has been possible
to sketch the picture of the community of England at the time by expanding
on its clauses. We can now examine the background to the document; and
something of the officials who had the job of realizing in written form the
agreement between the king and his barons.

Four copies survive. Two are in the British Museum, one in the care of
Salisbury Cathedral and the other, possibly the finest version, for centuries in
the cathedral at Lincoln, now in the castle there. It must be supposed that the
king and his officials scrutinized the finished document and this parchment,
in modern terms 'the original', was delivered to the barons sealed, possibly
in their presence and that of the king, on or before the 19th; whereupon the
barons formally renewed their allegiance. John, like his predecessors back to
the time of King Henry I, had used a charter to buy something. But whereas

the first Henry and Stephen had bought loyalty on trust, John had so conducted his affairs that after reigning for half a man's lifetime he had to purchase the loyalties of liegemen of sixteen years' standing.

Copies of liberty

A modern scholar has estimated that after the initial document another forty copies were made. The king of course did not sign any of the parchments, nor did he personally append his seal. This would be done by the professional officer whose job it was; it is highly doubtful whether John would have been present while the job was being done.

Not the least interesting thing about Magna Carta is the care that was taken to see to its publication to the country at large and the thoroughness with which this seems to have been carried out. On the 19th various writs attested in the name of the king at Runnymede were sent out to royal agents and officials in various parts of the country to let them know that peace had been restored between the king and his barons and his freemen.

Among these the most numerous single type was the *pro forma* directive to sheriffs and all royal officials with responsibilities in the counties, such as the bailiffs, warreners, foresters, and river wardens, as to how the document was to be publicized. In many cases they would have received these instructions before the arrival of their sealed official copy. The officials were directed to ensure that the charter be read in all the bailiwicks of the county, that all free men take the oath of loyalty to the Twenty-five, and that twelve knights be sworn in as an official committee of enquiry into all abuses of the king's officials within the county boundaries.

The copy of this *pro forma* on the Patent Roll (the official royal record of open charters) is followed by a dispatch list of the counties to which the charter itself had been sent. Unexpectedly, only thirty-three of the then thirty-nine counties of England are listed, yet Ralph Coggeshall, a usually reliable contemporary, states positively that every county received its copy. Moreover, the omissions include the great county palatinates of Durham and Chester. No satisfactory explanation of this conundrum exists.

Either we assume that one of the clerks in John's notoriously efficient administration made a colossal yet spasmodic oversight amounting in statistical terms to an error of some 15%, or that large and important areas of the country were left uninformed of the great righting of the wrongs of the community of England, or that the exemplification was not completed before it became apparent that the clerks had been overtaken by events, and that the virtual certainty of civil war made copies for the remaining counties redundant.

There is yet another possibility: that the list is accurate and that all the counties nevertheless received their copy. If the list on the Patent Roll is precisely what it is said to be, a *dispatch* list, then it could be that the copies of the 'missing' counties were taken to their destinations not like the others by official royal messengers but by some personality or official from the region, who happened to be at Runnymede and gave some token of receipt (now lost) to the recording clerk. This too unfortunately presents us with a problem, since the writ of instructions for Worcestershire appears to have been given to the bishop of Worcester on 19 June, who then received on the 24th *j. cartam*. Since, as has been seen, every attempt to solve this problem involves absurd assumptions, let us now assume that the bishop of Worcester was a pedant who insisted that the recording clerk put his county down on the 'dispatch' list even though he himself was acting as royal courier.

If all thirty-nine counties did indeed receive their own copy and we add to this number the one held for the royal archive and the one sent to the Cinque ports, we arrive at the probable total of forty-one copies. Since four are known to be still in existence, this gives a 10% survival rate over a period of 775 years. Taking into account that besides the charter itself we also have a near-contemporary copy in French translation, the enigmatic 'Unknown Charter' and also the 'Articles of the Barons', of which probably only one copy was ever made, and that all this material survives from a period when public administration, for all its comparative sophistication, was still in its infancy, historians really should think themselves extremely lucky.

If the four surviving examples of the Runnymede charter are typical, and there is no reason to suppose otherwise, the exemplifications were each on a single parchment sheet measuring some 15 by 20 inches (38 x 50 cm). They were written in a clear script, without a break from start to finish; the punctuation, division into paragraphs and numbering of the clauses in modern versions having been introduced by modern commentators.

The first batch of seven exemplifications was sent out on 24 June, that is, five days after the final agreement at Runnymede and the dispatch of the first writs, 21 in number. It is of course impossible to draw any certain conclusions from this. One merely observes that in the time it took the expert scriveners of the king's chancery to produce – and release, after the payment of due fees and bribes – 21 fairly short and standard documents, they were able to prepare one-third that number of charters of a new and comparatively lengthy type. The final dispatch given on the list (six charters) occurred on 22 July, more than a month after the agreement at Runnymede.

The style of a charter

The first thing in the preamble to a royal charter was the title of the king himself. A little later on in this chapter we shall be tracing the development of the regal title adopted by English kings; here let us look at how John described himself.

The style 'king of England' had been standard since the time of Stephen. Henry I had styled himself 'King of the English', the form commonly used by the Anglo-Saxon kings, in his coronation charter. Later in this clause John follows more recent precedent when he employs the royal 'we'. His father, the great Henry II, had been willing to settle for the businesslike and unpretentious first person singular. It was Richard, possibly influenced by continental practice, who modified the simple 'I' of ordinary men to the 'we' of kings. The innnovation that John did make was the incorporation of 'lord of Ireland' in the regal title.

The Norman incursion into Ireland had begun in the 1160s when Dermot McMurrough, king of Leinster, came to England looking for support in the recurrent power-struggles of his country. Some ten years before, ostensibly concerned for the state of the Irish church and in the hope that his young champion would conquer the place and force it into paths of reform, the English pope Adrian IV had conferred on Henry the title 'lord of Ireland'. Now, the Leinster under-king was offering a form of homage to Henry in exchange for armed assistance against his enemies at home. The English king was polite but unhelpful, and Dermot found the practical aid he was looking

The oldest item in the English royal regalia, the anointing spoon, shown here with the late-fourteenth-century eagle-shaped ampulla, dates from the late twelfth century and was almost certainly used at the coronation of King John. Both pieces were renovated for the coronation of Charles II in 1660.

Chess was a favourite game with noble men and ladies. Heavy sums were wagered on the outcome and players sometimes came to blows. The game was considered a model of war and courtly intrigue.

The ship shown on the seal of Winchelsea, one of the Cinque Ports, with its fore and after castles is clearly a ship of war; trumpet calls were standard parts of the signal system at sea.

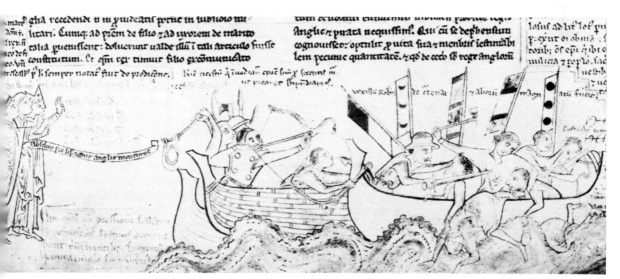

This near-contemporary picture of the Battle of Sandwich suggests that the ships of John's new royal navy were modelled on the classic longships of the Norsemen.

These two castles – Dover, above and Lincoln, below – were the key points in the battle for England in the civil war between John and his barons following Runnymede.

The Jew's House, Lincoln. This fine twelfth-century town house bespeaks the prosperity of its builder, at a time when most burgesses were content with wattle-and-daub, wood frame and thatch.

Even the villein finds his mention in the Great Charter, being guaranteed his 'wainage'. The term no doubt meant the tools of his trade of which the principal was the heavy plough and bullock team, often shared between two or three small peasant farmers.

The windmill symbolized a growing surge of power through the technology of Europe which heralded the Continent's industrial revolution. As this gathered strength Christian bankers encroached increasingly into the capital market and finally displaced the Jews, who were expelled from England in 1291.

Magna Carta Memorial erected by the American Bar Association in 1957. Nearby is the memorial to President Kennedy and the Commonwealth War Memorial.

for among a group of Norman lords from the Welsh Marches. They rapidly established themselves at the expense of their Irish 'master' and looked set fair to carve out independent principalities.

Up till that time the troublous island, engrossed in its own internecine conflicts, had made little impact on English affairs. Apart, that is, for a period during the tenth century when (soon after Scandinavian cousins of theirs had founded the duchy of Normandy) the Norse kings of Dublin irrupted successfully into the north of England against yet another Norse lordship, the Viking kingdom of York. The prospect of Ireland serving once again as a power base for independent regimes, ruled by descendants of the warlike Norsemen of the old school, looked a disturbing one for London. To scotch any such development, Henry bethought himself of his 'lordship' and, with the eager encouragement of a new pope, Alexander III (who issued a bull to the Irish clergy to mend their ways), sailed in the year 1171 with an imposing expeditionary force.

The pope may have been disappointed: the king's objective was clearly not the reform of the church. He wasted no time in establishing his authority in the matters that concerned the crown. The Irish had no interest in opposing him, since he was there to discipline their Norman rivals; the Normans had no interest in provoking the wrath of a notable soldier who was also their liege lord and master and, in addition, had a sizeable army at his back. After a token resistance they acknowledged his overlordship. The Irish formally did homage as vassals, while Henry asserted the crown's exclusive interest in the old Viking ports of Dublin, Waterford and Wexford. A viceroy was left in Dublin to hold the ring, while the Irish reverted to their rivalries and the Welsh-Norman incomers quickly learnt the rules and joined in.

Probably from the outset, Henry had earmarked the new island province as an appanage for his youngest, landless son. As is apparent from the wording of the document, Pope Adrian had supposed that his bull would provide the basis for the formation of a new kingdom of Ireland. When he was nineteen John was invested with the title 'lord of Ireland' until such time as he could be declared king, and was sent there with a respectable force of men-at-arms, a sizeable treasure and expert advisers. He was back in a matter of months, having incensed the Irish chieftains by his ill-mannered ribaldry at their expense and offended the Norman lords by slighting their hopes of patronage. His one achievement, an unusual one then as now, was to unite the Irish. After a humiliating defeat for his men in a skirmish John returned to England after only a few months in his new office. The crown of peacock feathers created for his coronation was never used.

But if John mishandled the historic opportunity of the kingship of Ireland, at least he retained a measure of effective power there for the English crown. The titles of duke of Normandy and count of Anjou were empty. All attempts to recover the great duchy had foundered and, to his even greater shame, he had been driven out of the ancestral county of the Angevins. His mother's great territory of Aquitaine remained to the English crown. Maybe it would have been better had John lost that too, for it would involve England and France in 300 years of intermittent but often bloody and destructive war, before the English were at last forced to withdraw.

The sense of proprieties

Such was the potentate who granted the Charter. The beneficiaries – 'the English church' and 'all the freemen of our kingdom' – appear several lines down, after the Charter has enumerated those to whom it is addressed and those to whom the grantor is indebted for their advice in the great matter of state with which it is concerned. These, apart from a select body of church-men, are a number of officials and a few noblemen – those, it is generally assumed, who were, so to speak, in the royal party with John at Runnymede. Unless the proprieties are properly observed, no public act can be properly conducted.

Magna Carta may be, as has been written, 'an unrewarding document for the general reader . . . bristling with technicalities of feudal law' and having 'no high-sounding statement of principle and no clearly defined political theory', yet it is fascinating for anyone interested in the history of human society. Since it is the only written constitution the English have ever had, the temptation to compare it with the other famous written constitution in the English language is irresistible.

By the nature of things, it is impossible in the 1990s to know whether in the 2200s anyone will be setting out to colonize a new world with a copy of the constitution of the United States in their cabin trunks, or whether having done so they will breed descendants who a further 200 years in the future will use that same constitution as the foundation stone of a new state, proudly independent of the United States. One supposes not, but then the stock of Magna Carta was not very high in the 1440s, as far away from Runnymede as we are from 1776. Nor can we know whether, in the year 2546, someone will be publishing a book on the history of the United States constitution. But we can be sure that if he or she is doing so that book will have nothing to say about the rights of widows in the America of the 1770s, or about the condition of Jews, or about the mayor of New York as specified in that constitution.

The weakness of Magna Carta is that apart from the pious generalities of what we now know as the preamble and the first clause 'having regard to God and for the salvation of our souls, and the advancement of holy church and for the reform of our realm', etc., it would not, in the immortal words of P. G. Wodehouse, recognize a high-sounding statement of principle or a clearly defined political theory if presented with them laid out 'on a plate surrounded with watercress'.

In the rhetoric and in-fighting that preceded Runnymede, there was much talk about the Laws of King Edward and the charter of Henry I. But when it came to the form of words that would establish their liberties beyond a peradventure, the barons fell back on the technicalities of the law – whether real or imagined. That, for a thirteenth-century Anglo-Norman baron, was the language of liberties. The meaning of the word 'liberty' still had to be conceived, let alone defined. In the meantime, Runnymede laid down a few useful, if primitive, benchmarks for future reference.

At a time when the debate over human rights is centre stage in the political arena and the question appears to be how best are they to be maintained, it is useful to look back at the struggle of the barons of Magna Carta. Their one strength was self-interest, intelligently if obsessively pursued. Even that is something to take note of. More important is their respect for the law as it was applied in their own day and in their own affairs. This led them to a respect for the law as it applied to the interests of others. Runnymede undoubtedly has its lessons for us today. Among them are matters so mundane as good government and decent administrative practice. The technicalities of the charter, fossilized to us, are the rock-hard foundation-stones on which it was built.

The beauties of routine

Among the reams of documents from the reign of King John which can still be consulted in the archives of England's public records is a simple formula of agreement between two litigants in a property dispute dated 15 July 1195. It is one of hundreds of such 'concords' to survive from the later twelfth century, and there is nothing extraordinary or noteworthy about the transaction it deals with. Even so, this nondescript piece of bureaucratic parchment has a special interest for us. On the back it carries a note to the effect that it is the first example of a new system of records instituted by the justiciar Hubert Walter. For a generation and more it had been standard practice in land disputes that the final settlement should be recorded in standard form and in two copies, one for each party to the dispute. In July 1195, it appears, the justiciar ordered that thenceforward a third copy be retained for the government records.

By the year 1200 government, both local and central, made regular use of a variety of instruments and documents. It was, if one may use the term, the dawning of the age of bureaucracy, and like anything new it was popular. This may seem a little odd today, when jargon, forms and paperwork are comprehensively deplored. But to a generation that was only just beginning to accept literacy as an accomplishment among educated lay people the developing use of documents signaled a growing sophistication of government.

One of the most popular innovations of Angevin government was the introduction of various types of writ, available to anyone who could afford the fee. The writ as such was as old as the early Anglo-Saxon monarchies. At a time when the rest of Europe was content to convey royal orders by word of mouth or ad hoc instructions, the English kings had established a system of more or less standard directives, bearing the seal of the king and binding on all who received them. For centuries, outside England only the papacy could boast such a system. But the writ was expensive and confined to the monarch except in special cases. Henry II introduced a range of standard formula writs drawn up in the royal chancery or exchequer and available to anybody who could afford the (not inconsiderable) fee and attendant bribe to the clerk.

The classic example, and probably the most popular of all these new-style writs was the writ *praecipe*. This was an instruction to the sheriff that he order the defendant in a case to restore property to the plaintiff – the man drawing the writ – or else appear before a royal justice to give his reasons for not doing so. At the time there were many types of case that were tried in the private courts of feudal lords. The right to hold a court was much valued because the fees and fines made the administration of justice very profitable. Litigants generally preferred royal justice because, at least in theory, it promised a fairer trial if the case were heard in the lord king's court rather than that of the big man of the local neighbourhood. The writ *praecipe* had the effect of taking a case out of such private jurisdiction causing the lord 'to lose his court' as the jargon had it.

No doubt in the Britain of the 1990s, or as soon as the government could bring the administration of justice within the scope of its enlightened measures of privatization, the writ *praecipe* would be pilloried as an unwarranted encroachment of government upon the legitimate province of free enterprise. In Clause 34 of Magna Carta, however, the government of King John agreed that in future the writ would not be issued to anyone 'regarding any tenement whereby a freeman may lose his court'. This has been variously condemned as one of the most reactionary clauses in the charter and explained away as merely a rationalization of procedures in the issue and use of the writ to avoid abuse. Whichever interpretation is correct it seems clear that the writ was a popular one, was regularly issued, and was seen, by the framers of Magna Carta at least, as a potential threat to private courts.

There would be much theorizing in later centuries about the origins of the Charter. One view much favoured by the Victorians thought its antecedents were to be found in the practices of the Anglo-Saxon kings. One scholar traced it to the Anglo-Norman writ charter, which he described as merely the Anglo-Saxon writ translated into Latin. An article in the *American Historical Review* suggested that it derived its form, at least, from Norman innovations – possibly from some Norman borough charter. In the 1980s historians tended to the earlier view.

The Victorians' view that Anglo-Saxon governmental procedures heavily influenced Norman practice is generally reinforced by recent scholarship. It has been suggested that the Domesday Book survey of 1086 was possible only because William I could draw upon the English royal administrative system. Although based in the royal household, in common with other European 'departments of state', it was far more sophisticated and in fact provided the foundation for the practices of the twelfth-century royal exchequer and chancery.

By the year 1200 the king's palace of Westminster had become the base for a group of administrative officers quite distinct from those of the royal household, while with the dramatic upsurge in the study of law during the twelfth century, following the continental fashion, this bureaucratic machine was well staffed with experts in every department of business that came within its province.

We can also trace something of the content found in the Charter to pre-Conquest practice. By the mid-tenth century it became standard practice for the archbishop officiating at the coronation to exact from the king an oath of good government. The oath comprised in essence three promises – to protect the church; to ensure the peace and repress violence among men of all ranks; and to combine justice and mercy in all judgements.

A history of royal obligations

The oath is first known to have been exacted from King Edgar at his coronation in Bath in the year 975. The first record of the words used are of the oath administered to the young King Aethelred II by St Dunstan in 978. William the Bastard of Normandy, who seized the crown by conquest in 1066, followed the practice of his English predecessors and thus gave sanction to a historic practice which would continue to be appealed to by successive generations.

William Rufus continued the practice and even, we are told, issued a brief charter of confirmation to reassure his understandably sceptical subjects. His brother Henry took the oath in due form and he too issued a charter – one which would achieve brief but historic importance, thanks, it appears, to the intervention of Archbishop Langton – on the day of his coronation. It was in surprisingly specific terms, promising not merely to 'make free the church of God' and to abolish 'evil customs', but also to permit heirs to succeed to their fathers' lands by a 'just and lawful relief' and covered a number of other technical points of feudal custom. Having seized the kingdom following the suspicious death of his elder brother William and from under the nose of his eldest brother Robert, King Henry needed all the support he could get from the English, of whom the charter proclaims him king. The charter ends with a promise to restore the laws of King Edward, together, be it noted, 'with such emendations as my father made with the counsel of his barons'. A surviving copy is addressed to 'Samson the bishop . . . and all [the king's] barons and faithful vassals, both French and English, in Worcestershire'. A chronicler reports that 'as many charters were made as there are counties in England, and by the king's command they were deposited in the abbeys of every county as a memorial.'

According to Roger Wendover, when Stephen Langton told the barons about the existence of Henry's charter he explained that it had just come to light, as though the idea of such a thing was a complete novelty. In fact, of course, most academic lawyers would have known about it and many others must have been aware that King Henry II had also granted a charter at the time of his accession. King Stephen, his predecessor, had granted two. The entire sequence of twelfth-century coronation charters provides an informative set of precedents for the historian.

King Stephen's first was a general charter of liberties; and was combined with a solemn oath securing generous liberties to the church. The two combined were granted as the price of support for his seizure of the crown and his consecration by the church. It was a good bargain. For the rest of his reign, no matter how parlous the state of his cause might become, no one could seriously contest his claim to the title of king: he, after all, really was the Lord's anointed, whereas his rival Matilda never received that recognition.

We next find Stephen conceding a charter some four months later, at Oxford. Again something had to be bought, this time the collaboration of Matilda's leading supporter, Geoffrey Earl of Gloucester. But the rights were still more handsomely confirmed. The charter not only made a general reaffirmation, but also made numerous specific concessions, notably that the crown would not claim rights of wardship of abbey lands during the vacancies in the headship of the houses. In fact the chief provisions were of interest to the church; a general clause promised to observe good ancient customs and to do justice. There was one specially valuable concession to the baronial interest – the renunciation of all land afforested since the death of William II. Otherwise the chief concession was the understanding that the barons' loyalty would be conditional on his future treatment of them and a group of charters to individual barons, granting specific rights.

With King Henry II's coronation charter we come to the first in the sequence not granted to buy the support of any specific individual or interest lobby. It was brief and vague. His succession had been secured by arrangements made with his predecessor. The country, if not so ruined by anarchy as once thought, was nevertheless glad of a smooth handover of power after the death of Stephen in December 1154. It might seem, then, as though the eighteen-year-old Henry issued the charter merely as a gesture to tradition.

But there was more to it than that. A few years into the reign one of Henry's admiring officers of state described his policy as 'renewing the golden days of his grandfather' (Henry I), while a chronicler spoke of 'the restoration of ancestral times'. From the outset of his reign Henry made it clear that all grants made by the 'usurper', as he termed his predecessor, were considered invalid. In practice of course many had to be allowed to stand if the kingdom were not to be reduced to a worse state of anarchy than that which he had replaced. But the principle, clearly established, gave the new king almost complete latitude as to what he would and what he would not confirm. The omission of all reference to the 'usurper' in the coronation charter was eloquent. It was reinforced by what the charter actually did say.

To the church and the barons the new king conceded only what his father had conceded. And herein lay the second reason for his granting any charter. Stephen's concessions to the church had been lavish to the point of excessiveness. By declaring the reign of his predecessor null and void as to precedent, Henry recovered the position of the monarchy vis-à-vis the church at a stroke.

It was also strong if blatant propaganda. Since he had been crowned, consecrated and anointed by the church Stephen could in no sense be termed a usurper. Indeed, since Henry had embarked on his English venture in the name of his mother and she was still alive at the time of his accession, he, if anyone, might be considered the usurper.

The little charter of Henry 'Curtmantle' had the dash and swing of his stylish short cape: it swept his predecessor from consideration and with the same gesture dismissed much of the mystique claimed by the church. Small wonder that when Langton began talking charters to the barons he drew their attention to the grant made by the *first* Henry. Why, it might be asked, did he not look at the coronation charters of John or Richard? The reason is simple; neither issued one. After almost a hundred years of struggle since the dubious accession of Henry I, the succession to the throne of England was so certain that the mere formality of the coronation oath was all the church could do in its own favour before discharging its duty and consecrating the king.

Nothing could more graphically demonstrate how far the question of the kingship of England had travelled than a quick survey of the titles borne by successive monarchs. Henry I terms himself merely 'Henry, king of the English . . .' and then explains: 'Know that by the mercy of God and by the common counsel of the barons of the whole kingdom of England I have been crowned king of this realm'. The wording tells it all. This is no assertion of divine grace upon the person of the monarch. It is, rather, a news report that a crowning has taken place with the agreement of the baronage. The fact that the 'mercy of God' receives first mention tends to expose the conventional nature of the invocation. The whole tenor of the announcement seems to be 'Take note, I have been crowned', with a barely suppressed 'Thank God' thrown in.

When we come to the second charter of Stephen insecurity is the keynote, so anxious does it seem to justify the event. He declares himself king 'by appointment of the clergy and people, by consecration of the archbishop and papal legate, and by the pope's confirmation'. This sounds like special pleading for the defence rather than an assertion of authority. In any case the last claim was unjustified; the pope had not given his formal confirmation. However, the church in England undoubtedly had, and this is what chiefly mattered to Stephen.

What a contrast with the giant self-assurance of Henry II, who called himself 'King by the grace of God'. So we find that when King John does, belatedly it must be said, come to grant his Charter it is as 'John, by the grace of God, king of England, lord of Ireland . . .' etc. that his clerks entitle him in the opening words.

One of the puzzles about the events of John's reign is why it took so long for the barons to raise the standard of revolt, if their wrongs were so great. Part of the answer lies in this high-sounding title. It was not that men were notably more religious than they are today, but they did tend to believe in God, and in such a thought-world it was difficult to shake off entirely the feeling that a duly consecrated king was someone special – perhaps as special as he claimed.

The history of the royal title as we have briefly traced it helps explain the awe in which even a monarch such as King John was held. The development of the charter as an instrument of government accounts in some measure for why the opposition barons, whether at the prompting of the archbishop or not, adopted it as their tool to tame the king. The coronation charter was only a special case of this development.

The routine of rights

It has been argued that the Angevin system of government was not so much an innovation as the codification and fossilization of existing practice thanks to the universal adoption of the technology of writing in secular administration. By the nature of the thesis it is almost impossible to put it to the test, but there are indications in the records that fill it out.

First of all, the bulk of those records themselves is much greater from the time of John onwards. Although his father reigned twice as long, John can show more than twice as many documents. The reforms of Hubert Walter played an important part, but thanks to the prompting by Henry II's legal reforms, 'paper' (i.e., of course, 'parchment') was simply becoming more popular. And men's attitudes were changing.

Earlier charters, from Henry's time for example, reveal the unlettered society they were drawn up for in their wording. They refer to grants already made which the charter merely confirms. The legal deed of transfer would be some public ceremony before witnesses, marked no doubt by the handing over of some token such as a hunting-dog or a knife to lodge it in the memory of those present. This had been the pattern for centuries. It was only at the period we are concerned with that the document itself, instead of being regarded merely as a record of an event, came to to seen as the actual deed of conveyance itself. Hence title 'deeds', once physical acts, would in the course of the development of the English language become merely pieces of paper.

The further back in time one goes, the more common it is to find charters which are undated. Validation of the deed came not from them but, if necessary, the convening of a jury or inquest of men of the neighbourhood able to testify from their own memory that such a deed of transfer had once been made in such a year and on such a day. The bulk of property titles had long rested on foundations such as this; many a cathedral chapter or monastic estates office could do little better if challenged than claim to have held land in question 'from a time when the memory of man runneth not to the contrary', track down some aged estate worker or member of the community, or point to its own chronicle or list of founders, and hope to be believed.

From the twelfth century onwards the forgery of documents became more frequent. Sometimes this was for the obvious reasons, but very often it was because property which had been in the community's possession literally since time immemorial was now coming into question. It was an age when literacy was leading to the expectation of memorials. At a time when the royal government was issuing charters merely as written records of arrangements which had been made orally months, perhaps years before, pious churchmen connived at creative recording in the form of documents produced generations after the event, rather than lose valuable endowments which were undoubtedly theirs by right.

Nor was it merely that writing was becoming the guarantee of reality which made John's barons favour the form of the charter. Such documents were the common currency of baronial as well as royal administration. A charter issued by the royal administration some three and a half months before the events at Runnymede is a case in point. On 1 March 1215 King John is recorded as granting to the abbey of Holmcultram in Cumberland the hermitage of St Kilda along with its clearing in the royal forest of Inglewood, for the monks to cultivate or keep pasture as they pleased. It was issued because the hermit of St Kilda had died and the abbey wished to be sure that it had the title as his successors. Without specific grant to cultivate, the pastureland of the clearing within the bounds of the royal forest would come under the rules of 'vert' (see page 85) and cultivation would be an encroachment of the royal rights of the forest.

This was just one of hundreds of such charters issued during the reign to confirm grants of all kinds to all kinds of petitioners. Like the king, barons, lords, churchmen and monasteries all issued charters for dozens of purposes. In the next century there would be teachers of business studies at Oxford giving instruction in the draughting of such charters to budding estate managers and estate stewards. The Great Charter of Liberties was in a recognized bureaucratic tradition. Its contents however, were not. From the care which was taken over its distribution across the country and the detailed instructions given to sheriffs and bailiffs for its publication, we can see just how important this particular royal charter was considered to be by John's contemporaries.

We are told that copies of the charter were carried through towns and villages (the sheriffs had been ordered to proclaim it throughout their baili-wicks) so that all might swear to observe its terms. Yet the reading of this screed of legal latin would have meant little to even educated laymen – when Archbishop Langton had presented Henry I's Charter to the barons at St Paul's (page 139) they had been perplexed by the language – to the average townsman or suitor at the county court it can have meant nothing. The Latin reading must surely have been followed by a viva voce translation. Langton's steward Elias of Dereham, was involved in the distribution of the charters in June to July, 1215 and, with the St Paul's assembly at the back of his mind, may have urged such a procedure. The translation would presumably have been in French, though in the greater towns English might have been used even at this early date – we have seen that one of the Londoners' complaints against Chancellor William Longchamp was his ignorance of the language. In the shires there would have been no need to pander to the sentiments of the lower orders, a French version for the benefit of the gentry and the more prosperous, upwardly mobile members of the English peasantry would presumably have sufficed. It seems that William Briewer, Hampshire's sheriff in June 1215, had just such a translation made for use in his county. A copy was made, for some reason, for transmission to French where it survived in a medieval document collection in the Norman town of Pont Audemer. Written in an early thirteenth-century hand, it preserves a remarkably accurate French version of Magna Carta. Possibly in some towns this was in its turn given in English by some prosperous peasant farmer for his neighbours. Forty years, on and English was coming into its own. A royal letter of October 1258 orders that the Provisions of Oxford, forced by barons from Henry III be issued in every county, 'both in French and English so that they might be read by the sheriffs and understood and observed . . . by all.'

A CHARTER
FOR WAR

As we saw in the last chapter, six of England's thirty-nine counties are unaccounted for in the list recording the copies dispatched, and it was suggested that one possible explanation lay in the sheer work-load of producing so many fair copies at such a high standard of penmanship in the time available. The last charters are recorded as having been sent out on 22 July. It was just over a month since the formal delivery of the document and the renewal of their allegiance by the opposition barons. John was still instructing his sheriffs and other officials to carry out the terms of the Charter and a great show was being made of restoring traditional liberties claimed by the more obstreperous of the barons. For example, in Durham royal foresters were instructed to restore his hunting rights in the royal forest to Eustace de Vesci. But these acts of compliance were probably intended to gain time while the king regrouped his position for a renewed confrontation.

On 20 June, the day after the solemn ceremony, the king had written post-haste to the pope with his own account of the events which had led to his predicament. On the baronial side, too, it seems there was less than straightforward dealing. We learn from a letter of protest by the leading churchmen that 'when the peace had been made between the Lord King John and the barons of England . . . those same barons promised to the Lord King in our presence and in our hearing that they would let him have whatever guarantee he required of them, except their castles or the giving of hostages.' What in fact John asked for was the issue of a personal charter by each baron, confirming his oath, whereupon, we are told by the bishops, the barons reneged on their promise.

Maybe the king had never intended to abide by the terms of the Charter: it seems equally clear that the more extreme of the opposition barons were equally unreliable. One or two, according to a contemporary account, even left Runnymede before the 19th so that they should be able to dissociate themselves from whatever should be agreed, on the grounds that it did not bind them since the terms had been settled in their absence. No names are named, but it is obvious from their subsequent behaviour that neither Eustace de Vesci nor Robert Fitzwalter, still vaunting himself as the 'Marshal of the Army of God', considered themselves obliged to observe the terms of the Charter until the king had discharged every last jot and tittle of his obligations. Others still more extreme had been bitterly frustrated by the decision of their colleagues to come to terms with the king at all. They had all along wished to carry the struggle on to the death.

In a sense they were right, for no matter how often the barons brought John to his knees he remained king and, as events were to show, could find a king's party willing and able to help his cause triumph over the opposition. In 1215 the argument was never followed through to its logical conclusion. The wild men on the baronial side merely wished to see the end of the enemy.

It is doubtful whether they saw the constitutional implications. Some four hundred years later, however, this precise question was debated in a discussion on parliament's military strategy during the Civil War when the army's fortunes were at a low ebb. The earl of Manchester lamented ruefully: 'Let us beat the king ninety and nine times, yet is he king still.' Such defeatism had to be nipped in the bud, and Cromwell put the case in a nutshell. 'My Lord,' he replied, 'if this be so, why did we take arms at first? This is against fighting ever hereafter. If so, let us make peace be it never so base.'

At the end of the Great Argument of the seventeenth century, Parliament followed the logic of the case and beheaded King Charles. In the civil war over the Charter the opposition barons were to prove as logical, when they made Louis of France the offer of England's crown. They had to. There was no way in which they could win the argument. Unless they could establish an alternative monarch in John's place theirs was by definition a lost cause. Oaths given under duress were not binding. No king, certainly not John, could willingly surrender powers: any forced concession would necessarily be merely a tactical withdrawal.

The struggle for Magna Carta was a classic example of the eternal problem of how to replace an established system. When the aim is to overthrow the law and the lawmaker himself, the traditional injunction of every establishment in history, 'Act within the law', becomes not only disingenuous but pointless. In the run-up to Runnymede, the barons had found their alternative law in precedents drawn from the ancient past and the reassuringly normal conventions of charter bureaucracy. During the months following the humiliation of John they found themselves, willy-nilly, in a fight to the death. In his *The Governance of Norman and Angevin England, 1086-1272*, W. L. Warren has written 'We should not suppose that Magna Carta was a set of demands imposed on a reluctant king made helpless in 1215 by the united opposition of an overwhelming majority of his barons. It was an attempt to find a formula for peace between the king and those of his subjects who had taken up arms against him made by those barons who wished to avert a civil war.'

While the first part of the assessment is undoubtedly correct – John had not been made absolutely helpless nor had he been brought to Runnymede by the action of the 'overwhelming majority of his barons' – and while the whole is carefully hedged with qualifications and while, finally, it might reasonably be said to apply to the body of the Charter, one must beg leave to differ if the judgement is applied to the notorious Clause 61 with its proposals for guaranteeing the discharge of the king's obligations. For that critical clause was, to all intents and purposes, a sentence of deposition. In the words of one later commentator, it made the king of England but the twenty-sixth petty monarch in his own dominions. Even her present Majesty, Queen Elizabeth II of the United Kingdom of Britain and Northern Ireland, shorn of power though she is, is not required by law to submit her every official act to a committee of minders appointed by her declared enemies.

The Twenty-five

As we have seen, the famous *forma securitatis* was in the form of a standard legal sanction to enforcement of a contract upon a defaulter. The wording of Clause 61 would not have been strange to any of the barons who attended the draughting sessions. Yet they may have been astonished at their own temerity when they considered that these words were being used against a king. The Clause provided for:

> five and twenty barons of the kingdom . . . who shall be bound with all their might, to . . . cause to be observed the peace and liberties we have granted . . . by this our present charter, so that if we . . . or any one of our officers, shall in anything be at fault toward anyone, or shall have broken any one of the articles of the peace or of this security . . . those twenty-five barons shall, together with the community of the whole land, distrain and distress us in all possible ways . . .

We shall examine the rest of the clause, but first it is worth noting that the king was to be penalized not merely for the breach of the charter he had just 'granted and confirmed' but for anything in which he might be at fault towards anyone. There was nothing general about the clause, in fact it was so precise in its provisions that all except the most hostile of John's opponents must surely have had doubts about its propriety. The procedures to be followed by any complainant are laid down in such detail that there was no loophole for compromise or adjustment on either side.

What is best described as a sub-committee of four was to be appointed by the Twenty-five. Anyone with a grievance against the king was to notify the Four; it was their job to go to the king, or to the justiciar if the king was out of the realm, and, 'laying the transgression before us, petition to have that transgression rectified without delay'. Should the royal government have failed to redress the injustice within forty days, the Four were then duty bound to lay the matter before the full committee of Twenty-five who would proceed about the business of distraining the king 'in all possible ways', which are spelt out in pitiless detail. With all the community of the realm they were authorized to seize royal castles, lands and possessions and to act generally as they saw fit with respect only to the person of the king, the queen and their children. '. . . And when the redress has been obtained,' the text blandly continues, 'they shall resume their old relations towards us.'

It has been called a licence to civil war: better call it a licence for mayhem. For these astonishing reprisals were to be levied on the king not only for his own misdemeanours or oppressions but for those of any of his bailiffs or officers anywhere in the country. Nothing is said about how serious must be the offence to set this awesome machinery in motion. As worded, the Charter left it open to any mischief-maker to raise any complaint, however trivial, if it was technically a breach of the Charter or an injustice, with the aim of raising the realm against the king. Nor does the Charter specify who was to adjudicate as to whether a wrong had been redressed or not. Given the creditworthiness of John's regime at the time, it could hardly have been left to the royal justices to determine that the plaintiff's case had been satisfied, should he himself not feel appeased. And if not the justices or the courts, who?

The only answer must be the Twenty-five, perhaps more aptly termed the Committee of Public Safety on the model of the French revolutionary committee of that name. For its powers were not merely conferred by the Charter, they were intended to be confirmed and buttressed by an oath of loyalty from every freeman in the land. And 'all those . . . unwilling to swear to the twenty-five to help them in constraining and molesting us, we shall compel to swear to the effect aforesaid'. This one provision is more radical than anything else in the Charter and can properly be called revolutionary. The oath it called for was of a kind never before heard of, though it had points of similarity with other types of allegiance.

Men were familiar with the idea of something higher than their feudal allegiances to lord or king. While kings and emperors claimed to be the vicars of Christ upon earth, they were also thought to hold their kingdoms of him just as men below the king held in tenure from him. Christ was the ultimate liege lord and, as such, in the last resort could demand service against the king. During the years of interdict and royal excommunication Englishmen had been reminded of this more forcibly than most people in Christendom. And, if it came to that, by John's own act of some two years back Englishmen quite literally acknowledged that their king had a feudal superior, namely the see of St Peter as embodied in the person of Pope Innocent III.

The idea of an oath levied on every man in the kingdom was also not new; John himself had used the device after the fall of Normandy. Nor yet was the idea of an oath jointly sworn against the authority of the king. The London commune of 1191 had called for such an oath, even if only for a short term and for a clearly defined purpose. What is so startling about the oath of Magna Carta's Clause 61 is the combination of all these elements to produce an oath which bound all the king's free subjects in allegiance to a *secular* authority which, given the range of its power as also specified in the Clause, was higher than he.

This authority was not an abstract notion nor yet a person embodying an abstract notion. Before John had given his kingdom into the hands of the pope and received it back from him as liege lord, Richard I had surrendered it to the emperor and received it back at *his* hands. Thus, feudal Europe could conceive of the possibility of an oath to a lay ruler higher even than one's king. What would have seemed inconceivable before June 1215 would have been an oath of ultimate allegiance, the highest bond known to society, given not to a liege lord but to a body of lords, all of whom were subjects of the king but who collectively were supposed to exercise an authority above the king. To the people of the time it must surely have seemed as startling and revolutionary as if today the Queen were to demand an oath of every man and woman on the electoral roll to uphold her authority against that of Parliament.

As if all this were not enough, the Charter provided for the continuance of the Twenty-five as a self-perpetuating oligarchy. Should their number be depleted by death or by the prolonged absence of one of them from the kingdom, the vacant place was to be filled not by canvassing the opinions of the baronage as a whole but by mere co-option of the existing members. It seems as though there was an absolute determination to make the new regime for the governance of England work if it was at all possible. Nothing suggests more clearly the degree of this determination than the provisions for the validation of the rulings of the committee of Twenty-five itself.

Given the diverse interests and opinions of those opposed to the king it must have seemed more or less certain to most participants in the draughting sessions that the brand new committee would be stopped in its tracks by the very first decision it was called upon to make or the first judgement it was called upon to render, simply by disagreement among the members. It was a world where community decisions were still expected to be unanimous. The supposition was that in any important matter there would be a right judgement revealed by God to the community through the deliberations of its representatives. At a less exalted level the very idea of majority voting, if considered at all, was seen as divisive. Unless those who held the minority view could be persuaded to agree with the general opinion, they would form a faction of discontent and, still more serious, the pattern of the divine or universal will would be frustrated. Until a few years back English and American juries were required to render a unanimous verdict, for reasons that stretched back to ancient tradition based on similar grounds. Similar considerations still obtain in the deliberation of the people's courts in modern China.

But with the development of workaday bureaucracy, where decisions had to be made if work were to proceed, the idea of decision by the will of the majority began to gain adherents during the twelfth century, and the first example of an institution regulating its affairs in this way appears to be, somewhat unexpectedly, the Roman conclave of the 1170s for the election of new popes by a bull. The first time we find the proposal described in an English source is at this point in the Great Charter. The relevant passage may be rendered thus: 'Furthermore, in all matters entrusted to these twenty-five barons for action, if by any chance when the twenty-five have been summoned and all being present are unable to agree on any matter, or if some of them even though summoned fail to attend, whether because they will not nor cannot, that shall be held to be fixed and established which the greater part of those present ordain or command.'

The selection of the Twenty-five seems already to have ensured that the 'greater part' were extremely hostile to the king; this provision was meant to ensure that the extremists should always have the upper hand and dictate the policy of the group, and through them the actions of the king. No monarch of whom the word could be used in any meaningful sense could accept as conditions of office such terms as the Charter sought to impose on John: he could not even entertain them. If Magna Carta, including the *forma securitatis*, seemed like a formula for peace to those in the realm 'who wished to avert a civil war', they must, one feels, have been excessively simple-minded. This one clause may have scuttled the Charter; it has been suggested that it was the sight of the *forma securitatis* that led Pope Innocent to absolve John from the obligations of his oath. If so, one can only agree that the pope was right.

The tournament, banned by more than one king because it provided ideal camouflage for raising armed rebellion, was in vogue in the summer of 1215. But the barons were nervous of the direction their actions were leading and fully aware of the importance of their hold on London in strategic terms. A tournament, scheduled to be held at Stamford, was moved at the last moment to Hounslow so as to be nearer the capital. The occasional meetings with the king were prickly affairs; the barons denied him the ordinary courtesies and absolutely refused to surrender London on one pretext or another. At length it was agreed that the Archbishop of Canterbury should be given custody of the Tower of London and the baronial leaders could hold the city itself, on the understanding that their conditions would be met by the middle of August when they would return it to the king. If their conditions were not met, they should be allowed to retain it until such time as they should be.

This apparently statesmanlike compromise in fact confirmed the barons in possession of what one of them had described as 'our refuge' while giving control of the Tower to the very man who was known to sympathize with them. Langton's position was ambivalent. If, as seems probable, it was he who had prompted the opposition to adopt the idea of a charter it is unlikely that he was any more confident of the king's honesty of purpose than the barons themselves. Nevertheless, as John's right-hand man according to the conventions of the time, and the pope's senior representative in the English church according to the facts of the case, he was obliged to accept at its face value the king's sworn oath to observe the Charter.

Reactions from Rome

For the time being, perhaps, he tended to agree with his fellow-bishops that the barons in fact were in the wrong. Certainly the archbishop joined in the letter of protest against them that we have referred to above. But if there was the beginning of a shift in his sympathies towards the king, it must have been badly jolted by the arrival of a papal letter based on Rome's understanding of events in England, which roundly condemned opposition to the king and upbraided the very bishops who had in fact been working to keep the peace and help the reconciliation between king and barons, for having shown him no 'favour against the disturbers of the realm'.

So far as Innocent was concerned John was not only a crusader but a crusader king who had surrendered his realm to St Peter, and the very king who, 'it was especially hoped, would succour the Holy Land'. But Innocent was no fool and must fully have recognized the advantages which his crusader vows would mean to a hard-pressed king. For John's oath to take the cross, made back in March at a time when the baronial opposition was building up unpleasantly, was very clever politics indeed. From the moment he took his vows, any crusader was considered to be under the special protection of the church – both his person and his property. Furthermore, he was allowed three years in which to meet all his secular obligations – which in the king's case could be taken to mean any commitments he might make to his barons.

At the time of the oath the pope was sceptical of the new crusader's sincerity, and even this most recent letter admits the possibility that the king might be lukewarm in his devotion or prove remiss. But Innocent was absorbed in his dreams for a crusade, and of all Europe's crowned heads John was so far the best bet for its leadership. He went on to proclaim excommunication as the penalty for any who still opposed the king and ordered the bishops, on pain of being suspended from office, to enforce the decree.

Written at a time before the meeting of Runnymede and the mutual undertakings there between John and his barons, it was long out of date. Accordingly Archbishop Langton refused to authorize the solemnities of excommunication against the recalcitrant barons. For their part, the legate Pandulf and the bishop of Winchester, together with the abbot of Reading Abbey whom the pope had also nominated as commissioner for the execution of his orders, pointed out that they themselves had been given the power to put through the sentences on the express authority of the bull: 'that Our mandate be not impeded by anyone's evasion'.

In so far as the papal letter had been written in ignorance of Runnymede and had applied itself to a situation that no longer existed, it was literally out of date. In this sense, no doubt, Langton was correct in rejecting its call to expel the opposition barons from the community of the faithful. In so far as they were still recalcitrant and even occupying the chief city of the realm in defiance of the king, it could be convincingly argued, as would certainly be understood by the pope to be the case, that they were, in the words of his letter, 'worse than Saracens' and 'were trying to unseat' a king who had pledged himself to full support for the cause of Christ and his apostles.

Acting on the authority conferred on them by the bull, the pope's commissioners declared the offending barons excommunicate, imposed the same sentence on all their supporters, naming the citizens of London especially, and announced the suspension of the archbishop of Canterbury himself from his office. Langton's appointment had caused a six-year interdict and his own exile; his intervention had prompted the imposition of the most humiliating charter upon the king; and now his resistance to the orders of his own master in God had caused his removal from office barely two years after his return to England. The trouble caused by this ecclesiastic certainly seemed to match anything achieved by the most famous of all turbulent priests, Saint Thomas Becket.

But the last thing John wished was for the death, let alone the murder, of his archbishop. With their most distinguished champion humiliated, the barons' cause was far more seriously compromised than it would have been by his removal from the scene. Outraged by what he considered the pope's ill-advised policy, Langton wearily took ship across the Channel, en route for Rome where he would put his case to the pope himself. As he made his way southwards, couriers were already on the road for England with letters of still heavier import for the baronial cause. In terms both outraged and explicit, they released the king from his oath to the barons and declared the Great Charter 'null and void of all validity for ever'.

If the proposers of Magna Carta seem a trifle simple-minded in expecting that John would accept a new-model monarchy which made him little better than the executive officer for a baronial cabal headed by his principal opponents, their ecclesiastical advisers (Langton included), who seem to have supposed that Innocent III, the most jealous advocate of papal monarchy to sit on the throne of St Peter for more than a century, would consent to the emasculation of his candidate, crusader, and liegeman John of England, must have taken leave of their senses. The king, wrote the pope, had been forced into an agreement, that was, 'not only shameful and base, but illegal and unjust'. If it were allowed to stand, not only would the king's legitimate interests be injured, but the apostolic see would be dishonoured and the crusade endangered. Churchmen in the opposition camp must have been brought rudely to their senses. Whatever the moral justification before the Great Charter, it was obvious that in the spiritual politics of Rome, King John had a special place.

The document revealed John's skill in surrendering England to the pope and then taking his vows as a crusader. He had won absolution from the interdicts on very modest terms of compensation to the church in England, now it appeared he had won the pope's unswerving support in perpetuity. Even if, continued Innocent, the king wished to honour the obligations incurred in such a way he would have had to abandon them in behalf of Almighty God and the Apostles St Peter and St Paul. John was not permitted to ignore the charter, he was ordered to ignore it on pain of excommunication and on the same sanction his baronial opponents were forbidden to insist on the fulfilment of its terms.

There was a large king's party with its own interests to defend, who rallied to John's cause over the ensuing months and so ensured that his child heir could secure the throne, but more than that, the common code of the great majority of the ordinary baronage would have been affronted by the proceedings at Runnymede. The most elementary convention recognized that oaths given under duress were not binding, irrespective of papal rhetoric. Given the expectations and assumptions of their times, the barons could not hope to win the argument; accordingly they had to win the war.

Civil war

Hostilities had already begun when the pope's letters arrived. Stephen Langton, though far from England by this time, was in spirit at least in the thick of it. Rochester, the second strongest castle in Kent after Dover, was part of the military responsibilities of the diocese of Canterbury and its castellan was one of Langton's appointees. Theoretically a king's man, he was in fact a calculating opportunist, so that when, in September, the baronial Army of God appeared before the walls of the castle and demanded its surrender he opened the gates with alacrity.

John was furious. It may be that his hatred for Langton dated from this event. Granted, the archbishop had been opposed to him more or less since the moment he returned to England. But even John could recognize that in the early days this had been to be expected, given his obligations as a servant of the church. But since then he had obstructed the king's will over the Charter and now his castellan had surrendered one of the key points on the approach to London to the rebels. However, the king was not over-impressed by the military capabilities of the garrison which the Marshal of God, Robert Fitzwalter, had installed before himself retreating to London. The idea was that Rochester should hold out until the arrival of the French prince Louis. John's vigour and military capabilities when roused were second to none and he forced the surrender of the garrison in a matter of weeks.

Meanwhile, the rebels in London were playing at government. In conformity with Clause 61 they called upon the kingdom as a whole to distrain upon the king's property; they called certain northern landholders to conference in London; they sent hopeful messages to the Welsh prince Llywelyn and the king of Scotland; above all, they awaited news from France. A delegation had been dispatched, offering the English crown to Prince Louis, son of Philip II. Only two years before Philip had been anticipating just such an addition to the crown of France; by the autumn of 1215, however, things had changed. He was at peace with King John and with the pope; to support his son's candidature would antagonize both of them. The prince however was eager for the adventure and sent a detachment of knights and men-at-arms who reinforced the garrison in London.

While his enemies passed the winter 'in camp' in traditional fashion, awaiting the advent of spring and with it the campaigning season, John led his army on a fearful punitive raid of waste and pillage through the lands of the hostile barons. He reached as far north as the then Scottish town of Berwick-upon-Tweed, which he captured and sacked before pushing on into the Scottish lowlands, Alexander II the new king of Scotland having retreated pell-mell from his own harrying raids into Northumberland on the approach of the royal army.

It was a terrible winter for the north country. Towns paid handsomely to avoid the fate of Berwick, rebels begged mercy – even the once arrogant Eustace de Vesci turned petitioner. Turning south again, the king meted out like vengeance on the rebel strongholds in the south and East Anglia until only London remained. But, of course, London was the key to England, and further reinforcements of French troops had arrived early in 1216. The arrival of their leader Prince Louis could only be a matter of time. In May, the prince set sail for England.

Following in the tradition of Stephen, Matilda and Henry II, Louis (later Louis VIII of France) was the fourth adventurer to bid for the English throne since the Conquest. Between 1216 and 1688, the year in which William of Orange frightened King James II out of his kingdom, there would be five more attempts backed with foreign money: in 1327, Queen Isabella overthrew her husband Edward II; in 1470 Henry VI and his French Queen Margaret of Anjou, financed by French gold, briefly recovered the Lancastrian crown; in 1485 Henry Tudor, another client of the French king, defeated the Yorkist Richard III to become Henry VII; only the Duke of Monmouth's rebellion of 1686 failed. It is one of the many myths entertained by the English about their history that the country has been free of invasion since the Conquest. As can be seen, there have been at least nine, six of which succeeded.

Statistically, and in the historical perspective, Louis had a good chance. Like William of Orange, he was invading at the invitation of a significant proportion of the disaffected English baronage. Louis's landing on the south coast late in May was the signal for a revival of the turmoil which John's terror tactics had so recently quelled. The Scots invaded once more, while Louis swept through the south winning support from defectors as important as John's half brother William, Earl of Salisbury. However, Dover, under Hubert de Burgh, held firm, while John's mercenary captains like Fawkes de Bréauté in the Midlands and Engelard de Cigogné at Windsor, and his trusted liegemen like William Marshal and Ranulph of Chester, remained loyal.

As summer turned into autumn, the rebel camp began to be embarrassed by its early success. The Frenchmen in Louis's train had come over in the expectation of rich pickings from the lands of the English baronage ranged against him. As more joined their master's cause, so their prospects declined. But then events began to run in John's favour. The Scots were defeated once again; William of Salisbury returned to the royalist camp, as did a number of other important lords. At the end of September John was able to bring relief to the loyal lady castellan of Lincoln, the redoubtable Nicholaa de la Haye. From there he went on to a royal welcome from the prosperous port of Lynn (now King's Lynn) on the north Norfolk coast, to arrange for victuals to be sent to various royal strongholds.

Between the 11 and 17 October, in extreme pain from dysentery probably brought on by food poisoning, John made slow and painful progress to the castle of Newark. On 12 October the lumbering royal baggage train, apparently trying to catch up with the king by taking a short cut through the treacherous lands skirting the Wash, lost a large number, possibly the bulk, of its packhorses and wagons in the quick sands of the Wellstream estuary. According to tradition it was a disaster which took the crown jewels with it. Certainly one set of regalia, that of his grandmother the empress Matilda, which John is known to have had in his possession, is never heard of again. But it is also the case that in the early hours of 19 October the king passed on from the realm of this world to that of the next, where one cannot lay up treasures, and that wayfarers on the roads around Newark reported men and packhorses leaving the city loaded with loot over the following twenty-four hours.

13

CHARTERS,
LIBERTIES AND POWER

THE death of King John of England on 19 October 1216 is one of those historical events which seem as important to posterity as they did to contemporaries. Roger of Wendover, the St Albans chronicler, welcomed England's deliverance from a monster of depravity: the Barnwell annalist mused on the passing of a great if unhappy prince. If we now incline to Barnwell rather than to Wendover in our estimation of John's qualities we share with them the conviction that his death was a major event. In fact, it was more important than either of them could have recognized.

Despite the death of the king, and despite the fact that his son Henry was still only a boy, the royalist cause had underlying strength. The west country was solidly for Henry and his advisers, while King John's last campaign in the east midlands had prepared the foundations of royalist superiority there. The Charter, which had seemed to set the seal on the rebel cause, was legally a dead letter since Pope Innocent had pronounced it null and absolved John and his successors from his oath. True, the rebel barons had required Louis of France to uphold its clauses, but the excommunication of Louis by the papal legate and the high-handed behaviour of the committee of Twenty-five established by the Charter as a monitor of John's behaviour weakened support for the rebels. Had John lived only a few years longer the affair at Runnymede might well have become one of the half-forgotten curiosities of history. Secure in papal support, backed by a large part of the baronage and a wily political operator when his back was to the wall, John could no doubt have overturned the Charter. His death made it once more centre-stage.

While Louis of France besieged Dover and his allies roamed the south-eastern counties and East Anglia, the royalists prevailed in the north and west. They were led by William Marshal, the papal legate Guala Biachieri, and a small group of powerful nobles and churchmen. These hardened and wealthy men of affairs owed their allegiance to a nine-year-old boy. Now he was brought to Gloucester, where on 28 October he was made king as Henry III.

The rebels held Westminster, but Gloucester, where the abbey church had been one of the venues for the crown-wearings of the Anglo-Saxon kings, had venerable royal associations. The ceremony was a modest and, according to witnesses, moving affair. First the 'pretty little knight' was given the accolade; next he took the usual coronation oaths to maintain the honour of the church and administer justice; then he did homage to the legate as the pope's representative for a kingdom which his father had surrendered to St Peter. He was crowned with a golden headband or circlet of his mother's by the bishop of Winchester.

Unconventional though it might be, the coronation was undoubtedly valid and opposition to Henry was now opposition to the Lord's anointed. The following day William Marshal accepted the post of regent by acclamation from his peers. A fortnight later, the day after counsellors, bishops and magnates had taken their oaths of allegiance to the boy king, the regent and his advisers played a trump card. On 12 November 1216 they made a solemn reissue of the Great Charter of Liberties in the king's name.

Everything possible was done to give weight to this ceremony. Each of the great lords and churchmen present was named separately as party to the act. Not only Marshal but also the legate authenticated the charter with their seals. Guala's decision, which reversed the pope's annulment of the document just a year before, cannot have been lightly taken. Nothing more tellingly demonstrates the impact of King John's death on the political situation. What had begun as a manifesto of rebellion was being transmuted into a government policy document.

It was sound politics in the king's cause, encouraging waverers to return to their allegiance, but there was more than an element of self-interest. Men like Ranulf of Chester and William de Warenne were fighting King John's war for his son as much to assure the continuance of their own grip on public affairs as to support any notion of constitutional rectitude, or to help the 'pretty little knight'. Nor was it merely cynics who observed that the king in whose name the new charter was promulgated was a minor. Who could know what he might do when he achieved his majority?

The Charter thus solemnly authenticated differed from that of Runnymede in important respects. Since the representatives of the barons now controlled the person of the king, it is hardly surprising that the clause establishing the Twenty-five was omitted, never to be restored. Other clauses such as the provisos against living off the country and commandeering livestock and pack animals were relaxed, others omitted or changed. But the royalists could now boast a crowned king who had reissued the Charter, whereas the rebels had merely a foreign pretender who had promised so to do if he should become king.

Even so, the winter of 1216-17 saw various advances by Louis. Local truces gave him local advantages, while concentration of force in the east midlands brought him the surrender of numerous royalist castles outside the radius of relief forces from the west country. But time was on the royalist side. The boy king had no personal enemies; and he undoubtedly represented the legitimate line of England. When in February 1217 William Marshal led his forces to the south-east, allegiances began to shift back to the king's cause. Louis, returning to France for consultations with his father, left an uncertain situation. The royalists took some important castles and south-coast ports, while royalist partisans in the Weald of Kent harried the rebel armies. Papal support was now firmly on the side of the royalists; Prince Louis was the excommunicate and his father, keen to mend bridges to Rome, was cool and unsupportive. Louis returned to England in April 1217 as an adventurer.

In England Louis's position was further weakened by the division of his force. While he continued to besiege Dover, a number of his baronial allies riotously garrisoned London while his chief French lieutenant, the constable of Arras, conducted a desultory siege against the castle of Lincoln, held once again by the redoubtable Nicolaa de la Hayc. When the constable was reinforced from London by the count of Perche the position looked threatening for the Lincoln garrison. But the rebel troops, comprising English northerners and French freebooters, both equally hostile to the southern English, ravaged the countryside and lost their cause much support. William Marshal marched northwards to Northampton, calling on royalist supporters to join him at Newark. There, on 19 May, 'in order to animate the army to battle', Legate Guala donned his white robes and, in the company of all the clergy, solemnly repeated the excommunication of Louis, his accomplices and abettors, 'especially those who were carrying on the siege of Lincoln'. The next day the royalist force reached the city.

They were accompanied by the warlike Bishop Peter des Roches of Winchester, while Fawkes de Bréauté captained a corps of hardened professional soldiers disdained as mercenaries by the barons but skilled fighting men nevertheless. The rebel force far outnumbered the royalists, and had the count of Perche chosen to fight in the open country around the city he could have expected victory. Instead he continued the siege, hoping to take the castle before the enemy could breach the walls.

For a time it seemed possible that Marshal's army in its turn would have to settle down to a tedious siege of the besiegers, when a weakness was found in the city's defences. Fighting in the narrow streets robbed the French of their advantage in numbers; the market place saw individual encounters between rival knights more like a tournament than a battlefield. Young Perche was slain in one such joust and his troops scattered. There were few other casualties in this 'Fair of Lincoln', but it was a royalist triumph none the less. The town and its great strategic fortress were secure against the rebels.

It was followed by a flood of *reversi*, former rebels anxious to return to the king's colours. In June Prince Louis abandoned his siege of Dover and moved up to London, which still held for him. He had high hopes of an expeditionary force mobilized by his wife Blanche of Castile and preparing to sail from Artois. On 24 August 1216, however, it was comprehensively defeated by English ships at the Battle of Sandwich, and on 12 September Louis made peace with the royalists on an island in the Thames, at the Treaty of Kingston.

By the terms of the treaty, Louis of France was not only allowed to leave the kingdom unmolested but was even paid a handsome subsidy for doing so. Years later, these generous terms would earn William Marshal accusations of treachery. In return for his pension, Louis promised to endeavour to persuade his father to return the lands which John had lost in France. Since Philip would never agree it was a meaningless undertaking. The treaty was well over-priced both in money and in concessions, but the country was at last free of foreign armies and rebellious magnates. With Henry secure on his father's throne the Angevin succession was assured and, it seemed, the *ancien régime* fully restored.

In reality, things were very different. The departure of the French was followed by the issue, in 1217, of another charter of liberties. Once more there were changes. From some of them it would appear that men with legal experience had been enlisted to reduce the demands of 1215 to manageable dimensions. The clauses on debts, for instance, were modified or omitted to suit the interests of the government. More important to many of the king's subjects, the clauses dealing with forest law and customs were consolidated with new provisos into a separate Forest Charter.

The 1217 charter, like that of 1216, was more an act of hope than an act of government. Grants made during the minority of a king could only be provisional, since they could not bind him. The version of the charter which would eventually be lodged in the statutes of England was the one which, along with its accompanying Forest Charter, was issued by Henry III in 1225 by the king's 'own spontaneous goodwill'.

It has been argued that Magna Carta, 'far from being the radical demands of rebels, reflects what reasonable men thought was amiss with Angevin government'. Its reissue, guaranteed by worthless promises, came to be almost a convention of thirteenth-century life. As Robert of Gloucester wryly observed in his chronicle, the Charter was 'as often granted as it was undone'; nevertheless, it became accepted as the legal yardstick of good government.

Central to the Charter was the idea that the law of England protected rather than restricted the liberties of the subject. For 'liberties of the subject' it is tempting to read 'freedom of the individual'. In fact, the differences, distinctions and discrepancies between the meanings of these two vibrant phrases occupy much of this book. Nevertheless, the equation of law and liberty, the idea that the man-made common law of England could bind even a king, that it was the champion of personal interests, an ally rather than an enemy, was central to the Charter and lay at the heart of English political thought until our own generation.

Although early thirteenth-century law concerned itself with many matters quite irrelevant to later generations, the fact that Magna Carta was framed as a legal document had great importance for the future. Feudal society was based on the idea of contract. Kings and lords held power because they had received the homage of their vassals in return for the promise to lead them in time of war. Land was held in return for military service, and both were hedged about by customary rights and obligations which could only be expressed in the language of contract. This was the language of Magna Carta.

It aimed to summarize the traditional obligations and duties which made the society of its own day function, but its legal character made it a rallying-point in the great constitutional debate that rumbled across England in the early seventeenth century during the generation which led up to the Civil War.

The power of the written word

The idea of Magna Carta, that is, the idea of a specific physical document which secured certain essential liberties of the subject, seems to have emerged about 1225, with the charter of Henry III. John's charter and those of 1216 and 1217, which we refer to as 'reissues', appear to have been viewed by contemporaries rather as three collections of liberties of the subject thought to be especially important. Royal charters were not new. Among the many things that distinguished 1215 was that a charter had been wrung from a king in the fullness of his power with provisos designed to ensure its terms were kept. The fact that the king died before he was able to overturn it and that he was followed on the throne by an infant at a time of civil war, when survival of the dynasty dictated a conciliatory policy, kept the momentum going. The fact that it acquired an identity gave it a powerful public-relations image.

The first recorded use of the words *magna carta* occurs in a document of 1218, when a clerk wished to distinguish it from the Forest Charter, physically smaller in size. Another clerk, recording how the distribution of the charters around the country was arranged in 1225 and wishing to make it clear that forest counties received two, one of each type, differentiated them as 'one concerning the liberties of the community [*libertatibus communibus*] and the other concerning the liberties of the forests [*libertatibus forestae*]'. The first was on the larger sheet of parchment, hence the 'greater charter', *maior carta*. The final stage in what we might call the grammatical evolution of the Charter came with the phrase '*magna carta communium libertatum Angliae*', by which was merely meant 'the large charter containing the liberties of the community of England' but which bears a striking resemblance to 'the Great Charter of English liberties'. In politics a name can become a potent talisman – a slogan. 'In the subtle psychology of human events the early possession of a simple but distinctive title perhaps helped to start the *carta libertatum* upon its unique career among the world's documents'.

In the lead-up to Runnymede, the laws of Saint Edward the Confessor had been a rallying call, and although they were not to be referred to by name in the charter everyone assumed that it embodied the customs which had ruled England in Edward's day. Thenceforward, any question as to what was meant by the liberties of England could be resolved by reference to the local archives. From 1225 nostalgic talk about the good old days gave place to quite concrete demands based on a written legal text.

To what extent this text recorded the actual state of the law before the reign of John was, however, another question. 'To penetrate beyond Magna Carta in search of substantive law is to discover not so much a body of established custom, still less a set of statutes, as an argument.' In other words, the barons' claim that John had infringed established laws and customs accepted by his predecessors was a political rather than an historical statement.

Precedents could be found for most of the clauses, but some were blatant innovations. The most obvious example of this concerned scutage, which had always been levied at the king's will, but which the barons at Runnymede claimed should only be raised with their consent. There are other instances where the Charter states as law what its supporters wished to pretend was law, and makes what we might call party-political points which had little regard for existing practice.

Within three months, thanks to its annulment by Pope Innocent III, the Runnymede charter was a legal dead letter. As we have seen, King John's death placed it squarely back in the political arena, but no one could have foreseen such a turn of events, and in the autumn of 1215 the great baronial initiative had failed. Intended to bring peace, the Charter in fact provoked war; proclaimed as a statement of customary law, it promoted fierce controversy. Even so, Runnymede changed the ground-rules of the debate by establishing a written document as the final arbiter.

At a time when few laymen were literate, custom and usage were more revered than any writing. But Magna Carta, by the standards of the day, was a long and explicit document, authenticated by the most solemn procedures and under the most dramatic circumstances. The idea of a written constitution was a long time in the future and, ironically, England almost alone among the nations of Europe would never have one. Yet from 1225 onwards a

177

charter with its royal seal would become the ultimate court of appeal on questions of constitutional law. In the 1290s the legal treatise *Mirror of Justices* put the matter in a nutshell: 'It is an abuse when the laws are not put in writing so that they might be published and known to all, whereas the law of this realm is founded upon the 40 Articles of the Great Charter of Liberties.'

Liberties, money and politics

Henry III's Charter of February 1225 tells us that 'in return for the concession and gift of these liberties the archbishops, bishops, abbots, priors, earls, barons, knights, free tenants, and all the people of the realm had given a fifteenth of their movables.' In short, the bastion of England's liberties was bought.

Henry had been growing up among councillors keen to exploit the powers of monarchy and to remind him of his rights. He was a willing pupil. Late in January 1223 writs went out in the king's name ordering sheriffs to enquire into the rights enjoyed by his royal father before the war. Alarm bells began to ring when, in April, the pope ruled that in certain matters the 16-year-old king could be considered of age. The royal favourites sought to appease baronial opinion by disclaiming any attempt to raise up evil customs. But in January 1224, as the winter court was coming to a close, Archbishop Stephen Langton asked that Henry confirm those liberties which had been won from his father and which he, as a boy, had confirmed by oath.

'Then William Briwere, one of the king's councillors, made reply for the king and said: "The liberties you ask ought not to be observed of right, because they were extorted by force."' It was a miscalculation to make explicit what everyone present remembered all too well. Only ten years ago men had gone to war for these liberties. The next words of the archbishop were a blunt reminder. 'William,' he retorted, 'if you loved the king you would not thus disturb the peace of the kingdom.' Watching as the hostility among his councillors heightened and 'seeing the archbishop excited to anger', the king intervened. 'We have sworn to observe these liberties, and what we have sworn to we are bound to abide by.' Tempers were calmed and the situation, for the time being, stabilized. Later that year money was needed and the king's advisers considered it wise to offer a confirmation of the Charters.

The fifteenth on movables was not the first instance of a tax on personal property – churchmen had long been familiar with such taxes and possibly the prominence of churchmen in the regency council, with Archbishop Langton at their head, may in part explain the council's decision to raise money in this way. But it would not become a regular source of revenue for another fifty years. Being something of an innovation, it could be levied only by consent and then in time of emergency (the immediate crisis in 1225 was war in Gascony). However, the 1225 Charter established a precedent that a council of the chief tenants of the crown could make consent on behalf of all the people of the realm, whether present at the council or not.

These arrangements foreshadowed the principle of taxation only with representation, but the idea that liberty belonged as of right to the subject was a long way in the future. Magna Carta was not concerned with human rights in the modern sense; it was a 'concession and gift' which made the payment of the agreed tax binding on the whole community of the realm. A special instruction to local justices ordered that anyone withholding the fifteenth, even on the plea of crusading, would 'have no share in the liberty granted to our worthy men by our charters'. Chartered concessions forced from King John were now being used by the councillors of his son as bargaining counters to extract new taxes.

In 1237, Henry III asked for a levy of a thirtieth – i.e., half that of 1225. There was immediate opposition from the barons. They repudiated responsibility for the king's financial difficulties and even charged him with seeking a private papal dispensation to absolve him from observing the terms of the Charters. The confirmation of 1225 had been made during his minority, and people suspected that he did not feel bound by concessions made on his behalf by councillors many of whom were now dead. In a dramatic gesture to rebut these accusations, Henry met with his barons under the auspices of the archbishop of Canterbury and with them pledged to observe the spirit of the Charter under pain of *ipso facto* excommunication in the event of any infringement. On 28 January Henry personally confirmed the Charter of Liberties – there could no longer be any question but that it was binding on him. In return he got his thirtieth.

Sixteen years later, with the blessing of the pope, Henry again applied to his magnates for money, this time on the pretext of a crusade. The barons grudgingly agreed an aid and the clergy the grant of a tenth on their movables. The money was specified as being 'for the succour of the Holy Land against the enemies', and granted only on condition that it was spent during the course of the crusade and under the supervision of baronial appointees. The grants were confirmed in solemn fashion in Westminster Abbey on 13 May 1253. They were linked to a confirmation of the Charters accompanied by a solemn sentence of excommunication pronounced against all who should transgress them. The Charters were formally confirmed on behalf of the king, while Bishop Grosseteste returned home and ordered the sentence to be read from every parish pulpit in his vast diocese of Lincoln. Once again the Charters were linked with the payment of tax, and their importance as constitutional documents was made public by the most effective medium of communication known at the time.

Another fifteen years elapsed before Henry troubled his lay magnates for money. Again a crusade was the pretext, this time one to be undertaken by his sons. This time, according to the London chronicler, the grant was made by all 'the free men of the realm of England, in townships as also in cities, boroughs and elsewhere.' Bishops, magnates and free tenants were summoned to Westminster, while in London the reconfirmation of the Charters was solemnly proclaimed at St Paul's Cross.

The link between the Charters and taxation was becoming almost traditional, but now the body summoned to grant the moneys and to witness the royal grant of liberties was something more than a council of magnates. Something very like parliament was beginning to emerge. The Charter of Liberties had long been coupled with royal finance; now it was coming to be linked with the wishes of the people. New constitutional equations were in the making and a power struggle between king and barons was once more a factor. The career of Simon de Montfort, Earl of Leicester and leader of baronial opposition to King Henry III, was for the Victorians one of the great episodes in the struggle for liberty in England and certainly his death at the Battle of Evesham in 1265 was a notable triumph for the royal party. That it was not total victory was thanks in part to Magna Carta and its companion from 1217 the Forest Charter.

In the latter part of the reign of Edward I the struggle for the Charters was a recurring theme waxing and waning in inverse proportion to the royal power. At the Michaelmas Parliament of 1297 the king, after a year in which civil war against his impervious methods had threatened grudgingly, promised a *Confirmatio cartorum* (Confirmation of the Charters) and actually did agree that henceforth he would take no aids or taxes 'except by the common consent of the whole kingdom'. Pieces of parchment, no more than pieces of paper, can bind powerful rulers against their will. But the charters of England and above all Magna Carta were to keep alive the idea that law should be paramount.

With the 1297 *Confirmatio*, Magna Carta was written into the statute book in its 1225 form. In 1300 King Edward promised yet again to observe the charters only to be absolved from his oath by the pope five years later. The baronial opposition to his son Edward II tried new tools. In 1311 The Ordainers concentrated on asserting the powers of the baronage in the royal great council and in the burgeoning institution called parliament. There were references to the Charter but they seem incidental at first sight. This was because they were now part of the law and might be thought beyond controversy; this was deceptive. The fact that the charters were firmly embedded in English constitutional thinking is fully confirmed since the Lords Ordainers reserved to themselves the right to interpret them and to settle obscure points. Still more telling is the fact that while no coronation oath, so far as we know ever referred to Magna Carta, by the 1340s legal opinion held that for a king to infringe the Charter was to infringe his oath. The youthful Richard II who acceded in 1377 was admonished by his first parliament '. . . to keep and observe the said Charter as at his coronation he had been charged to do'.

LAW LEGEND AND TALISMAN

Despite the fact that the 1225 version omitted various clauses from 1215 men soon came to look on Magna Carta as Unchangeable Law. The idea was already transcending the fact.

Clause 39 of the 1215 Charter guaranteed that no 'freeman' should be proceeded against save by the 'lawful judgement of his peers or by the law of the land'. The terms would be disputed for centuries, but in 1302 a royal justice allowed 'trial by his peers' to a simple knight. Then in 1354 a historic statute provided that no man 'of what state or condition so ever shall be put out of his land or tenement or put to death without being brought to answer by due process of law'. Many reckoned that the concept of 'freeman' now applied to all the king's male subjects but the words 'due process of law' would long be debated. In the 1360s, peasants of a manor of Christ Church cited the Great Charter in a petition to their Prior. In 150 years the sonorous pledge of the Liberties of Runnymede 'to all the freemen of our kingdom . . .' had seeped down to the grass roots. In the words of Max Weber (quoted by Max Rheinstein), the very idea of natural law derives in part 'from the idea particularly indigenous to England that every member of the community has certain natural rights. This idea of birthright arose essentially under the influence of the popular conception that certain rights confirmed in Magna Carta as the special status rights of the barons were the habitual Liberties of all Englishmen as such.'

14

MYTHS
OF LIBERTY

THE persistence of the Magna Carta legend is so much a part of the history of the English-speaking world that it may be at first difficult to realize how extraordinary it is. As we have seen, other countries in Europe had documents of a similar kind. Why should these have been forgotten, while John's and Henry's Charters persisted in popular as well as legal memory among the English? Why should people of later centuries have been interested in the Charter long after most of its clauses had ceased to have any actual legal application? And why, if it was to be recalled, should it have been surrounded by myth and misinterpretations? For in the early seventeenth century, the period when Magna Carta was to work its greatest influence on the English-speaking world as a whole, men's attitudes to it were shaped far more by myth and legend than by reality.

I have argued (Chapter 13) that the death of King John was a principal cause for the continuing life of the Charter granted at Runnymede. Had he lived just a year or two longer there is little reason to doubt that it would be remembered merely as a somewhat unusual example of the kind of royal charter not uncommon in contemporary Europe, or as an elaborate variant on coronation charters granted by most of John's predecessors.

Even so, the great charters granted by King John and his son Henry III were distinctly unusual in one most important respect. Unlike previous English royal charters, they were granted, to quote the words of 1225, 'to all the free men of the realm to have and to hold to them and their heirs from us and our heirs in perpetuity'. A charter granted by a king for his lifetime expired with him, whereas with the Great Charter, while few kings honoured its provisos unless pressurized to do so, the fact that the document was there, was even available for public consultation in some cathedrals, and was publicly read throughout the land from time to time was a constant reminder that a king had given his word, that his successors were bound by it and that, in consequence, there were principles of conduct and government above even the king himself.

As the middle ages advanced and the relevance of the charters at law diminished, so appeals to them decreased, and royal confirmations (the last by Henry V) were little more than pious statements of intent. But if their status as practical documents was under eclipse, the charters were on the threshold of a new life, thanks to a burgeoning of antiquarian interests which we can compare with the fascination with Edward the Confessor and pre-Conquest England at the time of Magna Carta itself. This time, however, in tune with the spirit of the times set by the humanists of Italy, the focus had shifted back in time to a remote classical antiquity. The early Renaissance generation saw the peoples of Europe looking for antecedents more venerable even than the fashionable antiquity of Greece and Rome. The result was a rich accession to the mythical material that existed in the world; and England, her people and her rulers found themselves richly endowed.

While German and French writers had to excavate and enhance pre-Roman Celtic and Germanic traditions, the English laid claim to an authentic classical ancestry as old as 'Homer the Greek' but far more splendid. In his exultant *Troy Book*, dedicated to Henry V, John Lydgate told a noble story. To us it seems a web of fantasy and myth; to his contemporaries it was a proud history they were heirs to. Britain took its name from Brutus, son of Priam, King of Troy. From him descended the royal house of England itself and Lydgate bitterly rejected as mendacious and slanderous the account of the fall of Troy as recorded in the pages of Homer. For him the Trojans were victims of Fate, defeated by a combination of treachery at home and the hostility of Mars the god of war. The disaster drove Brutus into exile and with twelve companions (the same number as Christ had apostles) he made landfall off the coast of Devon. And so it was that the kings of England could boast a more ancient and more noble lineage than any other.

The English church had equally venerable antecedents. In fact an Englishman might feel tempted to claim priority in conversion to Rome itself. For the Apostle of Britain was, supposedly, Joseph of Arimathea, who had laid Christ in the tomb. After the Crucifixion he had taken ship and found sanctuary in the south-west of Britain. There the local king had granted him and his companions twelve hides of land, and there they laid the foundations of Glastonbury. In this historic plot Arthur, King of Britain, had been laid to rest. The founder of chivalry and a greater paladin of the Faith than Charlemagne himself, Arthur was but one of the heroes of Christendom whom the English claimed as their own. St Helena, discoverer of the True Cross and mother of Constantine, the first Christian emperor, had been the daughter of King Cole of Colchester.

To this day otherwise quite sane people believe in the Glastonbury legends; while a few years back a supposedly reputable London publishing house put out a book on the Holy Grail which allowed its readers to assume it to be historical. Among other things the authors of the book solemnly advanced the theory that Jesus had survived the Crucifixion and escaped from Palestine to Marseilles. Here, apparently, he settled down with Mary Magdalen, a happily married man, to father a family whose descendants numbered the kings of France. The story, invented by the anonymous French author of a thirteenth-century collection known as *The Golden Legend*, had the not entirely subtle intention of enhancing the prestige of the royal house of France, and even contemporaries thought it a bit rich.

All this may seem a little remote from the theme of this book, but myths and the willingness to believe in them shape attitudes. They may even determine the course of history. It would be difficult to overemphasize the role of myth in the story of Magna Carta, and the atmosphere of legend and half-truth which provided the breath of life to Brutus the Trojan, Arthur and Old King Cole was the same in which flourished the misconceptions about John and those barons opposed to him, which so shaped the seventeenth-century struggle for liberties.

As the fifteenth century drew to its close, a century in which the realm had been troubled by civil wars, few people thought of restraining the royal power with charters. England was at the beginning of a period in her history which would see the monarchy advance claims for itself more extreme than ever before. At the end of that period Magna Carta, the myth not the reality, would prove a potent weapon against the myth of the divine right of kings. In the fullness of time Runnymede would achieve far more than the barons of John could have imagined.

The royal myth had deep roots. For centuries England's kings had enjoyed respect abroad as well as at home as the successors of Arthur. The fact that most of his legend had been made up virtually out of whole cloth by the twelfth-century Welsh writer Geoffrey of Monmouth mattered little. It received a new lease of life with the victory of the usurping Henry VII on the field of Bosworth in 1485. Having no hereditary right to the crown and dubious antecedents even as an English nobleman (his mother was an English descendant of John of Gaunt's mistress whom he later married, and his father a half-French Welsh gentleman), Henry Tudor, Earl of Richmond and client of the Duke of Brittany, made what he could of the fact that he had been born in a Welsh castle. By dint of patronizing Welsh harpers and calling his first son Arthur, after the epic British hero, he hoped to acquire vicarious virtue and perhaps even legitimacy-by-association. Tudor propaganda is often praised for the success with which it blackened the name of Richard III, whom Henry VII displaced, but the fact that he and his dynasty are still considered Welsh when few rulers before and none since were as truly English by birth and descent is still more a tribute to its skill. Myths, even medieval myths, continue to play their part in our idea of history.

The Tudors found publicists willing to embellish the tale further. Scholars revealed similarities between the Welsh and Greek languages, while others claimed to trace the story of Britain back even beyond the time of the mythical Brutus to 'Samothes' son of Japhet. The legend of England's conversion by Joseph of Arimathea encouraged the idea of an ancient British church independent of Rome. It matched well with Henry VIII's claims against Rome. Joseph, Brutus and Arthur and the whole 'matter of Britain' fed the swelling pretensions of monarchy. And the propagandists of the Reformation in England opened yet another chapter in historiographical revisionism. Not surprisingly, they excoriated Thomas Becket, Henry II's archbishop of Canterbury and formerly England's most loved and revered saint, as little better than a traitor who had sided with the pope against his sovereign and his own countrymen. Becket, enemy of the second Henry, received posthumous humiliation from the eighth of that name when his shrine at Canterbury was despoiled of its treasure. In a way the Henrician reformation was the culmination of a centuries-long struggle between the English crown and the church. Its apologists saw King John as a champion of the monarchical cause.

He acquired, indeed, semi-heroic status as a victim of papal intervention, as a faithful Moses withstanding the oppressions of the papal pharaoh yet forced by the power of the church, aided by the 'base rebellion' of the baronage, to surrender his kingdon. The quotation comes from John Bale's book *The Troublesome Reign of King John*, written in the 1530s when Henry VIII's struggle with Rome was reaching its climax. The king was, in Bale's view, a modern Joshua, fortunately destined to lead his people into the promised land of freedom from papal tyranny.

Tudor apologists of royal power contended that it was always wrong to take up arms against an anointed king. Memories of the conflicts of the past century were as powerful an argument as any ideological consideration. In this perspective the baronial opposition to John, far from being a brave resistance to tyranny, was but the prelude to a century of recurrent civil conflict painfully reminiscent of the 'Roses' wars still very vivid in men's memories. This royalist interpretation had a long life; even as late as 1611 John Speed could write in his *History of Great Britain* that the barons rebelled 'to attain the shadow of seeming liberties'. On the committee of Twenty-five appointed by the Charter to ensure John's conformity, Speed commented: 'Thus one of the greatest sovereigns of Christendom was now become the twenty-sixth petty king within his own Dominions.'

But Speed was unusual among his contemporaries in realizing that John actually had issued a Charter. In his Stenton lecture of 1968, '*Magna Carta in the Historiography of the Sixteenth and Seventeenth Centuries*', Sir Herbert Butterfield commented, 'It seems clear that for a considerable time even the more scholarly people . . . had come to be unaware of the fact that Magna Carta was connected with King John.' To theatre-goers one of the chief puzzles of Shakespeare's *The Life and Death of King John* is that it contains not one reference to the Charter. Since he probably used the Chronicles of Ralph Holinshed as one of his sources for the play, Shakespeare probably was aware of the Charter. Yet he clearly did not rate it as being of particular importance, in conformity with the received educated opinion of his time. Part of the explanation for this common establishment view seems to lie with the conventions of the law books.

The volumes of the statutes of England which began to appear in printed form in the sixteenth century opened with Magna Carta, but the text they used was given as that of 9 (i.e. the 9th year) Henry III, i.e. the issue made in 1225. Not unreasonably, perhaps, the lawyers assumed this to be the original grant. The historical sources for the reign were scanty and the discipline of history as we understand it still developing. Commenting on the statute in his *Interpreter* of 1607, Sir Henry Cowell wrote: 'I read in

Holinshed that King John, to appease his barons, yielded to lawes or articles of government much like this Great Charter, but we nowe have no ancienter written lawe than this.'

Shakespeare had a strong nose for box-office appeal. His long run of history plays is a perfect example of his writer's intuition. As we have seen, the vogue for national history went back at least a century and it was matched by the beginnings of scholarly interest in the past. As early as 1533 Henry VIII had appointed John Leland as the first King's Antiquary. His quarrel with the church gave Henry his own reasons for investigating the past. Magna Carta would have been especially objectionable to him, given the fact that its first clause guaranteed the liberties of the church and so could be looked upon as a charter of ecclesiastical freedom from royal control. The point was rather tactlessly emphasized by Catholic demonstrators at the time of the Pilgrimage of Grace, when they protested that Magna Carta was not receiving the respect it had previously enjoyed.

Forty years after Leland's appointment, royal patronage of antiquarian interests was matched by the foundation of the Society of Antiquaries in 1572. It held weekly meetings for discussions on old records and chronicles – the year before, the society's founding had seen the publication of the thirteenth-century *Chronicle* of Matthew Paris, destined to play its own influential part in the story of Magna Carta. Some years later, while imprisoned by King James I in the Tower of London, Sir Walter Raleigh wrote of 'digging from the dust the long-buried memory of the subjects' former contention with the king'. In 1604 that same James I suppressed the first Society of Antiquaries. As was well known to the regime of Orwell's *1984*, history can sometimes be subversive. 'He who controls the present controls the past, and he who controls the past controls the future.' As the sixteenth century drew to its close ideas ominous for the future of authoritarian monarchy were beginning to circulate, ideas of the liberties of old England before the Norman conquest, ideas which matched the notion of the Laws of Edward the Confessor so important to the formulators of the Articles of the Barons in the months before Runnymede, ideas which in harness with a reinvigorated Magna Carta would overturn the applecart of state.

By the early 1600s the myth makers had the bit between their teeth. Sir Henry Spelman called Magna Carta 'The most majestic and a sacrosanct anchor to English Liberties' and Richard Hakewill termed it 'The most ancient statute law . . . sealed and won with the blood of our ancestors.' The

Great Protestation of 18 December 1621 claimed that '. . . the Liberties . . . of Parliament are the ancient birthright of the subjects of England.' Speaking to the motion Sir Edward Coke MP, former chief justice, appealed directly to 'Magna Carta . . . called . . . the Charter of Liberty, because it maketh freemen'. King James I confined him to the Tower for seven months on a charge of treason. Then, in 1627, Charles I ordered the imprisonment of 'the Five Knights', gentlemen who had refused to pay a forced loan, 'by special mandate of the king'. Parliamentarians raged that this contravened Clause 39/29 of Magna Carta; the Attorney General countered that there was nothing explicit on the matter 'in all the statutes and records.'

The question of arbitrary arrest had been raised in fourteenth-century parliaments under King Edward III, while in the reign of his father the Ordainers, by reserving to themselves the exclusive right to interpret all doubtful passages in the Charter, hoped to pre-empt any awkward claims as to its meaning by the opposition. Of course, in their case, the 'opposition' meant the king himself, Edward II and his supporters. The Ordainers' attempt to return to Runnymede could hope to succeed only so long as they held secure military advantage in the civil strife they themselves had provoked. When Edward and his friends overthrew them all talk of the Charter, let alone its interpretation, ceased. As always, he who held the power determined the interpretation. In the seventeenth century the debate over the Charter led literally to an issue of life and death, as King Charles learnt to his discomfiture on 30 January 1649.

For the time being Parliament attempted to wrest the initiative, just as the Ordainers had done, from the king. A bill 'for the renewing of Magna Carta' had been proposed in 1621 but had failed to reach the Lords, let alone the statute book. Its purpose, though apparently to restore the whole ancient Charter to new vigour, was specifically aimed to reinstate clause 29/39 as part of the law of the land beyond a peradventure: to guarantee the subject against any arbitrary loss of his liberty. The case of the Five Knights added the question of non-parliamentary taxation to the issue of wrongful imprisonment, and now Edward Coke introduced a bill intended 'to explain Magna Carta and put it into execution'.

In the prolonged and heated debates which followed between the two houses and between Parliament and the king, Charles at first offered to confirm the Charter, like his medieval predecessors, but refused to consider any act of parliament which would aim to curtail his prerogatives as king.

Coke countered with what amounted to a compromise. While the procedure he proposed would not curtail the king's prerogative explicitly, it would declare the law in terms which would be binding on the judges. The result was the famous Petition of Right of 1628.

It should be noted that to many, of equal importance to the question of wrongful arrest was the very offence for which the five were being martyred. Their crime was refusal to pay a forced loan, a levy which in itself, many opined, infringed the terms of the ancient charters. This too was addressed by the Petition of Right.

Its chief clauses ensured against taxation in any form except such as was imposed by Parliament; against imprisonment without cause – this clause quoted not only Magna Carta but also the 1354 statute, the first to use the phrase 'due process of law'; and against martial law. The petition was read three times in each house of Parliament and the king responded, not with the time-honoured phrase '*le roi le veult*', 'the king wishes it', but with a formula unique to the occasion, '*soit droit fait comme est désiré*' – 'Let right be done as is desired'.

The granting of the Petition of Right should have relegated the Great Charter to the history books once and for all. It contained the essential freedoms thought to have been conferred or confirmed at Runnymede without the clauses, provisos and guarantees relevant to an outdated feudal society and by the 1600s merely anachronistic. Moreover, the very fact that the king had made his assent not to an assembly of barons whom later ages might come to see as the representatives of the whole community of the realm, but in Parliament which, in the 1620s, was, so far as anything could be, the actual representative of the whole community of the realm, meant that from now on Parliament became trustee for the liberties of the subject and the struggle for those liberties became the struggle for the survival of Parliament itself.

This issue was in the balance throughout the 1640s, a decade of civil war in which thousands of men died; for a sure and certain resolution of the issue the death of just one more man was needed, and that came on 30 January 1649 when Charles Stuart, 'that Man of Blood', stepped from a first-floor window in his palace of Whitehall on to a scaffold where waited an anonymous axeman and the executioner's block.

Why, to paraphrase Helen Cam, had the English gone historical and dug up the Charter? It is, as she commented, a fascinating problem, but perhaps not entirely opaque to analysis. A small number of barons in the opposition to John may have been content to make their *diffidatio*, go to war on the king and hang the consequences. But challenge to the royal power was a hazardous business, and remained so down to the seventeenth century. Prompted perhaps by Archbishop Langton, the majority of John's opponents had sought to gloss their temerity by an appeal to past precedents – to the charter of his revered ancestor Henry I and still more to the laws of the venerable Edward the Confessor. In a similar way the fledgling opposition to the Stuarts, parliamentary and legal, assumed the battledress of supposed precedents in what was shaping up for a systematic attack on royal claims, claims which were often of unchallengeable legitimacy. When he proposed the idea of a petition to the king to resolve the matter of the Five Knights, Coke asserted that it had been 'the ancient way, until the unhappy divisions between the houses of Lancaster and of Yorkshire'. Equally unhistorical was the claim that taxation without parliamentary consent was contrary to Magna Carta. In both cases the past was called in to redress the balance of the present and false precedents were used to cover the assertion of new rights.

The extent to which this practice was repeated sometimes prompts the thought that it was a conscious strategy of the opposition to James I and later his son. The origins of the House of Commons were fancifully found among the ancient Britons so that the monarchy could not claim seniority, and the fourteenth-century *Modus Tenendi Parliamentum*, 'How a parliament should be held', was attributed to the time of Edward the Confessor; trial by jury, indeed most of the liberties and institutions of England, were traced to an ever-receding antiquity. All were enjoyed as of right, none were owed to the concessions by the crown. In this scenario Magna Carta was not something new but simply a restatement of literally age-old privileges. The programme, for so it almost appears, of opposition by antiquarian research brought history to bear on the actual practices of the royal courts. But the technique could be worked in the reverse direction. An attack mounted in parliament against the institution of the episcopacy was countered by champions of the old order by an appeal to the first clause of the Charter and its guarantee of the rights of the church. But by this time the war of words was about to break out into fighting in earnest. The military triumph of parliament relegated the speculations of the antiquarian movement to scholarly debate and analysis. One outcome was a fundamental rethink. In his *Introduction to the Old English Liberties*, published in 1684, Robert

Brady described Magna Carta as merely a feudal document which was intended to serve the interests of the leading landholders. 'Sir Edward Coke,' opined Brady, 'hath a fine fetch to play off the Great Charter and interpret it by his modern Lawe.' More than three hundred years ago the veneration accorded to the Charter was coming under cold academic scrutiny; in place of heroic English noblemen struggling for their birthright and that of the nation, Brady introduced the notion of a squabble within a Norman ruling class.

With the Glorious Revolution of 1688 such cynicism went out of fashion. For more than 200 years the Charter in England remained a museum piece on a pedestal of semi-religious veneration. The fact that it continued in the front ranks of freedom's banners was largely due to the thousands of Englishmen who had flooded across the Atlantic to colonize the New World.

AN OLD CHARTER
IN A NEW WORLD

ENGLISH trading ventures to the New World date from the mid sixteenth century, but the first successful settlement was established at James Town, Virginia, in 1607. The pioneers set sail on the last day of December 1606 under the auspices of the Virginia Company of London and a royal charter granted by King James I. Draughted under the direction of Sir Edward Coke, Chief Justice of the Common Pleas and the seventeenth century's most influential commentator on Magna Carta, it declared that 'the persons which shall dwell within the colonies shall have all Liberties as if they had been abiding and born within this our realm of England or any other of our said dominions'. The guarantee, in one form or another, appears in the founding charters of Massachusetts (1629), Maryland (1632), Maine (1639), Connecticut (1662), Rhode Island (1663) and others, such as Georgia in 1732. The 'Liberties' thus conferred might sometimes be open to debate, but few doubted the Great Charter of Liberties to be their foundation. As we shall see, exposure to the air of America breathed new life into the old document.

For American history, it has been said, the influence of Magna Carta lay not in the encounter of King John and the barons at Runnymede in 1215 but 'in Coke's colourful version thereof and his equally inaccurate but highly palatable conception of the common law'. In 1647 the governor and Assistants of the young Commonwealth of Massachusetts ordered two copies of Coke on Magna Carta, along with various other books on English law, 'to the end we may have better light for making and proceeding about laws'.

It has been estimated that by 1640 some 20,000 British emigrants had settled along the eastern seaboard of the United States. Their leaders were early aware of the need to establish the rule of law on firm foundations. John Winthrop of Massachusetts noted in his journal how it was feared that without some recognized body of positive law the magistrates might, to use his pleasant euphemism, 'proceed according to their discretion'. Accordingly, it was agreed 'that some men should be appointed to frame a body of grounds of law, in resemblance to a Magna Carta, which . . . should be received for fundamental laws'. The 1641 Massachusetts Body of Liberties, while 'agreeable to the word of God', was also grounded in constitutional law. Inspired by clause 29 of Magna Carta, it guaranteed that 'No man's life shall be taken away, no man's honour or good name shall be stayned, no man's person shall be arrested, restrayned, banished nor anywayes punished, no man shall be deprived of his wife or children, no man's goods or estaite shall be taken away from him . . . unless by vertue of some express lawe of the country warranting the same.'

Given the Puritan persuasion of many of the founding fathers of English America, religious thought and language were central to much of this early constitution making. The first Massachusetts Body of Liberties has been called 'a curious conglomeration of theocratic principles joined with those of the Common Law', but in the revised version which shortly followed, religious content gave place in many sections to practical legal concerns. Other law codes followed the example, that of Rhode Island eschewing all use of Holy Writ in favour of Magna Carta.

By this time the very words 'Magna Carta' and 'Great Charter' had acquired an almost mystic incantatory quality. Instructions issued in 1618 by the Virginia Company to Sir George Yeardley, the colony's governor, came to be known as the 'Great Charter' by Virginian historians and writers. They required him to organize the election of a representative assembly, abolished martial law and made important changes in the terms and conditions of land tenure. Half a century later the proprietors of the colony of North Carolina authorized the governor to grant land on the same terms and conditions as the 'Great Deed of Grant' of Virginia, which they considered 'a species of Magna Carta'. The words became a common term for various documents of special constitutional significance. From the outset, American legislators were governed by the precept that fundamental legal principles should be embodied in written form.

In a sense, indeed, the early colonial charters were forerunners of the constitution of the United States. The colonists liked to regard their charters as solemn compacts between themselves and the king. For its part, the crown was always jealous of the royal prerogative. The colonial charters were more concise, sometimes more concrete documents than the cluster of ancient statutes and charters which the English at home could appeal to in their struggles with the crown. As British colonial and commercial policy developed, so the Americans came under increasingly tight imperial control through crown and parliamentary agencies.

In 1638 the assembly of Maryland agreed an Act whereby 'the inhabitants shall have all their rights and liberties according to the Great Charter of England'. The act was disallowed by King Charles I's Attorney General because, among other things, he considered it inconsistent with the royal prerogative. It was an early instance of that shift from chartered colony to royal province.

In Massachusetts, protests by leading citizens that, through high-handed actions of the governors, men could no longer feel secure in the enjoyment of their lives, liberties and estates as free-born Englishmen led to an order of the General Court that the Body of Liberties be thoroughly compared with Magna Carta and the principles of common law. The General Court sent an address to Parliament to prove that the government of the colony was framed in accordance with 'the fundamental and common laws of England and that rule by which all kingdoms and jurisdictions must render account of every act and administration in the last day'. This they did by presenting selections from the colony's law, English law and the text of Magna Carta itself in parallel columns.

In most colonies, the charters which conferred powers of local legislation were followed by moves in the written laws of these new dominions to establish their claims to rights under the common law independently. The Rhode Island charter defined Magna Carta's famous words '*lex terrae*', i.e. the law of the land, to mean the law of the General Assembly of Rhode Island and not the law of England unless this had been adopted by the Assembly as part of the laws of the colony. It was a forward-looking proviso, but the English Americans of this period were involved in a continuing struggle to maintain equality of liberties with the home country.

In 1692 William Penn, who while still in England had argued the rights of the colonials as Englishmen to the protection of Magna Carta as construed by Coke, published an edition of the Charter together with the confirmations of Edward I. The collection was prefaced with a heartfelt address to his readers, 'not to give away anything of Liberty and Property that at present they do enjoy, but take up the good example of our ancestors and understand that it is easy to part with or give away great privileges, which be hard to be gained if once lost.'

As American lawyers began to develop their own, independent traditions, the appeal to Magna Carta and the rights of 'every free-born English subject', perennially popular with defendants, occasionally provoked some asperity from the bench. Subjected to yet another harangue on ancient liberties one Massachusetts judge was moved to remark, 'We must not think that the laws of England follow us to the ends of the earth'. But in conflicts with the home government the Charter was sovereign. Almost exactly a century before the Declaration of Independence it featured in what has been called the 'first colonial rebellion against English taxation'.

In 1680, the New York state government confronted an angry opposition movement. Governor Sir Edmund Andros was well liked by James Duke of York for his profitable administration of the colony; New Yorkers protested against the regime as oppressive and high-handed, and charged mismanagement, extravagance and 'discrepancies in the financial reports'. Summoned to London, Andros embarked for England in October leaving instructions that the administration of the colony 'remain as then settled' until his return.

The duke's revenue derived from a long-contested customs duty levied under an order which expired in November and which Governor Andros neglected to renew. This aristocratic disregard for detail spelt trouble for his deputy William Dyer. When the order expired, New York's merchants, pleading the letter of the law, withheld payment of customs. Dyer, to cow the opposition, impounded a ship and its cargo and the storm broke. The owners brought suit against him in the colonial court of assize for unlawful seizure of property and further accused him of 'the subversion . . . of the ancient fundamental laws of the Realm of England contrary to the Great Charter of Liberties and the Petition of Right . . .' Nothing loth, the court ruled that so weighty a matter was beyond its competence and ordered that Dyer was to answer to the Privy Council in England. To no one's surprise, Dyer and Andros were both acquitted, though neither was returned to duty in New York. The colonists, pressing their advantage, now petitioned for an assembly elected by the freeholders, as was customary in the government of other colonies. The duke yielded the point and in October 1683 Thomas Dongan, an Irish gentleman, arrived as governor briefed to establish an elected assembly and frame a charter. Dongan's statute for New York's 'charter of liberties' embodied many of the principles of Magna Carta and was welcomed by the state legislature. It never received approval from London, where it was regarded as 'savouring too strongly of popular freedom and as counter to the prerogatives of the crown and the legal supremacy of parliament'. New York was still without an assembly. But the Charter of Liberties was not forgotten.

All legislation in the American colonies required the assent of the crown. Whereas the royal veto had long been discredited in British affairs, the imperial veto exercised by the crown in parliament and applied by the colonial governors was used by the government at Westminster to safeguard the authority of parliament. That was the intention, but eighteenth-century colonial legislatures frequently by-passed the veto, re-enacting or rewording measures as they saw fit, to preserve what they conceived as their liberties, among which provisions based on Magna Carta were prominent.

As the eighteenth century progressed the Charter was called on in the most unexpected causes. In Virginia in the 1750s the legal profession had sunk so low in popular estimation that moves were made to expel all lawyers from the state, or at least to prohibit any person pleading in any judicial proceedings for reward. Bowing to public opinion, governor and council approved the measure but only on condition that the proposed legislation did not infringe the terms of Magna Carta.

In his 'Rights of the American Colonies' published in 1764, James Otis reiterated the appeal to Coke and Magna Carta. Benjamin Franklin observed that Englishmen had not lost their rights by coming to America. Even the great battle cry, 'No taxation without representation', would be justified by appeal to the Great Charter. That it was bad history is neither here nor there. Almost every appeal to Magna Carta over the past two centuries had been in the same category. English liberties had been won by parliamentary opposition to arbitrary taxation, and seventeenth-century English parliamentarians had traced the tradition back to Magna Carta. As a matter of sober historical fact, the very word 'parliament' was unknown to King John and his barons, but 'history' in the sense of what actually happened in the past had little to do with the power of Magna Carta to shape the British constitution. 'Magna Carta-ism', as we might call it, continued as creative in the New World as it had been in the old. Myth-making was at the heart of the process, and the American revolutionaries proved worthy heirs to the tradition.

By the eighteenth century it was accepted as a principle of that tradition that no Englishman could legally be taxed except by his consent, given by his representative in parliament. The Great Charter, which was held to guarantee the principle, had been text for a civil war, the execution of one king and the expulsion of another, and the usurpation of the powers of monarchy by parliament. In America, where Englishmen were denied representation, Magna Carta gave inspiration in a struggle which ended with the overthrow of parliament itself. 'In England', it has been said, 'the powers of the king, said to be founded on legal foundations, were destroyed. In America the powers of parliament, unquestionably legal in character, were repudiated.'

In one sense, it could be said that the American War of Independence was fought to vindicate rights won in England and embodied in the doctrines of Common Law, the principles of the Bill of Rights and the idea of Magna Carta. Fuelled by the tradition of English constitutionalism, the war was sparked by that fiery pamphleteer Tom Paine, whose writings, above all the *Rights of Man*, provided the touch-paper. Paine belonged to the age of Enlightenment, the age of Jean-Jacques Rousseau, an age enthralled by that amorphous notion, the natural rights of man. Rooted ultimately in the medieval concept of natural law, it was wedded also to the idea of a people's birthright, and Magna Carta came into play here too as 'the essential proof of the natural law that attested the rights of the people against the government'.

In the American environment the idea of Magna Carta gave rise to revolutionary attitudes to government and the concept of liberty. From an early date the fact that the Charter had been forced from the king (ironically the very fact which invalidated the original grant of liberties) was seen as more important than almost any of the actual clauses of the document. A dissident group of barons and churchmen were mythologized into champions of the people. This, combined with a flattering history of the power of parliament, made Magna Carta a symbol of the concept of the sovereign power of the people to impose their will on the government. In the American context this gave rise to the idea that the expression of the people's will concerning the fundamental rights retained by them was to be recorded in a written document.

From this it was perceived that the document of fundamental liberties, because it embodied the will of the people and the concepts of fundamental law, must be superior not only to the executive but even to the legislature. In England, which removed the supremacy of the monarchy only to replace it with the supremacy of the monarch in parliament, the idea of a constitution supreme over the powers that be at any one time in the state has still to be accepted. The point was made by the US Supreme Court in the case of Hurtado *v*. California in 1884. 'The concessions of Magna Carta were wrung from the king as guaranties against the oppressions and usurpations of his prerogative. It did not enter into the minds of the barons to provide security against their own body or in favour of the Commons, so that . . . in English history . . . the omnipotence of Parliament over the common law was absolute, even against common right and reason. In this country written constitutions were deemed essential to protect the rights and liberties of the people against the encroachments of power delegated to their governments, and the provisions of Magna Carta were incorporated into the Bill of Rights.' Thus it was America that gave to the world the idea of a written constitution, a formula adopted by almost every nation in the world except Britain.

The final transformation of the Charter into a truly mystic instrument of government was the proposition, embodied in the Ninth Amendment of the US Constitution, that the written document, though it specified the limits of government power, was merely recording rights that had existed prior to the promulgation of the charter, and in so far as the writing was deficient in stating all those rights, those not stated were still retained by the people.

Within a few years of the signing of the constitution itself a series of amendments was added which have come to seem so important to generations of Americans that they are collectively termed the Bill of Rights. Just as the final version of the Charter was a 'revised version', that of 1225, so the definitive statement of American rights came in amendments to the Constitution. But whereas the advisers of King Henry III aimed to safeguard the authority of the legislature and executive by their work, the Fathers of the Republic sought to strengthen popular liberties. And whereas the ultimate interpreters of the medieval statute came to be the legislature/executive itself, in America the final arbiter was the Supreme Court, held to be above both legislature and executive.

Of the role of Magna Carta in the United States, it has been said that it 'provided the starting-point for framing standards appropriate to safeguarding the liberties of a people living under a regime socially, economically and politically about as far from 1215 as it is possible to conceive. Having served its function of having put law on the right track, it receded into the background.' And yet the ancient document continued to exert its spell over the Supreme Court judges, tempting them, from time to time, into flights of rhetoric as soul-stirring and unhistorical as anything conceived by Lord Coke. Delivering judgement in the case of Murray's Lessee *v.* Hoboken Land and Improvement Company in 1855, Mr Justice Curtis lyrically described Magna Carta as 'the affirmance of the ancient standing laws of the land as they existed among the Saxons ere the power of Norman chivalry, combined with the subtlety of Norman lawyers, had deprived the Saxons – who then formed and whose descendants still form the mass of the English nation – of their ancient political institutions'.

In 1941, summing up in the case of Bridges *v.* California, Mr Justice Frankfurter opined that 'The administration of justice by an impartial judiciary has been basic to our conception of freedom ever since Magna Carta'; while in 1963 Mr Justice Goldberg, in the case of Kennedy *v.* Mendoza Martinez, commenting on the Fourteenth Amendment, observed: 'Dating back to Magna Carta, it has been an abiding principle governing the lives of civilized men that no freeman shall be taken or imprisoned or disseised or outlawed or exiled . . . without the judgement of his peers or by the laws of the land.'

Both learned judges took liberties with history as understood by the annalist, and yet, such was the power of these two medieval Latin words, both clearly felt their views were given authority by the incantation. Although the principle took centuries to establish and although in our own day it is maintained only by constant vigilance, the goal of constitutionalism is 'freedom under the law', and so long as this remains true, in the Anglo-American world Magna Carta will be its prime symbol.

APPENDIX 1

The Charter of Liberties granted by King John at Runnymede in
1215.

In medieval Latin and dealing with many concerns which have long since
lost their relevance, in some cases even their meaning, the text of the Great
Charter can nevertheless have resonances even today. What follows is a
summary of the contents of the entire document, parts being given in free
translation others being merely summarized *in italics*. The actual text runs
unbroken but by long established modern convention it is divided into 63
clauses (some historians make only 61 divisions, running what are here given
as the final three clauses into one).

For treatment of topics in the main body of the text see index headings.
There are some more detailed comments in this summary, between square
brackets and *in italics*.
Asterisk [*] indicates clauses not in the Issue of 1225.

John by the Grace of God, king of England, lord of Ireland, duke of
Normandy and Aquitaine, and count of Anjou [*it was eleven years since
King Philip Augustus of France had driven John from Normandy and the
Angevin family's ancestral lands of Anjou, but titles die hard – to this day,
Queen Elizabeth II is 'duke of Normandy' in the Channel Islands*], to the

archbishops, bishops, abbots, earls, barons, justiciars, foresters, sheriffs, stewards, servants, and to all his bailiffs and liegemen, greeting [*the document is addressed not only to those who are to benefit from it but also to those of the king's officers who are to implement its provisions*]. Know that, with respect for God and for the salvation of our souls and of all our ancestors' and heirs', and to the honour of God and the advancement of Holy Church, and for the emendation of our realm, by advice of Stephen Archbishop of Canterbury, Henry Archbishop of Dublin, bishops William of London, Peter of Winchester, Jocelyn of Bath and Glastonbury, Hugh of Lincoln, Walter of Worcester, William of Coventry, and Benedict of Rochester, of master Pandulf [*the papal legate*], of brother Aymeric [*master of the Knights Templar in England*], and of the noble men William Marshal, earl of Pembroke [*the most honoured knight in Europe*], William, earl of Salisbury [*the king's half brother*] . . . *14 other 'noble men' [at this time the words mean 'men of note or distinction' rather than aristocrats of technical rank] are named, among them Hubert de Burgh whose defence of Dover would be vital to the royal cause in the looming civil war and who was destined for a prominent role in the next reign . . .*
we have granted

[1] that the English church shall be free . . . and shall have her liberties inviolate [*notably*] . . . the freedom of elections, which is reckoned most important . . . and which we of our pure and unconstrained will [*this is no cliché. The rights to the church are described as given voluntarily, those granted to the lay freemen pointedly are not leaving the king free to claim, as he did, that the Great Charter had been extorted under duress*] did grant . . . by charter before the discord arose between us and our barons . . . And we have also granted to all freemen of our realm, for us and our heirs forever, all the underwritten liberties to be had and held by them and their heirs, of us and our heirs forever.
[2] *'Relief' payments (the feudal equivalent of death duties) shall be* according to the ancient custom of fiefs
[3] *An heir who is under age at the death of his father shall have his inheritance without the payment of a fine.*
[4] *The guardian administering the lands of an under age heir is to take only reasonable customs and services and is not to 'waste' (i.e. overexploit) men or goods on the estate. If the unscrupulous administrator is a royal appointee,*

for example a sheriff, or someone who has bought the right to administer the lands from the king, the king will extract compensation from him on behalf of the heir and appoint two scrutineer administrators.

[5] *Moreover the guardian is enjoined to return the property,* its houses, parks, fishponds, stanks, mills and other things pertaining to the land *in good repair and fully stocked with* ploughs and wainage (p.ooo) according as the season of husbandry shall require and the revenues of the land can reasonably be expected to yield.

[The meaning of the word 'stank' is debated by scholars – it may signify merely a specific type of fishpond, fish farming being much more widespread in the middle ages than it is today, or the standing pond of a water mill. It would be interesting to know whether the clerks who framed the Charter meant 'mills' to include the comparatively modern windmills as well as watermills. The American historian of technology . . . places the invention of the horizontal axle windmill in twelfth-century England, probably East Anglia some time in the 1130s-50s]

[6] *Heirs shall be married without disparagement with due notice given to the next of kin*

[7] *A widow henceforward to be assured of the rights in her 'dower' (**dos**) – the portion of her husband's lands specifically set aside for her widowhood; her 'marriage portion' (**maritagium**) – that portion of his lands which her father had made over to her at the time of her marriage; and her inheritance (**hereditas**) – any lands bequeathed to her personally, by relations or friends perhaps, after her marriage. She was also guaranteed 40 days' (in legal jargon the widow's quarantine, from the Latin word for '40') residence in the house of her husband after his death, during which time the dower had to be made over to her. The 1217 issue of the Charter also provided for a widow to receive **estovers** from the estate, i.e. supplies for her daily maintenance, during the quarantine period.*

[8] *No widow shall be compelled to marry, though if she does marry she must have the consent of the lord from whom she holds her lands*

[9] *Neither we nor our bailiffs shall seize any land or rent for any debt, if the chattels of the debtor are sufficient to repay the debt . . .*

* [10] *If one who has borrowed from the Jews . . . die before that loan be repaid, the debt shall not bear interest while the heir is under age . . . [During the heir's minority he who held the wardship of the estate drew its revenues. Since the heir had nothing with which to pay the interest this clause was*

certainly fair to his interests – equally it was unfair to the moneylender]

* [11] And if anyone die indebted to the Jews, his wife shall have her dower and repay no part of the debt; any children of the deceased who are under age shall receive maintenance in keeping with the holding of the deceased; the debt shall be paid out of the residue of the estate, . . . and the same shall apply to debts owed to others than Jews

* [12] Neither aid nor scutage shall be imposed on our kingdom without the common counsel of the kingdom *except for ransom of the king, knighting his eldest son, or for one marriage of his eldest daughter . . .* Let aids from the city of London be decided in the same way.

[13] And the city of London shall have all its ancient liberties and customs by land and water; *the same to apply all other cities and towns.*

* [14] And to obtain the common counsel of the kingdom on the assessment of an aid or a scutage, we will have the archbishops, bishops, abbots, earls, and greater barons individually summoned by our letters; *others holding in chief (i.e. directly from the king) would receive a general summons through a royal officer such as the sheriff. The summons was to give at least 40 days' notice, but the meeting would go ahead on the given day even if not all those summoned appeared.*

* [15] *Conditions governing aids levied by the king are to apply also to those levied by lords on their tenants*

[16] *Demands for military service shall not exceed what is legally due by terms of the tenure*

[17] *The court of common pleas shall have a permanent venue and no longer follow the royal court on its travels across the country.*

[18] *Certain assizes concerning local landowning titles are to be decided by the king's travelling justices in the county court.*

* [19] *The clause provides for assizes covered by 18 which for any reason cannot be settled on the day of the county court*

[20] *A freeman shall be amerced only reasonably for a small offence and even in the case of a grave offence shall not be penalized so heavily that he cannot maintain himself in a fitting way of life; a merchant must be left with sufficient stock to continue in business and even a villein shall not lose his 'wainage'. No amercement can be imposed except by the oath of honest men of the neighbourhood*

[21] *Earls and barons are to be amerced through their peers*

[22] *The clause deals with the amercement of clerics*

[23] No village or individual shall be compelled to make bridges at river banks, except those who of old were legally bound to do so

[24] Pleas of the crown shall not be held by our sheriffs, constables, coroners or other bailiffs.

* [25] *The clause forbids sheriffs to raise rents and levies arbitrarily*

[26] *The clause concerns debts owing to the king by the estate of a deceased landowner*

* [27] If a freeman die intestate, his chattels shall be distributed by . . . his nearest kinsfolk and friends, under supervision of the church . . .

[28] No bailiff of ours shall take . . . provisions from anyone without immediately tendering money therefor . . .

[29] *Knights owing castle-guard cannot be compelled to give money in lieu if they wish to serve in their own persons or to provide a competent substitute.*

[30] *No bailiff of ours, or other person, shall requisition the horses or carts of any freeman*

[31] *. . . nor wood . . . for castle building or any other work*

[32] *The lands of convicted felons, which by tradition fell to the crown for a period, are henceforth to be returned to the lord of the fief in which they lie after a year and a day*

[33] All kydells [*i.e. fish weirs*] shall be removed from the rivers Thames and Medway, as throughout all England, except from the seashore.

[34] *The government writ* praecipe, *which concerned property disputes and effectively removed such cases from the jurisdiction of the territorial lord to the king's court,* shall not in future be issued to anyone concerning any tenement whereby a freeman may lose his court.

[35] Let there be one measure of wine throughout our whole realm; and one measure of ale; and one measure of corn, namely 'the London quarter'; and one width of cloth – whether dyed or russet, or halberget [*possibly a heavy material used for the haubergeon body vest worn by knights under a coat of mail*], namely, two ells within the selvedges; let it be the same for weights as for measures.

[36] In future no payment shall be offered or accepted for a writ of inquisition . . .

[37] *In this clause the king agrees that where a man may hold small parcels of land from him, or owe service by minor feudal obligations known as 'small or petty serjeanties', but holds the bulk of his land from another lord by major obligations, the royal government will not exploit these petty*

dues to claim the right to administer the land during the minority of an heir.

[38] *The clause forbids royal officials to put a man to his 'law' on their own unsupported complaint and requires them to back it up with credible witnesses.*

[*Historians differ as to what the word 'lex' i.e. 'law' means in this context, which is hardly surprising since the term was causing trouble for commentators as early as 1300. However the clause opens yet another window into the world of fear and intimidation presided over by petty officialdom*]

[39] No freeman shall be taken or [*'vel', the Latin word used here, can also mean 'and', a fact which has caused endless debate among historians and lawyers*] imprisoned or [*here the unambiguous 'aut' is used*] disseised or exiled or in any way destroyed nor will we go upon him nor send upon him, except by the lawful judgement of his peers or [and] by the law of the land.

[40] To no one will we sell, to no one will we refuse or delay, right or justice.

[41] *The clause guarantees freedom of movement to foreign merchants in time of peace and provides that in time of war they shall be held safe but secure until the government can discover how English merchants are being treated by the belligerent power*

* [42] It shall be lawful in future for anyone . . . to leave our kingdom and to return, safe and secure by land and water . . . reserving always the allegiance due to us.

[*The clause excepts convicts and restricts its terms in time of war, but the modern tourist licensed to travel with a passport which remains the property of his government should perhaps look back on the good old days of King John with nostalgia.*]

[43] *A technical clause concerning land held of an escheated estate.*

* [44] Men who live outside the forest need no longer attend before our Justiciars of the Forest on a general summons . . . [*exceptions include anyone who has offered himself as surety for someone charged with a forest offence*]

* [45] Only men who know the law of the realm and mean to observe it well shall henceforward be appointed as justices, constables, sheriffs or bailiffs

[46] All barons who have founded abbeys, for which they hold charters . . ., or of which they have long-continued possession, shall have the wardship of them, when vacant . . . [*The clause is to protect a baronial right against the king, not to protect the abbeys in question*]

* [47] *All land afforested in our time shall be immediately disafforested, all* river banks put 'in defence' are likewise to be returned to their former state. *[To 'defend' a river meant to fence off bridal paths and make other provisions to give the royal hunt free course in following hawks and falcons.]*

* [48] All evil customs connected with forests and warrens, foresters and warreners, sheriffs and their officers, river-banks and their wardens, shall immediately be inquired into in each county by twelve sworn knights . . . and shall, within forty days of the said inquest, be utterly abolished . . . provided we have intimation thereof

* [49] We will immediately restore all hostages and charters delivered to us by Englishmen, as sureties of the peace or of faithful service.

[A glimpse of the unacceptable face of royal 'protection'.]

* [50] We will entirely remove from their bailiwicks, the relations of Gerard of Athée . . .

[The men in question, who are named in the clause, were professionals, foreigners, low-born and well hated by the Anglo-Norman baronage]

* [51] As soon as peace is restored we will banish from the kingdom all foreign-born knights. . . and mercenary soldiers

[Probably John's most loyal as well as most effective servants, like the mercenary captain Fawkes de Bréauté.]

* [52] If anyone has been dispossessed or removed by us, without the legal judgement of his peers, from his lands, castles . . . or from his rights, we will immediately restore them to him; and if any dispute arise let it be decided by the Twenty-five barons to be mentioned below. . . Moreover, for all those possessions from which anyone has . . . been removed by our father, King Henry or our brother King Richard, and which we retain in our own hand . . . we shall have respite until the usual term of crusaders . . . but immediately on our return we shall grant full justice

* [53] *The respite of the Crusader is extended to afforestations, wardships, and abbeys on other lands than those of the king*

[54] No one shall be arrested or imprisoned upon the appeal of a woman, for the death of any other than her husband

[Women could appoint a champion in the trial by battle, men had to fight for themselves]

* [55] *All fines and penalties [i.e. amercements] made and imposed unjustly and against the law of the land are to be remitted or otherwise dealt with as shall be decided by the Committee of Twenty-five barons set up by Clause 61 of the Charter to see that its terms are carried out.*

* [56] If we have dispossessed any Welshmen of lands or liberties or other things without the legal judgement of their peers in England or in Wales, they shall be immediately restored to them . . . *disputes to be settled by judgement of peers according to English law, Welsh law or the law of the Marches, according to the location of the tenement.*

* [57] *This, the second of three clauses concerning the opposition barons' Welsh allies headed by Llywelyn, provides that they shall be restored to any lands or liberties unjustly taken from them by John's brother [Richard I] or his father [Henry II], with the proviso that the king shall enjoy the respite allowed a crusader in all cases concerning which proceedings were not instituted before he took the cross.*

* [58] We will immediately free the son of Llywelyn and all the hostages of Wales, and charters made over to us as securities for the peace.

* [59] *Alexander II King of Scots is to be treated on the same terms as the barons of England in the matter of his sisters and the hostages he gave as security and concerning his franchises, unless it ought to be otherwise according to charters which John had received from Alexander's father William the Lion (died 1214), the questions to be settled by the judgement of the king's peers in John's court.*

Although the seventeen-year old Alexander II of Scotland was not a party to the Charter, the barons wanted all the allies they could get and included this as a bait to the northern monarch. The question naturally arose, how could the King of Scots have peers, i.e. equals in rank? The issue revolved around the question of the homage which the kings of England reckoned was owing to them from the Scottish ruler – just as the kings of France reckoned the English ruler owed them homage. William had in fact done reluctant homage to John with the saving clause 'reserving always his own right'. Then in August 1209 Alexander did homage on behalf of his father in regard to other castles and lands, while his sisters Margaret and Isabel were handed over as wards of John, being held in close but honourable confinement in Corfe Castle, Dorset. Needing John's military help against a pretender to the Scottish throne, in 1212 William even made the 14-year-old Alexander a ward of England to be married at John's discretion over the next six years. Finally, in October 1213, Pope Innocent ordered both William and Alexander to do homage to King John.

[60] . . . the customs and liberties aforesaid, the observance of which we have granted . . . as pertains to us towards our men, shall be observed by all of our

kingdom, clergy as well as lay, as pertains between them and their men.

* [61] . . . moreover . . . we give and grant to our barons the under-written security, namely, that the barons shall choose Twenty-five barons of the kingdom they wish, who must with all their might observe, hold and cause to be observed, the peace and liberties which we have granted and confirmed to them by this present charter of ours, so that if we, or our justiciar, or our bailiffs or any one of our officers offend in any way against anyone or transgress any of the articles of the peace or the security and the offence be notified to four of the aforesaid Twenty-five barons, the four shall report to us or our justiciar and petition to have that transgression without delay. And if we shall not have corrected the transgression within forty days . . . the four barons shall report to the rest of the Twenty-five and [*they*] together with the community of the whole land, shall distrain and distress us in all possible ways, as by seizing our castles, lands, possessions, and in any other way open to them, *though without violence to the king, queen or their children* until they deem that redress has been done, . . . *this astonishing clause goes on to enjoin everyone in the realm to swear loyalty to the Twenty-five in helping them* to 'molest' *the king* 'to the utmost of their power' *and any who do not take the oath will be compelled to do so by the king himself. Finally, the clause provides for the then very modern proceeding of majority decision to govern the actions of the Twenty-five.*

* [62] We completely remit and pardon to everyone any ill will hatred and bitterness that has arisen between us and our men during the time of discord between us. . . And on this head, we have caused to be made for them letters testimonial patent of the lord Stephen Archbishop of Canterbury, or the lord Henry Archbishop of Dublin, of the bishops above mentioned and of Master Pandulf [*the papal legate*] concerning this security and the concessions aforesaid [*i.e. in fact, the Charter*]

Letters, containing the text of the charter, were issued.

* [63] Wherefore it is our will, and we firmly enjoin, that the English church be free, and that the men in our kingdom have and hold all the aforesaid liberties, rights and concessions . . . for themselves and their heirs, of us and our heirs . . . for ever . . . An oath, moreover has been taken as well on our part as on the part of the barons, that all these conditions . . . shall be kept in good faith and without evil intent. Given under our hand . . . in the meadow which is called Runnymede, between Windsor and Staines, on the fifteenth day of June, in the seventeenth year of our reign.

APPENDIX 2

The European Dimension

Chapter 11 showed that Magna Carta was part of an English bureaucratic tradition of charter making and heir to a series of coronation oaths and charters that stretched back over the generations. But England was by no means the only country in Europe where rulers granted liberties and concessions to their subjects, guaranteed by charter. To some it was merely a matter of common sense. In the preamble to a Charter she granted to the commune of Ghent in the year 1192, Countess Matilda gave her view that it was not only in accordance with the law of God, but also with 'human reason that lords who wish to be honoured and well served by their subjects will maintain their rights and customs for them'.

On the Continent, cities enjoyed something of a favoured status when it came to security of traditions and liberties. The great cities of Northern Italy, Flanders and the German cities of the empire were all centres of immense power and wealth whose friendship was courted by kings, dukes and emperors. In the 1180s, indeed, Emperor Frederick I, 'Barbarossa', bought peace in a long drawn out struggle with the cities of Lombardy with a generous charter.

Best known of Magna Carta's Continental contemporaries was the Golden Bull granted by Andrew II of Hungary in 1222. It had some striking points of resemblance. Where Magna Carta looked back to St Edward the Confessor, the Golden Bull purported to restore the customs of Hungary's first Christian king, St Stephen (d. 1038), and like the Charter of John it guaranteed freedom from harassment without due judicial process. The appeal to tradition is found elsewhere. In 1266 Charles I of Sicily was required to restore the customs of William the Good (d. 1180 and, incidentally, an uncle to John of England) while in 1314 Philip IV granted a raft of concessions 'to the barons and nobles of the realm of France as they had been enjoyed at the time of St Louis IX' (d. 1270).

But in the words of the modern German historian Ferdinand Seibt, 'English institutions were much more advanced' (*viel weiter gediehen*) at this period. The circumstances of Andrew's Golden Bull tell the story. It was forced on him by members of the lower nobility angered by royal connivance at the oppressions of the great magnates. In full, the crucial clause reads 'no noble shall be arrested or destroyed to please any powerful lord unless he has been first summonsed and convicted by judicial process.' Among other European charters at this period was that granted by King Alfonso VII of Leon to 'all of my realm lay and clerical' in 1188.

But as the 13th century advanced, while the English continued their stubborn struggle for Charters which could benefit all classes of society and in due course did, other European countries found these grants of liberties increasingly limited to restricted and privileged groups of the community. A Sicilian charter ensured that 'no services shall be demanded from counts, barons and other nobles and knightly men such as may not become their station.'

Thirty years later, in 1314, King Philip IV of France, urged by his barons and nobles, granted concessions and liberties as they had been enjoyed at the time of St Louis (d. 1270). In fact this amounted to the revival of feudal jurisdictions, the right to private war and the exemptions of the nobility from royal jurisdiction. It was, in essence the foundation document of the French noblesse, which met its Waterloo in 1789.

SELECT BIBLIOGRAPHY

APPLEBY, JOHN T., *John King of England* (New York, 1959)
— *England Without Richard 1189–1199* (London, 1965)
BAGGLEY, J.J., *Historical Interpretation 1066–1540* (Harmondsworth, 1965)
BARKER, J.R.V., *The Tournament in England 1100–1400* (Woodbridge, 1986)
BARLOW, FRANK, *The Feudal Kingdom of England* (London, 1955)
BAZELEY, M., 'The Extent of the English Forest in the Thirteenth Century', *Transactions of the Royal Historical Society*, 4th series, iv (1921)
BECHMANN, ROLAND, *Des arbres et des hommes: La forêt au moyen-âge* (Paris, 1984)
BERESFORD, M.W., *New Towns of the Middle Ages* (1967)
BUTT, RONALD, *A History of Parliament: The Middle Ages* (London, 1989)
BUTTERFIELD, SIR HERBERT, 'Magna Carta in the Historiography of the Sixteenth and Seventeenth Centuries' (Reading, 1969)
CAM, HELEN M., *Magna Carta – Event or Document?* (Selden Society Lecture, London, 1965)
CHENEY, C.R., *From Becket to Langton* (Manchester, 1956)
— 'The Eve of Magna Carta', *Bulletin of the John Rylands' Library*, XXXVIII (Manchester, 1955)
— 'The Twenty Five Barons of Magna Carta', *Bulletin . . . Rylands'*, I (Manchester, 1968)
CHURCHILL, WINSTON S., *A History of the English Speaking Peoples* (New York, 1956)
CLANCHY, M.T., *England and its Rulers 1066–1272* (London, 1983)
COLLINS, A.J., 'The Documents of the Great Charter of 1215' (Proceedings of the British Academy, xxxiv, London)
CRONNE, H.A., *The Reign of Stephen* (London, 1970)
DAVIS, G.R.C., *Magna Carta* (London, 1963)

DAVIS, R.H.C., *King Stephen* (London, 1967)

FRAME, R., *Colonial Ireland 1169–1369* (Dublin, 1981)

GILLINGHAM, J., *The Angevin Empire* (London, 1984)

HOLT, J.C., *Magna Carta* (Cambridge, 1965)

— *The Making of Magna Carta* (Charlottesville, 1965)

— *The Northerners: a Study in the Reign of King John* (Oxford, 1961)

— *Magna Carta and Medieval Government* (London, 1985)

HOWARD, A.E. DICK, *The Road from Runnymede* (Charlottesville, 1968)

JEFFREYS, STEPHEN, *Tourney and Joust* (London, 1973)

JENNINGS, I., *Magna Carta: its influence on the world today* (London, 1965)

JONES, J.A.P., *King John and Magna Carta* (1971)

KEEN, M.H., *Chivalry* (New Haven and London, 1984)

KEENEY, B.C., *Judgement by Peers* (Cambridge, Mass., 1949)

LABARGE, M.W., *Gascony, England's First Colony* (London, 1980)

MCFARLANE, K.B., *The Nobility of Later Medieval England* (Oxford, 1973)

MCKECHNIE, W.S., *Magna Carta: A Commentary on the Great Charter of King John* (Glasgow, 1914)

MCKISACK, MAY, *The Fourteenth Century 1307–1399* (Oxford, 1959)

MADDICOTT, 'Magna Carta and the Local Community', *Past and Present 102* (1984)

NEALE, J.E., *Elizabeth I and her Parliaments* (London, 1953)

PAINTER, SIDNEY, *William Marshal* (Baltimore, 1933)

— *The Reign of King John* (Baltimore, 1949)

PALLISTER, ANNE, *Magna Carta: Heritage of Liberty* (London, 1971)

POOLE, A.L., *From Domesday Book to Magna Carta* (Oxford, 1955)

POWELL, W.R., 'The Administration of the Navy', *English Historical Review*, lxxi (1956)

POWICKE, F.M., *King Henry III and the Lord Edward* (Oxford, 1947)

— *The Loss of Normandy* (Manchester, 1961)

PRESTWICH, MICHAEL, *Edward I* (London, 1988)

RHEINSTEIN, MAX, *Max Weber on Law in Economy and Society* (Cambridge, Mass. 1954)

RICHARDSON, H.G., editor, *The English Jewry under Angevin Kings* (London, 1960)

ROTH, C., *The History of the Jews in England* (Oxford, 1964)

ROUND, J.H., 'An Unknown Charter of Liberties', *English Historical Review*, viii (1893)

RUTLAND, ROBERT A., *The Birth of the Bill of Rights* (Chapel Hill, 1983)

RUSSELL, C., *The Crisis of Parliaments . . . 1509–1660* (Oxford, 1971)

SEIBT, FERDINAND, *Glanz und Elend des Mittelalters* (Berlin, 1987)

SMITH, ELSIE, *The Sarum Magna Carta* (Salisbury, 1967)

STENTON, D.M., *English Justice between the Norman Conquest and the Great Charter* (London, 1965)

STOEL, CAROLINE P. & CLARKE, ANN B., *Magna Carta to the Constitution* (Portland, 1986)

THOMPSON, FAITH T., *The First Copy of Magna Carta. Why it persisted as a Document* (Minnesota, 1925)

— *Magna Carta: its Role in the Making of the English Constitution 1300–1629* (Minneapolis, 1948)

THORNE, SAMUEL E., ET AL. *The Great Charter. Four Essays on Magna Carta and the History of Our Liberty* (New York, 1965)

WARREN, W.L., *King John* (Harmondsworth, 1966)

— *Henry II* (London, 1973)

— *The Governance of Norman and Angevin England 1086–1272* (London, 1987)

WICKSON, R., *The Community of the Realm in Thirteenth Century England* (London, 1970)

WILLIAMS, G.A., *Medieval London from Commune to Capital* (London, 1963)

YOUNG, C.R., *The Royal Forests of Medieval England* (Leicester, 1979)

INDEX

Under the heading 'Magna Carta' in this index will be found page references to the text discussion of the individual clauses where relevant. An asterisk (*) placed before a word indicates that the index entry is to be found under that head: thus, for 'Adhemar of *Limoges' see Limoges, Adhemar of